P9-APQ-053

VOLUME 531   JANUARY 1994

THE ANNALS

of The American Academy *of* Political
and Social Science

RICHARD D. LAMBERT, *Editor*
ALAN W. HESTON, *Associate Editor*

THE EUROPEAN COMMUNITY:
TO MAASTRICHT AND BEYOND

Special Editor of this Volume

PIERRE-HENRI LAURENT

Tufts University
Medford
Massachusetts

 SAGE Periodicals Press *THOUSAND OAKS LONDON NEW DELHI*

ABA1564

THE ANNALS

© 1994 *by* The American Academy *of* Political *and* Social Science

Editorial Office: 3937 Chestnut Street, Philadelphia, PA 19104.

For information about membership* (individuals only) and subscriptions (institutions), address:

SAGE PUBLICATIONS, INC.
2455 Teller Road
Thousand Oaks, CA 91320

From India and South Asia, write to:
SAGE PUBLICATIONS INDIA Pvt. Ltd.
P.O. Box 4215
New Delhi 110 048
INDIA

From the UK, Europe, the Middle East and Africa, write to:
SAGE PUBLICATIONS LTD
6 Bonhill Street
London EC2A 4PU
UNITED KINGDOM

SAGE Production Staff: LINDA GRAY, LIANN LECH, and JANELLE LeMASTER
*Please note that members of The Academy receive THE ANNALS with their membership.
Library of Congress Catalog Card Number 93-85874
International Standard Serial Number ISSN 0002-7162
International Standard Book Number ISBN 0-8039-5585-5 (Vol. 531, 1994 paper)
International Standard Book Number ISBN 0-8039-5584-7 (Vol. 531, 1994 cloth)
Manufactured in the United States of America. First printing, January 1994.

The articles appearing in THE ANNALS are indexed in *Book Review Index, Public Affairs Information Service Bulletin, Social Sciences Index, Current Contents, General Periodicals Index, Academic Index, Pro-Views,* and *Combined Retrospective Index Sets.* They are also abstracted and indexed in *ABC Pol Sci, Historical Abstracts, Human Resources Abstracts, Social Sciences Citation Index, United States Political Science Documents, Social Work Research & Abstracts, Sage Urban Studies Abstracts, International Political Science Abstracts, America: History and Life, Sociological Abstracts, Managing Abstracts, Social Planning/Policy & Development Abstracts, Automatic Subject Citation Alert, Book Review Digest, Work Related Abstracts, Periodica Islamica,* and/or *Family Resources Database,* and are available on microfilm from University Microfilms, Ann Arbor, Michigan.

Information about membership rates, institutional subscriptions, and back issue prices may be found on the facing page.

Advertising. Current rates and specifications may be obtained by writing to THE ANNALS Advertising and Promotion Manager at the Thousand Oaks office (address above).

Claims. Claims for undelivered copies must be made no later than three months following month of publication. The publisher will supply missing copies when losses have been sustained in transit and when the reserve stock will permit.

Change of Address. Six weeks' advance notice must be given when notifying of change of address to ensure proper identification. Please specify name of journal. Send address changes to: THE ANNALS, c/o Sage Publications, Inc., 2455 Teller Road, Thousand Oaks, CA 91320.

Origin and Purpose. The Academy was organized December 14, 1889, to promote the progress of political and social science, especially through publications and meetings. The Academy does not take sides in controverted questions, but seeks to gather and present reliable information to assist the public in forming an intelligent and accurate judgment.

Meetings. The Academy occasionally holds a meeting in the spring extending over two days.

Publications. THE ANNALS is the bimonthly publication of The Academy. Each issue contains articles on some prominent social or political problem, written at the invitation of the editors. Also, monographs are published from time to time, numbers of which are distributed to pertinent professional organizations. These volumes constitute important reference works on the topics with which they deal, and they are extensively cited by authorities throughout the United States and abroad. The papers presented at the meetings of The Academy are included in THE ANNALS.

Membership. Each member of The Academy receives THE ANNALS and may attend the meetings of The Academy. Membership is open only to individuals. Annual dues: $42.00 for the regular paperbound edition (clothbound, $60.00). Add $9.00 per year for membership outside the U.S.A. Members may also purchase single issues of THE ANNALS for $13.00 each (clothbound, $18.00). Add $2.00 for shipping and handling on all prepaid orders.

Subscriptions. THE ANNALS (ISSN 0002-7162) is published six times annually—in January, March, May, July, September, and November. Institutions may subscribe to THE ANNALS at the annual rate: $132.00 (clothbound, $156.00). California institutions: $141.57 paperbound, $167.31 clothbound. Add $9.00 per year for subscriptions outside the U.S.A. Institutional rates for single issues: $24.00 each (clothbound, $29.00). California institutions: $25.74 paperbound, $31.10 clothbound.

Second class postage paid at Thousand Oaks, California, and additional offices.

Single issues of THE ANNALS may be obtained by individuals who are not members of The Academy for $17.00 each (clothbound, $26.00). California residents: $18.23 paperbound, $27.89 clothbound. Add $2.00 for shipping and handling on all prepaid orders. Single issues of THE ANNALS have proven to be excellent supplementary texts for classroom use. Direct inquiries regarding adoptions to THE ANNALS c/o Sage Publications (address below).

All correspondence concerning membership in The Academy, dues renewals, inquiries about membership status, and/or purchase of single issues of THE ANNALS should be sent to THE ANNALS c/o Sage Publications, Inc., 2455 Teller Road, Thousand Oaks, CA 91320. Telephone: (805) 499-0721; FAX/Order line: (805) 499-0871. *Please note that orders under $30 must be prepaid.* Sage affiliates in London and India will assist institutional subscribers abroad with regard to orders, claims, and inquiries for both subscriptions and single issues.

Printed on recycled, acid-free paper

THE ANNALS

of The American Academy *of* Political
and Social Science

RICHARD D. LAMBERT, *Editor*
ALAN W. HESTON, *Associate Editor*

——————————— **FORTHCOMING** ———————————

FOREIGN LANGUAGE POLICY:
AN AGENDA FOR CHANGE
Special Editor: Richard D. Lambert

Volume 532   March 1994

TRENDS IN U.S.-CARIBBEAN RELATIONS
Special Editor: Anthony P. Maingot

Volume 533   May 1994

STRATEGIES FOR IMMIGRATION CONTROL:
AN INTERNATIONAL COMPARISON
Special Editor: Mark J. Miller

Volume 534   July 1994

See page 3 for information on Academy membership and
purchase of single volumes of **The Annals.**

CONTENTS

BOOK DEPARTMENT CONTENTS

PREFACE

Some fifteen years ago, *The Annals* published an entire volume on the European Community (EC). That issue, entitled *The European Community after Twenty Years*, attempted to examine and analyze the history of the then new regional institution of nine Western European nations. A decade and a half later, it is necessary to revisit this most important European integration venture of twelve states because of the numerous significant developments both within it and outside it that have affected it. The Community is now undeniably an international actor of major consequence.

The eleven essays in the present collection are devoted to reviewing the historical evolution of the Community and its future prospects. They all inspect the 1978-93 period and the EC movement from Eurosclerosis and economic malaise to *relance* with the Single European Act, the 1992 Project, Iberian expansion, and the Delors Plan through to the collapse of communism in Central and Eastern Europe and the Soviet Union, along with the turbulence of the Maastricht Treaty (the Treaty on European Union), and then back to the economic recession and Europessimism of the 1990s. Specifically, the overall historical context is set by the first article, written by Dinan, and the final article, a concluding overview by Hillenbrand. Two major member-state case studies by Gardner Feldman and George place Germany and the United Kingdom at the very center of EC continuity and change before and after the fall of the Berlin Wall. The studies by Wallace and Lodge explore the evolving roles of three EC institutions—Council of Ministers, Commission, and Parliament—with emphasis on the contests over national, intergovernmental, and supranational distribution of power and authority. Central economic issues are at the heart of two other contributions, the one by Overturf concentrating on the financial and monetary integration process and the Pelkmans work being a detailed exploration about the meaning of the single unified market.

The remaining three articles are specific studies about Community activities of critical significance for the 1990s and the next century. The Rummel presentation focuses on transnational foreign and security policy construction as it emerges from the Maastricht agreement but also as it reflects previous Community efforts to elaborate and practice common policy formation in the defense and foreign policy areas. In the Laurent article, enlargement as the paramount integration experience is reviewed in terms of its past consequences and appraised in terms of its forthcoming implications, particularly in the projected 1996 intergovernmental conference. The realm of trade competitiveness and questions of technology between the three global titans are the focus of the contribution by Zysman and Borrus. In their case study of electronics, the inadequacies of the European responses are detailed and evaluated.

It should be noted that these articles were all completed in April or May 1993. The reader, seeing and reading them almost a year later or beyond, should be aware of that fact.

PIERRE-HENRI LAURENT

ANNALS, *AAPSS*, **531**, January 1994

The European Community, 1978-93

By DESMOND DINAN

ABSTRACT: The European Community underwent a remarkable transformation in the mid-1980s. The Single Market Program (1992) became synonymous with a revitalized Community moving rapidly toward greater political and economic integration. The end of the Cold War, to which the Single Market Program undoubtedly contributed, posed enormous internal and external challenges. The most common concern was that Germany's preoccupation with unification, and the Community's preoccupation with Germany, would derail the Single Market Program and the most recent initiative for economic and monetary union. Instead, German unification spurred renewed interest in European integration, culminating in the Maastricht Treaty of February 1992. Yet growing popular concern about the Community's development sparked the Maastricht Treaty ratification crisis. In the past, crises have acted as a catalyst for deeper European integration. The Maastricht ratification crisis could have a similar impact, especially by focusing attention on the Community's democratic deficit.

Desmond Dinan is an associate professor of history and director of the Center for European Community Studies at George Mason University. His most recent books are the Historical Dictionary of the European Community *and* Ever Closer Union? An Introduction to the European Community.

THE period covered by this article began and ended with the European Community in crisis. Yet between the crisis of Eurosclerosis and Europessimism in the late 1970s and the political, economic, and currency crises of the early 1990s, the Community experienced a remarkable metamorphosis. The Single European Act (SEA) of 1986 and the Maastricht Treaty of 1992 (also known as the Treaty on European Union) are striking landmarks in the Community's development, presaging completion of the Single Market Program, achievement of economic and monetary union (EMU), and closer coordination of member states' foreign and security policies.

For historians of European integration, the Community's development in the 1980s and early 1990s poses challenging questions of causation and interpretation. Early integration theorists developed such concepts as spillover, forward linkage, and system transformation.[1] Spillover is the supposedly inexorable extension of cooperation into associated areas because of linkages and interconnections between economic sectors; forward linkage is a process whereby spillover causes a marked increase in the scope of integration or in its institutional capacities; and system transformation means going beyond the obligations of the original

1. See, for instance, Ernst Haas, *The Uniting of Europe: Political, Social, and Economic Forces, 1950-57* (Stanford, CA: Stanford University Press, 1958); Leon Lindberg, *The Political Dynamics of European Economic Integration* (Stanford, CA: Stanford University Press, 1963); Leon Lindberg and Stuart Scheingold, *Europe's Would-Be Polity* (Englewood Cliffs, NJ: Prentice-Hall, 1970).

agreement concerning integration and taking on new commitments, either geographically or functionally. System transformation involves a conscious decision to take additional action, and it usually requires a new constitutive bargaining session, in the form of an intergovernmental conference (IGC) leading to a treaty. Successive enlargements of the European Community—in 1973, 1981, and 1986—are obvious examples of system transformation affecting the Community's geographical scope.

System transformation may require an IGC, but IGCs do not necessarily result in system transformation. The IGC that gave rise to the SEA is a striking example. The SEA was a landmark in the Community's history. It incorporated the most important revisions to date of the Treaty of Rome, the original agreement to establish the European Economic Community. Although the SEA increased the Community's institutional capacities and functional scope, however, it did not extend the Community's activities beyond the obligations of the original treaty. By committing the Community's member states to achieve a single, barrier-free market, and enhancing the Community's policymaking powers to buttress the marketplace in areas such as social, environmental, and industrial policy, the SEA sought to achieve objectives that were either clearly stated or unambiguously implied in the treaty.

Is the Community's development since the SEA, culminating in the Maastricht Treaty, an example of forward linkage or system transformation? Undoubtedly, there was spillover from the Single Market Program into the Community's latest initiative for EMU. The title of the Commission's cost-benefit analysis of EMU, *One Market, One Money*, explicitly proclaims forward linkage. For political reasons, however, the Commission overstated the connection. There is an undoubted logic to having a single monetary policy and a single currency in a single market, but its automaticity should not be taken for granted.

EMU would most likely represent system transformation because it involves a major new Community action, one that is only ambiguously implied in the Treaty of Rome. By moving toward EMU, the Community is also moving from the low politics of market integration into the high politics of monetary integration, an issue much closer to the core of national sovereignty. The Community attempted such a move in the early 1970s, partly as a response to changing international economic circumstances and partly as a deliberate effort to deepen integration while simultaneously extending its geographic scope. Deep economic recession and ensuing Eurosclerosis during the remainder of the decade put paid to the first EMU initiative.

As well as grappling with EMU in the early 1970s, the Community's member states launched European Political Cooperation, a tentative process of foreign policy coordination. Like monetary policy, foreign policy is a core competence of the nation-state; transferring responsibility for it—and ultimately for security and defense—to the Community would represent a major transformation of the system. But member states have been extremely slow to do so. European Political Cooperation remained an intergovernmental process, with minimal Commission and European Parliament involvement in it.

Profound shocks to the international political system in the late 1980s changed the context in which European integration had hitherto taken place. Revolution in Eastern Europe and the Cold War's sudden end immediately raised the prospect of a further increase in the Community's geographic scope. What about their impact on the Community's functional scope? Building on the perceived success of the European Monetary System (EMS) and on momentum generated by the Single Market Program, the Community was already re-exploring the EMU option. Fallout from events in the East, and the sudden prospect of German unification, strengthened the Community's interest in EMU and, to an extent, caused spillover from EMU into European political union (EPU). German Chancellor Helmut Kohl made a clear connection between EMU and EPU; his Community colleagues' concerns about a united Germany's role in the new Europe sparked additional interest in the subject.[2] Consequently, in 1991 member states conducted parallel IGCs on EMU and EPU that ended at the Maastricht Summit, resulting in the Treaty on European Union.

2. See Finn Laursen, "Explaining the Intergovernmental Conference on Political Union," in *The Intergovernmental Conference on Political Union*, ed. Finn Laursen and Sophie Vanhoonacker (Maastricht: EIPA, 1992), pp. 229-48.

The spillover from EMU to EPU was not in the obvious or logical sense of the spillover from a single market to a single monetary policy; having produced *One Market, One Money*, the Commission did not produce a sequel entitled *One Monetary Policy, One Government*. EPU was not an attempt to establish a single European government responsible for managing a single monetary policy and a single market; instead, EPU was a mixed bag of forward linkages involving the Community's functional scope and institutional capacities. The high political issues of foreign, security, and, ultimately, defense cooperation remained outside the Community's supranational framework, subject only to intergovernmental agreement.

The 1992 Maastricht Treaty ratification crisis revealed much popular concern about policy formulation and decision making in the Community. People in the Community perceive a huge democratic deficit: the Commission appears remote and democratically unaccountable, and national governments seemingly run the Community like a cartel. The Community has responded by developing the imprecise principle of subsidiarity—a federalist-type doctrine to delineate the proper level at which decisions should be made, either in Brussels, in national capitals, or in regional centers—and by promoting openness and transparency in the Community's legislative process.

There is similar popular concern about the Community's attempted move into the high politics of EMU and about the projected Common Foreign and Security Policy. Regardless of what the Maastricht Treaty really stipulates, it appears to most people to represent a huge advance on the Community's existing functional scope. The popular backlash against it shows a clear need for better communication between Brussels and national governments, on the one hand, and Community citizens, on the other. It also demonstrates genuine concern about further loss of national sovereignty and proves that popular acquiescence in system transformation within the Community can no longer be taken for granted.

Creeping economic recession in 1992 was not an auspicious background against which to transform the Community system. Currency turmoil later in the year, and especially the ongoing Bosnian conflict, had a similar deleterious impact on the Maastricht Treaty ratification process. Economic recession, currency turmoil, and war in Bosnia are seemingly unrelated developments. Nevertheless, to some extent each was caused by the profoundly altered international system, and to some extent each contributed to the Maastricht Treaty ratification crisis.

The ratification debacle and related crisis of confidence hardly represent a threat to the Community's survival. There is no talk of dismantling the single market or of rolling back existing levels of integration. Moreover, the Community has a long list of applicant and potential applicant countries, and in 1993 it began accession negotiations with Austria, Sweden, Finland, and Norway. A more pertinent concern relates to the Community's functional scope: will it become a high-politics Community? Regardless of the impact of economic recession and currency turmoil on EMU, is there sufficient popular support for that level of system transformation?

The 1992 crisis was the most recent in a series of crises that have characterized the process of European integration. Indeed, the concept of crisis is central to the Community's experience. Frequently, economic and political crises have catalyzed the Community and its member states to intensify intergovernmentalism and strengthen supranationalism. The Maastricht Treaty ratification crisis may have a similar effect, although the profound change in the international system since the end of the Cold War makes it doubly difficult to predict the Community's future.

REVIVAL AND TRANSFORMATION

There were few outward signs at the beginning of the 1980s that the Community had survived the serious setbacks of the 1970s. The Community's problems were legion: a paralyzed decision-making process, a feeble Commission, agricultural expenditure out of control, a new French President—Mitterrand—pursuing a "dash for growth" that further strained Community solidarity, and a new British Prime Minister —Thatcher—who rebuked her colleagues with incessant demands for a budget rebate. Under the circumstances, the Commission's 1979 report on progress toward European union was unusually upbeat.[3] Three

3. *Bulletin of the European Communities*, supp. 1, pp. 12-13 (1979).

events that year held out the prospect of a modest improvement in the Community's fortunes: the Treaty of Accession with Greece, the first direct elections to the European Parliament, and the inauguration of the EMS.

In view of the Community's first experience with enlargement, Greece's impending accession and the imminent membership also of Spain and Portugal were dubious grounds for confidence. Nor did direct elections, delayed for many years and openly unwelcome by a number of member states opposed to a stronger Parliament, seem a likely source of Community resurgence. Even the EMS, an initiative launched with unusual speed to establish a degree of exchange rate stability, appeared to have little potential for the Community's long-term growth. Cumulatively, however, these three developments marked the beginning of the end of the Community's lingering malaise.

If only to prevent greater sluggishness in Community decision making once further enlargement took place, the accession of Greece and the impending accession of Spain and Portugal prompted badly needed institutional reform and was one of a number of factors that gave rise to the SEA. By the same token, direct elections did not cause a radical redistribution of power in the Community but brought a new breed of Europarliamentarian to Strasbourg and noticeably improved the European Parliament's morale. From the first directly elected European Parliament came a Draft Treaty Establishing the European Union, which played an important part in the Community's subsequent revival.[4] In that sense, the Commission's 1979 report on European union was prophetic.

The EMS, an initiative to establish a zone of relative monetary stability in a world of wildly fluctuating exchange rates, owed a great deal to Roy Jenkins, Commission President between 1977 and 1981, and to Franco-German leadership in the Community. After an uncertain beginning, the EMS was a striking success and helped participating member states fight inflation and recover economic growth. The EMS also provided a vital underpinning for the Single Market Program. As Peter Ludlow has observed, "The EMS was a precondition for . . . 1992. Had the EMS not been created and functioned so well, the White Paper strategy could not have been contemplated, let alone implemented."[5]

The beneficial impact on European integration of enlargement, direct elections, and the EMS became apparent only in the mid-1980s, when the Community emerged from the debilitating British budgetary question. Margaret Thatcher's abrasive personality and hostility to European integration help to explain why a relatively straightforward issue turned into one of the most complex and divisive disputes in the Community's history and filled a reservoir of ill feeling toward Britain in Brussels. Thatcher's demand for a British budgetary rebate dominated

five years and 15 European summits. It was eventually resolved at the June 1984 Fontainebleau Summit, thanks largely to François Mitterrand's commitment to finding a way out of the budgetary impasse and relaunching the Community.

In a press conference after the Fontainebleau Summit, Thatcher said she now looked forward to " 'pressing ahead with the development of the Community.' "[6] Thatcher's Community colleagues could not have agreed more. At Fontainebleau, Mitterrand had spoken eloquently about the need to revive the Community's policies and institutions and instill a new sense of European identity. In a famous speech to the European Parliament the previous month, he had called for reform of decision making in the Council, extensive treaty revisions, and a new agenda for European integration. Although France would no longer hold the presidency, the Fontainebleau Summit created a favorable environment in which to push Mitterrand's pro-Community agenda and especially to promote completion of the internal market.

The ideological shift then sweeping Western Europe was one of the most important factors that fueled renewed interest in the Community's long-proclaimed goal of a single market. Thatcher's election victory in 1979 was an obvious manifestation of it. Across the Channel, by contrast, President Mitterrand pushed a socialist agenda of state intervention and regulation after his election victory in 1981. The consequences were

4. *Bulletin of the European Communities*, point 1.6.1 (Feb. 1982).

5. Peter Ludlow, *Beyond 1992: Europe and Its World Partners* (Brussels: Center for European Policy Studies, 1989), p. 25.

6. Quoted in *Financial Times*, 28 June 1984, p. 14.

catastrophic. In an effort to reduce unemployment and stimulate economic growth by a policy of national independence, Mitterrand caused inflation to soar and investment to slump. The value of the franc plummeted, forcing devaluation within the EMS and prompting a tough domestic austerity program.

By 1983, pragmatism had overcome principle when Mitterrand, at the urging of Jacques Delors, his Finance Minister, abandoned a disastrous doctrinaire approach to economic recovery. Mitterrand began to bend with the prevailing wind, blowing from the United States and the United Kingdom, of deregulation and neoliberalism. The implications for France and the European Community were striking. Mitterrand's U-turn influenced other socialist leaders, notably Gonzalez in Spain and Soares in Portugal, two countries then on their way to Community membership.

The Commission played a key role both in encouraging technological collaboration in the Community and in championing the cause of the single market. Concern about declining European competitiveness in the late 1970s had prompted Etienne Davignon, Commission Vice President with responsibility for industrial affairs, to cultivate the chief executive officers of major European manufacturers in the high-technology sector. His so-called Round Table discussion group included leaders of the Big 12 electronics companies in the Community.[7] Davignon gradually

7. See Margaret Sharp and Clare Shearman, *European Technological Collaboration* (London: Routledge & Kegan Paul, 1987), p. 46.

succeeded in getting these industrial giants to reconsider the virtues of cross-border collaboration, something that the failure of national champions and the persistent economic recession predisposed them to do in any case.

Davignon's initiative led to the ESPRIT program for "pre-collaborative" research between major European manufacturers, smaller firms, and universities throughout the Community. Whatever else about their impact on European competitiveness, ESPRIT and other Community-sponsored initiatives at least satisfied European industrialists that the Commission was a constructive and competent partner. That partnership, in turn, led to awareness on both sides of the Community's potential for economic revival in Europe. If the Commission could bring industrialists together to try to improve Europe's competitiveness, why could it not help to end the fragmentation of Europe's own market by breaking down the plethora of nontariff barriers that impeded intra-Community trade? Why not use the Commission's authority to promote liberalization, harmonization, and standardization? In the same way that industrial policy might help Europe's global competitiveness, why not use competition policy to pry open public procurement in Europe? Thus Davignon's endeavors to promote industrial competitiveness in the Community contributed to the momentum gathering in the early 1980s for completion of the internal market.

The Commission's strategy for reviving interest in the internal market involved putting forward concrete proposals, notably on standardization, and politicizing the issue by prodding the European Council into action. The Commission's efforts contributed to the consensus in Brussels and the member states on the need to achieve a genuine single market, involving as much deregulation as possible at the national level coupled with as little reregulation as necessary at the Community level, and culminated in the 1985 White Paper, a legislative blueprint for achieving a single market by the end of 1992. The white paper is often caricatured as a typical Commission product: unintelligible, obtuse, and tedious. Indeed, the highly technical nature of the internal market hardly lends itself to lively prose. Yet the white paper is a surprisingly lucid piece, containing a ringing defense of market liberalization and a clear exposition of how and why the Community should complete the internal market.[8]

Ideological, political, and economic transformations had paved the way for an imminent breakthrough. Other developments—notably, tension in the transatlantic relationship, the assertiveness of the first directly elected European Parliament, and the impending accession of Spain and Portugal—directed attention also on institutional reform and constitutional change in the Community. These objectives—completion of the single market and a revision of the Treaty of Rome—were not unconnected. Each gave added impetus to the other and paved the way for the IGC that resulted in the SEA.

8. White Paper on Completing the Single Market, COM(85)210, May 1985.

THE INTERNAL MARKET, THE SEA, AND EMU

Jacques Delors, who became Commission President in January 1985, is generally credited with the Community's metamorphosis. Yet Delors's importance should not be exaggerated. Undoubtedly, he possessed an abundance of ambition, competence, and resourcefulness. The new President sought to infuse the Commission with a renewed sense of purpose and set the Community on the road to European union. But Delors could not possibly have realized those objectives had the economic, political, and international circumstances been unfavorable. It was his good fortune to have become Commission President at precisely the time when internal developments and external factors made a dramatic improvement in the Community's fortunes almost inevitable. Without Delors, the Single Market Program and the acceleration of European integration might not have happened exactly as they did, but that is not to say that they would not have happened at all.

At the beginning of his presidency, Delors was torn between a number of priorities: the single market, institutional reform, a new monetary initiative, and extending Community competence in the field of foreign policy and defense. The political advantages of the internal market option soon became apparent. By going back to basics and emphasizing one of the original objectives of the Treaty of Rome, to which the heads of government unequivocally subscribed, Delors could hardly be accused of overweening ambition. Moreover, Delors believed, a single market strategy would indirectly but inescapably result in improved decision-making procedures and renewed interest in economic and monetary union. Political will to complete the internal market could never translate into action unless unanimity gave way to qualified majority voting in the Council of Ministers. Without reform of the legislative process, single market proposals would ultimately bog down in disputes between member states. Furthermore, a successful single market strategy would most likely fuel interest in EMU. How could the market be fully integrated without monetary union and a common macroeconomic policy? The political if not the economic logic of a large, vibrant internal market pointed inexorably, Delors thought, toward currency union.

Negotiated by the member states in late 1985 and early 1986 to amend the Treaty of Rome, the SEA was much more than a device simply to achieve a single market by the end of 1992.[9] Instead, the SEA was a complex bargain to improve decision making, increase efficiency, achieve market liberalization, and, at the same time, promote cohesion in the Community. The SEA made possible what French President Georges Pompidou had sought at an earlier stage of the Community's existence: "completion, deepening, enlargement." As Helen Wallace remarked, "The 1992 goal was clearly intended as completion, but new policies had been substantively embraced and institutions had been strengthened, thus deepen-

ing was in hand, and widening had occurred for a third time without momentum being lost."[10]

Moreover, the SEA had real potential for the Community's rapid development. First, provision for qualified majority voting could not only expedite the internal market but also encourage the Council of Ministers to be more flexible when legislating in areas where unanimity remained the norm. Second, a successful Single Market Program might advance European integration in related economic and social sectors. Third, the SEA's endorsement of the white paper and formal extension of Community competence could strengthen the Commission's position. Fourth, the introduction of legislative cooperation could help close the Community's supposed democratic deficit and boost the European Parliament's institutional importance. Finally, the SEA's incorporation of European Political Cooperation into the treaty framework and agreement on new procedures to coordinate foreign policy might enhance the Community's international standing.

By the late 1980s, much of the SEA's potential had been realized. Thanks partly to the optimistic conclusions of the Cecchini Report,[11] a cost-benefit analysis of the Community's existing fragmented market,

9. *Bulletin of the European Communities*, supp. 2 (1986).

10. Helen Wallace, "Widening and Deepening: The European Community and the New European Agenda," Discussion Paper no. 23 (London: Royal Institute of International Affairs, 1989), p. 6.

11. Commission of the European Communities, *Research on the "Cost of Non-Europe": Basic Findings* (Luxembourg: Office of the Official Publications of the European Communities, 1988).

the private sector immediately embraced the Single Market Program. On another level, "1992" caught the popular imagination. Yet widespread enthusiasm for the single market disguised the program's slow legislative progress. The problem lay not only with the complexity and sensitivity of many of the white paper's proposals—the Council of Ministers dealt swiftly and easily with the least controversial measures—but also with a festering dispute over the Community's budget. In an effort to meet the greater expenditure implicit in the SEA—notably the obligation to promote economic and social cohesion between the rich North and poor South—in January 1987 the Commission unveiled a five-year budgetary plan. Agreement on the budgetary package in early 1988 was a landmark in the Community's internal development and resulted in a generous transfer of resources to the Community's poorer regions.

The budgetary agreement and the single market's popularity allowed the Commission and sympathetic member states to focus on EMU. At the Hanover Summit in June 1988, Community leaders recalled their commitment in the SEA eventually to realize monetary union, and they asked a committee of experts, chaired by Delors, to study the issue. The committee produced a report, the Delors Report, in April 1989,[12] which Community leaders endorsed at the Madrid Summit two months later.

The heads of government agreed with the committee's three-stage approach to EMU and decided that Stage I, involving greater coordination of member states' macroeconomic policies, the establishment of free capital movement, and membership of all Community currencies in the EMS, should begin on 1 July 1990. Moreover, the heads of government agreed that an IGC to determine the treaty revisions that would be needed to launch the subsequent stages would meet after Stage I had begun.

For the understandable reason that only if monetary policy decisions were taken on a Community-wide basis could France hope to regain some of the influence lost to Germany in the EMS, President Mitterrand was a strong supporter of the Delors Report. For the same reason, Chancellor Kohl was indifferent about EMU, although the Bundesbank seemed surprisingly open to the idea. Alone among Community leaders, Margaret Thatcher unequivocally opposed EMU, which she saw as an unacceptable abrogation of national sovereignty and an effort to aggrandize power in Brussels. Opposition to EMU had led in part to Thatcher's infamous September 1988 speech in Bruges, a brilliant articulation of her understanding of European integration and of Britain's contribution to it.[13] But Thatcher's hostility toward the Community in general, and EMU in particular, lacked widespread support within both the Conservative Party and the British Cabinet and contributed to her ouster in Novem-

12. Commission of the European Communities, *Report of the Committee for the Study of Economic and Monetary Union* (Luxembourg: Office of the Official Publications of the European Communities, 1989).

13. Margaret Thatcher, Speech at the College of Europe, Bruges, 20 Sept. 1988.

ber 1990 as party leader and Prime Minister. This was the first time in the Community's history that Community affairs had impinged so dramatically and directly on domestic politics.

THE ACCELERATION OF HISTORY

What Jacques Delors called "the acceleration of History"[14]—the quickening tempo of developments in Eastern Europe that culminated in the revolution of 1989—coincided with and initially contributed to a huge boost in the Community's fortunes. Yet the inexorable rate of reform in the Soviet Union and Eastern Europe, and the consequent transformation of the international system, quickly called into question several of the assumptions underlying European integration, as well as many of the Community's policies, programs, and procedures.

The most immediate issue in late 1989 and early 1990 was the sudden prospect of German unification, which throughout the Community's existence had remained a remote aspiration. The challenge for the Community was both procedural—how to absorb the underdeveloped German Democratic Republic—and political—how to prevent a resurgent, united Germany from tipping the institutional balance and subverting the Community system. The challenge for Germany was to reassure Community partners of its commitment to European integration. And the challenge for other member

14. Jacques Delors, Speech at the College of Europe, Bruges, 20 Oct. 1989.

states was to overcome latent fear of Germany's size in the Community: a united Germany would account for 27 percent of the Community's gross domestic product and, with 77 million people, 25 percent of its population. The solution to most of these problems seemed to lie in deeper European integration.

The period between November 1989 and March 1990, when German unification seemed probable but not imminent, was especially testing for the Community and its member states. This was when Kohl seized the initiative, dealt directly with Gorbachev, and forced the pace of unification. It was also the time when Mitterrand, Council President until the end of 1989, expressed serious reservations about Kohl's haste and unilateralism, thus straining the much-vaunted Franco-German relationship; when Thatcher displayed deep distrust of German motives, thus alienating herself further from the Community; and when Delors enthusiastically endorsed unification and deeper European integration, thus ensuring the Community's centrality in the events that unfolded.

The relationship between German unification and European integration was a constant theme in official German pronouncements at the time. Yet Kohl's earliest articulation of it failed to reassure all his Community colleagues. Torn between an instinctive antipathy toward German unification, which increasingly appeared inevitable, and an equally instinctive affinity for European integration, Mitterrand forged a link between both. The implicit agreement at the December 1989 Strasbourg Summit to deepen European integration manifested itself immediately in a decision to hold an IGC on EMU. Moves toward European political union were further evidence of the momentum generated by German unification. In an act of Franco-German reconciliation and Community leadership, Kohl and Mitterrand called in April 1990 for a separate IGC on EPU. The Franco-German initiative led to a decision to convene both IGCs in December 1990 "to transform the Community from an entity mainly based on economic integration and political cooperation into a union of a political nature, including a common foreign and security policy."[15]

In retrospect, the summer of 1990 can clearly be seen as the high point of the Community's transformation and resurgence since its revival in the early 1980s. Western Europe's economy was buoyant, the Single Market Program was successful, the Community's role as an anchor of stability in the new Europe and as a pole of attraction for newly independent Eastern European states was unquestioned, and German unification in the context of deeper European integration was imminent.

Yet in the run-up to the two IGCs, member states' understanding of EMU came into sharper focus while their understanding of EPU became more blurred. This reflected the concrete nature of EMU and the inherently imprecise nature of EPU. The ultimate goal of EMU was obvious, whereas the definitive objective of EPU was far from certain. Most

15. *Bulletin of the European Communities*, point 1.10 (June 1984).

member states agreed on what EPU could or should include—closing the democratic deficit, strengthening subsidiarity, improving decision making, increasing Community competence, reforming European Political Cooperation, and developing a Common Foreign and Security Policy —but disagreed on the extent of these changes and how to bring them about. With the approach of the IGCs, a consensus on EPU seemed more remote than ever.

At the December 1990 Rome Summit, the heads of government launched the IGCs, a yearlong process of intensive bargaining in which the lowest common denominator often prevailed but which nonetheless marked a decisive turning point in the Community's development. The Commission was a formal participant; the Council Secretariat played a crucial behind-the-scenes role; and the Parliament had little input. Of the larger member states, Germany was the most committed to EMU and EPU, although on EMU the Bundesbank, rather than the government, determined the country's position. Unencumbered by an independent central bank, France wanted EMU at almost any cost but had reservations about many aspects of EPU. Britain was profoundly skeptical of both EMU and EPU. Only late in the negotiations did the British government subscribe to the prevailing conception of a single currency and abandon its alternative proposal on a hard European currency unit.

External factors impinged directly on the IGCs. The end of the Cold War and the start of the Persian Gulf and Yugoslav wars not only impressed on member states the need for effective joint positions on international security issues but also demonstrated the difficulty of harmonizing their notoriously discordant positions on foreign policy and defense. Thus an apparently irreconcilable dispute over foreign and security policy decision making, between proponents of unanimity and majority voting, persisted throughout the IGCs. A compromise reached at Maastricht provided for unanimity on decisions of principle and majority voting on implementing decisions.

The most striking feature of the Maastricht Treaty was its unusual design for the European Union.[16] Instead of a single structure, the Union would consist of three pillars: the Treaty of Rome, including provisions for EMU and other new competences agreed in the negotiations on political union; the Common Foreign and Security Policy; and cooperation on home affairs, such as immigration and internal security. Keeping the Common Foreign and Security Policy and cooperation on home affairs on an intergovernmental basis, outside the Rome Treaty, reconciled the two extremes of Community opinion epitomized by Germany, Italy, and the Netherlands on the pro-federalist side and by Britain and Denmark on the antifederalist side. A last-minute dispute at the Maastricht Summit resulted in a fourth, freestanding pillar, when Britain's refusal to accept the draft treaty's Social Chapter led the others to create a new Social Com-

16. Commission of the European Communities, *Treaty on European Union* (Luxembourg: Office of the Official Publications of the European Communities, 1992).

munity of 11 member states. This set a dangerous precedent for European integration and reinforced the emergence of a multispeed Europe, already inherent in the Maastricht Treaty's provisions for EMU.

A COMMUNITY IN CRISIS?

The year 1992 was to have been the *annus mirabilis* of the single market's completion. Instead, growing popular concern about further loss of sovereignty and about secretive and undemocratic decision making in Brussels, compounded by creeping economic recession, the high cost of German unification, and intense frustration over the Community's inability to broker a lasting cease-fire in Yugoslavia, shook confidence in the Community's future. Failure to ratify the Maastricht Treaty by the end of 1992, due to a narrow no vote in the Danish referendum and the British government's mismanagement of the issue in the House of Commons, epitomized for many a new Community crisis.

At the heart of the Maastricht ratification debacle lay doubts about the Community's relevance in the post–Cold War world. What was the Community's feasibility and utility in a radically altered international environment? From the outset, the Community had considered itself synonymous with Europe. With the Cold War over, could the Community foster a sense of pan-European solidarity and a genuinely all-European integration? Despite the Commission's leadership of the Eastern European assistance effort, by 1992 the Community's *Ostpolitik* seemed to have lost direction. The opening of enlargement negotiations with Austria, Sweden, Finland, and Norway in 1993 raised the perennial question of whether wider would also mean weaker.

It is easy to exaggerate the Community's difficulties in the post-Maastricht period, although some serious problems undoubtedly exist. One is the Commission's retreat in the face of a sustained onslaught from national governments and the media. The Commission's unpopularity increased dramatically during the ratification debacle. Ironically, the Commission had neither played a prominent role in negotiating the Maastricht Treaty nor benefited greatly from its provisions. Yet journalists and politicians caricatured the Maastricht Treaty as the Commission's doing, from which the despised Brussels bureaucracy would derive even greater authority. The Commission's defensiveness does not bode well for the Community's immediate development. As this survey has shown, a strong Community needs a strong Commission.

Another problem, potentially more serious, is a lack of national leadership in the Community because of a growing divergence between France and Germany. The original Franco-German bargain, struck in the late 1950s, hinged on the Common Agricultural Policy (CAP). Thirty-five years later, disputes over CAP reform and over oil-seed subsidies in the context of the Uruguay Round of the General Agreement on Tariffs and Trade suggest that the original bargain has unraveled. In the future, France and Germany are likely to be at loggerheads over a host of other Community issues. And as this survey has also shown, the Community has not progressed in the past without decisive Franco-German leadership.

Yet the notion of a Community in crisis could be misleading and need not be entirely disadvantageous. The history of the Community's development is a history of overcoming crises: the crisis of German reconstruction in the late 1940s, leading to the European Coal and Steel Community; the European Defense Community crisis in the mid-1950s, leading to the relaunch of European integration; the crisis of declining competitiveness and decision-making paralysis in the 1970s and early 1980s, leading to the SEA; and the crisis of German unification in the late 1980s, leading to the Maastricht Treaty.

The Maastricht Treaty ratification crisis may have a similar beneficial impact. Already it has obliged member states to tackle the democratic deficit, both in the narrow sense of institutional accountability and in the broad sense of "the absence of a genuine European political culture and discussion of key policy matters outside of elite circles."[17] Hence the European Council's frenzied efforts at the Birmingham and Edinburgh Summits in late 1992 to make the legislative process more transparent.

Without a doubt, circumstances in the early 1990s seem unpropitious for the future of European integra-

17. Sophie Meunier-Aitsahalia and George Ross, "Democratic Deficit or Democratic Surplus: A Reply to Andrew Moravcsik's Comments about the French Referendum," *French Politics and Society*, 11(1):63 (Winter 1993).

tion. The last three years have seen a steady deterioration in Western Europe's economic and political situation. As for Maastricht, the December 1992 Edinburgh Summit may have saved the treaty as a symbol of the member states' commitment to further integration, but the opt-outs granted to Denmark, together with continuing turmoil in European currency markets and the Community's impotence in Yugoslavia, undermined its concrete achievements. Whatever the depth of the Community's current crisis, however, it is reassuring to observe that the Community is far better off in the early 1990s than it was in the late 1970s. Of course, today's Community is markedly different from what it was 15 years ago. Nevertheless, the Community's revival and transformation in the early 1980s suggest that, even in the radically altered environment of the post-Cold War period, the future of European integration is far from bleak.

ANNALS, *AAPSS*, **531**, January 1994

Germany and the EC: Realism and Responsibility

By LILY GARDNER FELDMAN

ABSTRACT: This article compares the place of realism and responsibility as motivations for Germany's policy toward the European Community (EC) before 1989 and after. It argues that while the context and style have changed, there remains basic continuity in Germany's EC policy. Germany is characterized as interdependent partner and not as dominant leader or preoccupied spoiler in the EC. The assessment of continuity and partnership assumes that promotion of national interest, together with the pursuit of integration as an ideal, has been a fundamental element since the early 1950s and not a motive suddenly discovered with German unification. The full range of Germany's goals in the EC—economic, political, cultural and societal, regional, international—is examined.

Lily Gardner Feldman is research director of the American Institute for Contemporary German Studies at Johns Hopkins University and former associate professor of political science at Tufts University. She is author of The Special Relationship between West Germany and Israel *and more than a dozen articles on the European Community as an international actor, federalism and foreign policy, and German foreign policy.*

IN his March 1993 *tour d'horizon* of Germany's foreign policy for a new world, Foreign Minister Kinkel identified the twin challenge of synchronizing responsibility with realism and of fine-tuning continuity with respect to change.[1] The delicate balancing act Germany faces in its overall external policies is doubly required in Germany's relationship to the European Community (EC), which Foreign Minister Kinkel ranked at the top of the Federal Republic's priorities.

For the last 15 years, and indeed since the inception of Chancellor Adenauer's policy of integrating the Federal Republic into the West, Germany has balanced its historically determined special obligation to the European idea with its domestically inspired pragmatic needs. The relative stability of the Cold War meant large doses of continuity, particularly after 1959, when the Social Democratic Party (SPD) accepted the centrality of the EC and thereby made consensus on European policy a fundamental precept of German foreign policy.

The process of German unification initiated by the November 1989 breach of the Berlin Wall, which produced a Germany of 80 million as a bridge between East and West in a new Europe, has raised the question for Germans and outsiders of whether there is today more realism than responsibility, more change than continuity in Germany's EC policy. This article will examine these two dimensions—of realism and re-

sponsibility and of continuity and change—by comparing trends in German EC policy in terms of goals, interests, and behavior in the decade before unification and in the five years since the autumn of 1989. It will focus on government policy but will also refer to the attitudes of various segments of German society. It will consider both content and context.

The conclusion about continuity and change will depend on the perception of the nature of Germany's post-1989 EC policy but, just as important, on the characterization of German activity before 1989. If we assess the earlier period as one of uniform, unflinching support of the EC by a self-abnegating, dependent Germany, then any signs of either assertiveness or introspection after 1989 will be viewed as a departure signaling major change. If, however, we have a more nuanced historical interpretation, involving Germany as interdependent partner, then post-1989 behavior will be seen more readily as combining continuity and change. Not only the behavior but also the current debate about whether Germany is dominant leader, interdependent partner, or preoccupied spoiler has pre-1989 origins.[2]

1978-88: DIVIDED GERMANY IN A DIVIDED EUROPE

The premise and practice of Germany's partnership in the EC re-

---

1. See Klaus Kinkel, "Verantwortung, Realismus, Zukunftssicherung: Deutsche Außenpolitik in einer sich neu ordnenden Welt," *Frankfurter Allgemeine Zeitung*, 19 Mar. 1993.

2. See the response to Carl Lankowski in Simon Bulmer and William Paterson, *The Federal Republic of Germany and the European Community* (London: Allen & Unwin, 1987); Dieter Buhl, "Leichtfertig ins europäisches Abseits," *Die Zeit*, 5 July 1985.

volved around its relationship to France. By the mid-1970s, as a result of a greater power symmetry between the two countries and a superb personal chemistry between the German Chancellor and the French President, the Franco-German couple had institutionalized further and recaptured its earlier function of spearheading integration, a role that could survive changes in leadership in both countries at the beginning of the 1980s. The European Monetary System (EMS), the decisive proposals for political union, and the expansion of the EC's international profile were all attributable to the Franco-German friendship, which Kohl deemed in 1987 "the dynamic force in the process of European unification."[3]

Beyond the Franco-German centerpiece are the five main goals of Germany's European policy. Outlined by Foreign Minister Kinkel for the 1990s, they resemble those of previous decades, but the radically changed context has sharpened the focus, made intentions more transparent, and reordered priorities. Germany's goals are both functional (economic, political, cultural/societal) and geographic (regional and international).[4] All of Germany's goals

in the decade before unification contained elements of realism and responsibility, of individualistic national interest, and of collective European interest. The analysis presented here, then, combines the national-preference perspective of neorealism with the ideals approach of neofunctionalism.[5]

Economic goals

Historically, Germany's economic goals with respect to the EC related to its pursuit of economic liberalism abroad and growth, a social market economy, and stability at home. As Bulmer and Paterson have carefully demonstrated, by the beginning of the 1980s, Germany had established a pattern of balancing contradictory pragmatic needs resulting from different domestic political, economic, and bureaucratic pressures.[6]

3. "Policy Statement by Helmut Kohl, Federal Chancellor, to the Bundestag," 18 Mar. 1987, reprinted in Federal Republic of Germany, Press and Information Office of the Federal Government, *European Political Co-operation* (Bonn: Press and Information Office, 1988), p. 378.

4. For an overview, see Lily Gardner Feldman, "1992 and the Federal Republic's European Identity: Implications for Relations with the United States," in *German-American Relations Yearbook 1*, ed. James A. Cooney, Wolfgang-Uwe Friedrich, and Gerald R. Kleinfeld (Frankfurt/Main: Campus Verlag, 1989). For

detailed treatments of Germany and the EC, see Roger Morgan, "The Federal Republic of Germany," in *Building Europe: Britain's Partners in the EEC*, ed. Carol Twitchett and Kenneth Twitchett (London: Europa, 1981); Werner J. Feld, *West Germany and the European Community: Changing Interests and Competing Policy Objectives* (New York: Praeger, 1981); Bernhard May, *Kosten und Nutzen der EG-Mitgliedschaft* (Bonn: Europa Union Verlag, 1982); Rudolf Hrbek and Wolfgang Wessels, eds., *EG-Mitgliedschaft: Ein vitales Interesse der Bundesrepublik Deutschland?* (Bonn: Europa Union Verlag, 1984).

5. See Andrew Moravcsik, "Negotiating the Single European Act: National Interests and Conventional Statecraft in the European Community," *International Organization*, 45(1) (Winter 1991); Wolfgang Wessels, "Staat und (westeuropäische) Integration: Die Fusionsthese," in *Die Integration Europas*, ed. Michael Kreile (Opladen: Westdeutscher Verlag, 1992).

6. Bulmer and Paterson, *Federal Republic*, chap. 2.

As an export-dependent trading state—one-third of gross domestic product derived from exports by the early 1980s, up from one-fifth in the early 1970s[7]—the German government (specifically the Ministry of Economics) vigorously espoused an open global economy yet urged renewal of the trade-regulating Multi-Fiber Agreement in the early 1980s. Similarly, while staunchly supporting completion of the internal market,[8] it clung to certain nontariff barriers such as standards. Germany opposed industrial policy, except in the case of steel. Most significantly, the Ministry of Agriculture—often to the consternation of the Ministry of Economics, the Finance Ministry, and the Foreign Ministry—promoted protectionist interests in the Common Agricultural Policy, notably during the mid-1980s in the cases of dairy quotas, Monetary Compensation Amounts, and cereal prices.[9]

The market element of Germany's social market concept was clearly met in the decade before 1988 through the EC. Markovits and Reich have noted that "Germany proved to be the primary beneficiary from the free trade arrangements as measured by increased exports in the 1970s and 1980s," with the growth amounting to some 15 percent.[10] The EC continued to be Germany's main market, a trend established already in the 1960s. By 1981, 45.7 percent of Germany's exports were destined for the EC and 47.4 percent of Germany's imports derived from the EC.[11] By 1985, exports from Germany to the EC had grown to 15 percent of gross domestic product, an almost 200 percent increase since 1972, and by 1980 Germany had come to account for 26.1 percent of intra-EC exports. In the decade through 1989, Germany accumulated a trade balance of $208.4 billion, approximately twice as much as the next highest country, the Netherlands.[12]

The social dimension of the concept was not totally lost in the EC, even though opposition to EC involvement was fierce by Britain. Germany vigorously pursued a "social-protectionist interpretation"[13] of the EC's social dimension after its tentative inception in the form of Articles 118A and 118B of the 1986 Single European Act (SEA).

The search for social and economic stability, grounded in the German dread of inflation, was further manifested in Chancellor Helmut Schmidt's championing, together with Valéry Giscard d'Estaing, of the EMS in the

7. Andrei S. Markovits and Simon Reich, "Deutschlands neues Gesicht: Über deutsche Hegemonie in Europa," *Leviathan*, 1/1992, p. 32 (Mar. 1992).

8. See, for example, the speech of Chancellor Kohl, "The European Market 1992—Implications for European-American Relations," *Statements and Speeches* (German Information Center, New York), 16 Nov. 1988.

9. See Bulmer and Paterson, *Federal Republic*, chap. 3.

10. Markovits and Reich, "Deutschlands neues Gesicht," p. 33.

11. Bulmer and Paterson, *Federal Republic*, p. 12.

12. David Cameron, "The 1992 Initiative: Causes and Consequences," in *Europolitics: Institutions and Policymaking in the "New" European Community*, ed. Alberta M. Sbragia (Washington, DC: Brookings Institution, 1992), tab. 2-11, p. 69.

13. Peter Lange, "The Politics of the Social Dimension," in *Europolitics*, ed. Sbragia, p. 243.

late 1970s. As an intermediate union of exchange rates, the EMS reflected both the divisions within the German bureaucracy about whether monetary union should be a cause or a consequence of integration and the German Chancellor's combination of deep "European proclivities" with a "sense of realism,"[14] a balanced view replayed in Germany's position on monetary matters during the negotiation of the SEA.[15]

The widespread German commitment to Europe, coupled with recognition of the market benefits that EC membership afforded Germans, accounted for Germany's continuing willingness during the 1980s to be the paymaster of the EC, but increasingly within well-specified limits.[16] Between 1979 and 1989, Germany contributed between 26.2 and 30.7 percent of the EC's budget, with most years showing contributions over 28.0 percent. In the same period, Germany received between 14.0 and 21.4 percent of the EC's structural funds, with most years revealing payments under 17.0 percent.[17] The discrepancy between contributions and benefits of member states was a major

issue for the United Kingdom, culminating in the February 1988 budget deadlock that the German presidency of the Council resolved, leading, in part, to Commission President Jacques Delors's July 1988 statement: "We have managed to do more in six months than in ten years."[18]

Germany's idealistic attachment to the EC as a new form of international governance and cooperation had shaped its policies from the beginning of the European Coal and Steel Community, but now in the 1980s that goal became more open. It was expressed in Germany's definition of the EC's political purpose both internally and in the international arena.

Political goals

In a 1979 interview with *The Economist*, Chancellor Schmidt rejected the common dual conception of Germany as economic giant and political dwarf.[19] Germany's economic attributes amounted to neither the hegemony nor the hubris of a giant, but, as already suggested, it clearly outranked its fellow members; and the political reticence of dwarfdom was still real but was beginning to yield, as in other areas of German foreign policy, to greater self-assertion. As in the economic and monetary sphere, it moved now beyond proof that it could

14. Wolfram F. Hanrieder, *Germany, America, Europe: Forty Years of German Foreign Policy* (New Haven, CT: Yale University Press, 1989), pp. 302-3.

15. See Moravcsik, "Negotiating the Single Act," p. 29.

16. One might argue that trade benefits far outweigh Germany's contribution to the EC budget, but the lack of correspondence between initial beneficiary (the private sector) and ultimate donor (the government) renders the calculation more complicated.

17. *Official Journal of the European Communities*, Court of Auditors, 31 Dec. 1982, pp. 166-67; ibid., 15 Dec. 1987, pp. 176-77; ibid., 13 Dec. 1991, p. 66; ibid., 15 Dec. 1992, p. 46.

18. Statement to the European Parliament, 6 July 1988, in *Official Journal of the European Communities*, Debates of the European Parliament, 1988-89 session, no. 2-367, p. 138.

19. For the text of Schmidt's interview, see Wolfram Hanrieder, ed., *Helmut Schmidt: Perspectives on Politics* (Boulder, CO: Westview Press, 1982), p. 209. The original characterization came from Willy Brandt.

play by the rules to a leadership role, shaping both the content and the framework of European Political Co-operation (EPC), the most visible demonstration that the EC was more than a common market and customs union. The 1981 Genscher-Colombo initiative, the 1983 Stuttgart Solemn Declaration on European Union, and the 1985 Kohl-Mitterrand Milan pro-posals all contributed to the conclu-sion of the SEA that set the EC's agenda for the 1990s by reiterating the commitment to political union and crafting institutional, structural, and substantive changes to achieve the completion of the internal market and progress toward "solidarity," "consistency," and "one voice" in for-eign policy.

The benefits of the SEA were not undisputed in Germany, especially by the *Länder*, which feared erosion of their authority in the SEA's provis-ions on the environment and the in-ternal market. Their assent to the SEA was exchanged for an increase in and formalization of the informa-tion exchange procedures instituted in 1979.[20] The SEA's foreign policy provisions were welcomed at home, notably by the SPD, which, in its consistent calls for a "self-assertive" Europe, shared the government's preference for a more pronounced in-ternational profile for economic and technological reasons—vis-à-vis Japan and the United States—and

for peace and stability reasons, par-ticularly in the Third World.[21]

The SEA's commitment to coordi-nating the political and economic as-pects of security, to preserving inter-national peace, and to developing ties with other regional groupings were particularly important for Germany and Foreign Minister Genscher as a confirmation of Germany's political and moral rehabilitation in Western Europe, as an opportunity for Ger-many to contribute internationally without arousing fear of German uni-lateralism, and as a cloak behind which to hide when there were chal-lenges to its foreign policy, for exam-ple, by Israel.

The EC's incipient penchant for projecting itself internationally as a model for regional integration and conflict resolution was reflected in German leaders' references to the "peace initiatives," "peace commu-nity," and "role model" of the EC.[22] Germany's active pursuit of EPC and political union reflected the dual goals of national political and eco-nomic interests, satisfied through an internally coherent and externally assertive EC, and an idealistic con-viction, based on German history, that the EC represented an antidote to excessive nationalism.[23]

---

20. On the history of the relationship be-tween the *Länder* and the EC, see Rudolf Hrbek and Uwe Thaysen, eds., *Die Deutschen Länder und die Europäischen Gemeinschaften* (Baden-Baden: Nomos Verlagsgesellschaft, 1986).

21. Gardner Feldman, "1992 and the Fed-eral Republic's European Identity," pp. 111-12, n. 39.

22. Press and Information Office, *Euro-pean Political Co-operation*, pp. 343-44, 349; Werner Ungerer, "EC Progress under the Ger-man Presidency," *Aussenpolitik*, 39(4) (1988).

23. Morgan, "Federal Republic of Ger-many," pp. 61, 65-66; Rudolf Hrbek and Wolf-gang Wessels, "Nationale Interessen der Bun-desrepublik und der Integrationsprozess," in *EG-Mitgliedschaft*, ed. Hrbek and Wessels.

*Cultural and
    societal goals*

The idea of the EC as an international actor presupposed a separate European identity that could differentiate the Community from other actors in the international system. In their calls for "European patriotism," Chancellor Kohl and Foreign Minister Genscher amplified the goal of the 1983 Solemn Declaration on European Union to coordinate cultural activities in third countries and to develop the sense of a common cultural heritage among the member states.[24]

The EC was viewed by both officials and scholars as a way for Germans to retain their own cultural identity—as *Kulturnation* or *Staatsnation* or both—and to develop loyalties that went beyond the nation-state.[25] Broad acceptance of the EC could be detected also in the German public, although support for what was seen as financial altruism began to decline in the early 1980s, manifesting what was visible at the governmental level as a balance of realism and responsibility. In the decade before 1989, public support for unification (combining "very much" and "to some extent") ranged between 70 and 80 percent with some stark variations between years and within.[26] A large majority, compared to those against the EC, saw membership as a "good thing"; this majority was between 49 and 66 percent, again with some wide fluctuations.

The general public's support was also evident in the private sector's attachment to the EC. Umbrella organizations, such as the Federation of German Industry and the Confederation of German Employers' Associations, as well as specific sectors of the economy and prominent firms largely endorsed the government's advocacy of the EC. At times they went beyond endorsement to initiative, as, for example, on the Single Market Program.[27] The Federation of German Trade Unions was also supportive of the EC, although, as with business, there was disagreement between specific unions regarding the benefits from completion of the internal market.[28]

Whether in economic, historical, or spiritual terms, increasingly during the 1980s, the sense of cultural identity also embraced the eastern half of Europe, including the German Democratic Republic, to which

---

24. Press and Information Office, *European Political Co-operation*, pp. 349, 378.

25. Werner Weidenfeld, ed., *Die Identität der Deutschen* (Bonn: Schriftenreihe der Bundeszentrale für politische Bildung, 1983); Günter Gaus, *Wo Deutschland liegt: Eine Ortsbestimmung* (Hamburg: Hoffmann & Campe, 1983); Eberhard Schulz, *Die deutsche Nation in Europa* (Bonn: Europa Union Verlag, 1982); Eberhard Schulz, "Unfinished Business: The German National Question and the Future of Europe," *International Affairs*, 60(3) (1984); Richard von Weizsäcker, *Die deutsche Geschichte geht weiter* (Berlin: Siedler, 1983).

26. See *Eurobarometer: Public Opinion in the European Community*, no. 28, tabs. B4 and B5, pp. B40, B55-56 (Dec. 1987); ibid., no. 29, tab. A1, p. A5 (June 1988); Bulmer and Paterson, *Federal Republic*, chap. 5.

27. See Bulmer and Paterson, *Federal Republic*, chap. 4; Maria L. Green, "The Politics of Big Business in the Single Market Program" (Paper delivered at the Third Biennial International Conference of the European Community Studies Association, Washington, DC, May 1993), p. 34.

28. Andrei S. Markovits and Alexander Otto, "German Labor and Europe '92," *Comparative Politics*, 24(2) (Jan. 1992).

Bonn's EC policy had always been addressed.

Regional goals

The major parties differed on the relationship between *Westpolitik* and *Ostpolitik*, but all saw an inextricable link. By the beginning of the 1980s, Adenauer's "policy of strength," which assumed that the EC's magnetic attraction would dissolve communism, had long given way to the policy of "change through rapprochement," implemented first by Chancellor Brandt, who believed that the EC was a catalyst for creating an all-European peace order to ameliorate the human consequences of Europe's division.

Chancellor Schmidt continued the notion of Western Europe's "windows, doors and passageways to the East Europeans," a theme central to the 1988 elaboration by Chancellor Kohl and Foreign Minister Genscher of Gorbachev's concept of the "common European house." As a "cooperative partner" for Eastern Europe, the EC could help retrieve the "common roots of European history and culture." The "sense of wholeness" included all Germans; after all, it was Kohl's chancellorship that revived politically the commitment to national unity.[29]

29. See Helmut Kohl, "Healing the Wounds of the Past to Build a Better Future," *Statements and Speeches* (German Information Center, New York), 25 Oct. 1988; Hans-Dietrich Genscher, "Nicht Schranken sondern offene Türen müssen die neue Ordnung auszeichnen," *Die Zeit*, 28 Oct. 1988; Dorothee Wilms, "Konzept der Deutschlandpolitik im Rahmen der europäischen Einigung," *Bulletin* (Presse- und Informationsamt der Bundesregierung, Bonn), 27 Jan. 1988.

While German leaders disagreed in the 1980s over the interpretation of the EC's realistic opportunities regarding the East—overwhelming communism versus co-opting it—all exhibited a sense of responsibility toward the peoples of Eastern Europe, particularly East Germans. The crafting, during the German Council presidency in 1988, of a joint declaration on normalization of relations between the EC and the Council for Mutual Economic Assistance and the initialing of a trade agreement with Hungary were clear indications of Eastern Europe's priority for Germany and its faith in the EC's "community building capacity."[30]

Germany's all-European perspective on how to achieve national, if not state, unity also accounted for its long-standing commitment to the Conference on Security and Cooperation in Europe (CSCE) as a central focus of EC foreign policy coordination through EPC. It was in the CSCE forum, valued by Kohl and Genscher as a contribution to a "European peace order," that the cleavage in U.S. and European perspectives on the Soviet Union and on the very definition of security became obvious in the 1980s.

International goals

In the 1980s, German leaders still viewed the transatlantic relationship and European integration as two sides of the same coin, as relatively equal elements of *Westpolitik*, but as in the old Atlanticist-Gaullist debate

30. Werner Weidenfeld, "Die Europäische Gemeinschaft und Osteuropa," *Aussenpolitik*, 38(2):142 (1987).

of the early 1960s, potential contradictions were reemerging. At the same time that Kohl and Genscher were insisting on the natural security link between the United States and the EC, fears of decoupling and increased vulnerability provoked by the Intermediate-Range Nuclear Forces Treaty, the Strategic Defense Initiative, and the Discriminate Deterrence Report led them to emphasize in 1987 and 1988 the need for greater coordination of European security interests and the realization of a European pillar both militarily through the Western European Union and in political and economic terms through the provisions of the SEA.[31] In the face of American concerns about a "Fortress Europe," German officials were at pains to stress the internal market's contribution to world trade, but they could hardly ignore the growing threats of U.S.-EC trade wars.

1989-94: UNIFIED GERMANY IN A UNITING EUROPE

The formal process of German unification, of structurally integrating the former German Democratic Republic with the old Federal Republic, lasted less than a year, from Chancellor Kohl's 10-point plan of 28 November 1989 until 3 October 1990. Legal absorption of East Germany into the EC was just as rapid, revealing astounding technical depth, administrative flexibility, and political agil-

ity, despite genuine differences between EC institutions and member states.[32] Yet the longer-term maturation of German unity and digestion by Europe of a larger Germany are by no means as clear-cut five years later, even though the parameters are becoming more fixed.

The context of the relationship between Germany and the EC has now changed completely, and the style of Germany's approach shows signs of alteration. Until 1989, Germany's national unity was connected to its EC focus but was also separate from it. Since spring 1990, with Kohl's February reaffirmation of Europe as "every German's future" and the EC's April 1990 acceptance of unification, the two have become densely interwoven. When Germany was divided, some EC issues had special German dimensions; now that Germany is unified, almost every topic on the EC's agenda is Germany specific. During the Cold War, Germany's perspective on the EC was shaped by its domestic, regional, and international environments, which registered changes periodically but nonetheless had become by the 1980s recognizable, predictable, and comfortable. Now, in the post-Cold War era, change occurs at all levels simultaneously, is kaleidoscopic, and requires creative, nontraditional responses.

In the past, despite the reality of regional systemic constraints, Germany could afford a flexible, mag-

31. See Kohl's speech at the Feb. 1988 Wehrkunde conference in *Statements and Speeches* (German Information Center, New York), 10 Feb. 1988; Genscher's Mar. 1988 speech, reprinted in Press and Information Office, *European Political Co-operation*, p. 382.

32. See Lily Gardner Feldman, "The EC and German Unification," in *The State of the European Community: Policies, Institutions, and Debates in the Transition Years*, ed. Leon Hurwitz and Christian Lequesne (Boulder, CO: Lynne Rienner, 1991).

nanimous, relatively limitless set of policies on the EC. Now, at a time of systemic fluidity, Germany has begun to face real limits in its EC policies financially and politically. Before the earthquake of 1989, Germany could paper over or ignore domestic fissures and inconsistencies in specific areas of policy toward the EC. Now Germany must squarely confront cleavages and contradictions. Divided Germany had managed to either clothe the nakedness of self-interest or, where it was obvious, not suffer suspicion about its intentions. United Germany is forced, for reasons of domestic and EC credibility, to make its objectives more transparent and then to be scrutinized about its ulterior motives.

A new German role and purpose?

During the last five years, two earlier opposing images of Germany's role in the EC have crystallized and vied for superiority: Germany as hegemon, as shown, for example, in its initiatives in the EC with respect to Yugoslavia, the former Soviet Union, and East Central Europe, and Germany as spoiler, as shown, for example, in public, political, and economic opposition to the Maastricht Treaty (also known as the Treaty on European Union) during the ratification debate. On balance, however, while Germany has exhibited elements of both images, since unification Germany has, in the aggregate, continued to play the role of partner. As its weight in the EC clearly has grown, so, too, has its dependence: in terms of the EC's twin function as a mirror

of fundamental commitment by Germany and as a source of relative stability for Germany.[33]

National unity and a reconfigured international system have provoked, on one level, a basic redefinition of realism and responsibility, but they remain balanced in a way that still engages Germany centrally in the EC. In the past, realism meant active pursuit through the EC of German domestic interests; responsibility denoted commitment to the concept and practice of European integration and belief that Germany must be a constrained, nonmilitary power. At least from the government's perspective, the terms have in part reversed. Responsibility to the regional and international system now means activism, including international military involvement, whereas realism with respect to domestic needs suggests restraint, as Foreign Minister Kinkel explained in his review of German foreign policy:

In the third year of German unification, it is becoming urgent that the question as to the international role to be played by united Germany be answered. As a nation of 80 million and a major economic power in central Europe we have a special and, in part, a new responsibility, whether we like the idea or not. We will have to adapt the full range of our foreign policy activity to this fact. However, realism and moderation will be needed. As long as we are not "over the hump" at home, we will not be able to act with full strength abroad.

33. For these two approaches, see Barbara Lippert, Dirk Günther, and Stephen Woolcock, "Die EG und die neuen Bundesländer—eine Erfolgsgeschichte von kurzer Dauer?" *Integration*, 16(1):2-6 (Jan. 1993).

Yet constancy thrives in Germany's "commitment to . . . historical responsibility [through] an unconditional 'yes' to European union." The EC remains the vehicle for achieving equilibrium between realism and responsibility, even as those terms take on new meaning: "Only if we are firmly anchored in Europe can Germany find domestic balance and full capability to act," asserted Kinkel.[34]

France and Germany:
Enduring partnership?

As in the decade prior to 1989, France is a critical part of the equation for Germany in the years after 1989, as Kinkel has noted: "[Our] future lies in a European union that is close to the people and open to the world . . . together with our closest friend and partner, France, we will continue to be the driving force for European unification."[35] Despite the inauspicious outset of Kohl's surprise November 1989 plan and Mitterrand's initial hesitation and vexation, France, after the German Democratic Republic's first free election in March 1990, adopted a realistic stance that assumed the inevitability of unification, whose long-term impact could be molded through the EC's deepening.

The monumental task of making EC integration strong enough to embrace German unification and to vivify all-European unity depends on agreement (as in the past, not harmony), coordination, and initiative by the Franco-German dyad. Despite

differences over the strength of the European Parliament, the independence of the economic and monetary union's central bank, and the speed and scope of East European countries' new relationship with the EC, at critical junctures since 1989 France and Germany have demonstrated unequivocally the capacity for compromise and conviction necessary to propel the EC. The major examples were the 1990 initiatives on political union, the 1991 plans on foreign and security policy, the creation of the Franco-German corps, the joint attempt to support the Exchange Rate Mechanism after the September 1992 currency crisis, and the combined effort after the close French referendum on the Maastricht Treaty to make the process of integration more democratic, responsive, and transparent.[36]

Economic goals

Domestic interests are hardly new for Germany's EC policy, but they are more pronounced, immediate, and unavoidable. Unification's financial implications are gargantuan: net transfers to eastern Germany amounted to DM50 billion in 1990, DM120 billion in 1991, and DM170 billion in 1992, with future annual transfers estimated at approximately $100 billion. By 1993, many of the structural, economic, social, and environmental dif-

34. Kinkel, "Verantwortung."
35. Ibid.

36. See Christian Deubner, "The Role of the French-German Couple in European Integration in the 1990s: Disruption or Continuity?" (Paper delivered at the Third Biennial International Conference of the European Community Studies Association, Washington, DC, May 1993).

ficulties foreshadowed in the European Parliament's 1990 assessments of unification had become real, and Germany had joined the ranks of recession-ridden countries.[37] Stability, growth, a social-market orientation, and trade liberalization remain the driving principles for Germany, but some of the mechanisms for their realization have changed.

Germany's new economic environment has noticeably affected its EC policies in four areas: the budget, economic and monetary union, agriculture, and the internal market. Past German concerns about the EC budget have become anxieties, as demonstrated in Germany's opposition to the Delors II package to finance the Maastricht goals. The discrepancy between contributions and payments still exists: Germany contributed 25.1 percent of the total budget in 1989 and received 12.8 percent; in 1990, the figures were 25.0 percent and 12.9 percent. In addition, there is no certainty about the actual impact of EC resource transfers to eastern Germany—a minuscule 1 percent of German transfers—or of the exceptions from the *acquis communautaire* contained in the three-stage integration of the eastern German economy into the EC.[38] The reality that the federal budget will increase by less than 3 percent has rendered the EC budget's proposed 10 percent annual increase practically untenable, and the suggestion of a ECU6 billion increase in Germany's contribution between 1992 and 1997 politically impossible.[39]

In budgetary as well as economic and social terms, the agricultural sector in eastern Germany stands out as a particular challenge, reaffirming agriculture's prominence in Germany's EC preferences. Unification increased Germany's population by 27 percent and its land mass by 44 percent, but its agricultural population by 70 percent and its utilized agricultural land by 51 percent.[40] The old opposition to price cuts in the Common Agricultural Policy has become more vigorous; an example is the 1991 negotiations on this policy.

Another traditional German trait —economic and financial stability and discipline—has reasserted itself since 1989, particularly in official responses to Maastricht's plans for economic and monetary union and in the insistence on high interest rates by the Bundesbank that helped precipitate the September 1992 Exchange Rate Mechanism crisis. In both cases, long-established concerns and behavior had broader effects than in the past because of the changed context and higher stakes. The Finance Ministry, the Bundesbank, and some parts of the Economics Ministry still share concerns about the overall relationship between economic and monetary union, the independence of

37. See Gardner Feldman, "EC and German Unification," pp. 319-21.

38. For the EC's impact on eastern Germany, see Lippert, Günther, and Woolcock, "Die EG und die neuen Bundesländer."

39. See Anita Wolf, "Bundesrepublik Deutschland," in *Jahrbuch der Europäischen Integration 1991/92* (Bonn: Europa Union Verlag, 1992), p. 315.

40. See Stefan Tangermann and David Kelch, "Agricultural Policymaking in Germany: Implications for the German Position in Multilateral Trade Negotiations," *Working Paper*, no. 91-8 (Washington, DC: International Agricultural Trade Research Consortium, 1991).

the central bank, and the wisdom of a common currency.[41]

At Maastricht and since, Kohl and Genscher have sought to reduce some of the consternation by insisting, unsuccessfully, on a coupling of economic and monetary union and political union. Kinkel has renewed the linkage and, like the Chancellor and his predecessor in the Foreign Ministry, has underscored the other connection between trade benefits and dependencies, economic and monetary union, and the Single Market Program.[42]

Political union retained its old promise of enhancing the EC's capacity to act coherently in the international economy and thereby to improve Germany's position in world markets, but its political significance was more than reconfirmed with unification.

Political goals

German unification has required Germany to demonstrate anew its commitment to universal values, democratic principles, and international rules. What West Germany had spent forty years proving via the EC and other Western and international institutions now has to be repeated in short order for a larger Germany. For other member states, German unification has accelerated the process of European political union; for Germany, it has become an

absolute priority, as Chancellor Kohl has clearly recognized.[43]

Germany's push at Maastricht for a federal Europe, for increased supranationalism through a strengthened Parliament and Commission, and for common foreign and security policy reflected Germany's undented capacity to blend self-interest with dedication to a larger vision. The fact that it could accomplish only some of its objectives reinforces the notion of Germany as a partner that is required and able to compromise.[44]

Political union represents at once the enshrinement of Germany's postwar ideal of muted national power and the opportunity nonetheless to exert international influence, as the German domestic debate over peacekeeping, peacemaking, and Germany's international role made clear. EC deliberations over both the Persian Gulf war and the Yugoslav conflict indicated that Germany would define the parameters of the Common Foreign and Security Policy through its political and/or constitutional reluctance to use military force, a sentiment embedded also in eastern Germany. But just as much as Yugoslavia showed German leadership in military inaction, it also revealed Germany's setting the tone for political action through its effective persuasion or arm-twisting in mid-December 1991, which resulted in Slovenia and Croatia being granted recogni-

41. See W. R. Smyser, "The Bundesbank and Europe" (Paper delivered at the Third Biennial International Conference of the European Community Studies Association, Washington, DC, May 1993).

42. Kinkel, "Verantwortung."

43. See Helmut Kohl's speech to the Christian Democratic Union party convention, Düsseldorf, 25-27 Oct. 1992.

44. For Kohl's analysis of Maastricht's achievements and weaknesses, see his speech of 3 Apr. 1992 to the Bertelsmann-Forum in *Bulletin* (Presse- und Informationsamt der Bundesregierung, Bonn), 8 Apr. 1992.

tion.[45] Germany had played a leadership role before 1989—for example, in establishing the 1980 Venice Initiative's limit on the Palestine Liberation Organization's inclusion in a Middle East peace process—and it also had been prone to unilateralism—for example, in the continuation of its preferential relationship to Israel in the 1980s when the EC was trying to develop a common Middle East policy—but without fanfare. Now the style involved open threats and triumphalism.

Domestic pressure with respect to European union has not been confined to the foreign policy arena. In the Maastricht process, the German emphasis on federalism, subsidiarity, and a Committee of the Regions partially derived from the energetic work of the *Länder*. While Maastricht enhanced the role of the *Länder* in one direction, the treaty's expansion of competences to the EC level also challenged their domestic position.

As a quid pro quo for the *Länder*'s acceptance of the Maastricht Treaty, therefore, Germany has expanded and institutionalized their involvement in EC policy, already won at the time of the SEA, through revision of the Basic Law's Article 23 that had become obsolete with unification. The powers of the Bundesrat and Bundestag were also increased. The federal government will need the consent of the Bundesrat—the Parliament's upper chamber, representing *Länder* interests—for further

transfers of sovereignty. The actual creation of European union will require the support of a two-thirds majority of the Bundestag and Bundesrat. In areas of *Länder* legislative jurisdiction that come before the EC, and even in areas where they are affected administratively, the *Länder* and the Bundesrat are to participate in the EC decision-making process. Future transfers of *Länder* competence to the EC will occur only with their approval.[46] The *Länder* have shown their further commitment to the issue by creating a conference of the *Länder* ministers responsible for Europe.

Policymakers and analysts predict that Germany's negotiating style in Brussels will change substantially because of the increased role of the *Länder*, probably in the direction of fragmentation with uncertain consequences for German influence. One of the positive functions the *Länder* play is as a conduit for the articula-

45. James B. Steinberg, *The Role of European Institutions in Security after the Cold War: Some Lessons for Yugoslavia*, N-3445-FF, A RAND Note (Santa Monica, CA: RAND, 1992).

46. For the text of the July 1992 cabinet proposal, see *Frankfurter Allgemeine Zeitung*, 22 July 1992. For the ultimate formula hammered out between the Bundestag, Bundesrat, *Länder*, and federal government, see "Kontroverse um den neuen Europa-Artikel im Grundgesetz," ibid., 11 Nov. 1992; "Der Bundestag soll Anfang Dezember über Maastricht entscheiden," ibid., 14 Nov. 1992; "Verständigung in Bonn über die Konsequenzen von Maastricht," ibid., 21 Nov. 1992. For details of *Länder* activities and positions, see Franz H. U. Borkenhagen and Rainer Godry, "Die deutschen Länder in einem neuen Europa," *Deutschland Archiv*, no. 25 (1992); Franz H. U. Borkenhagen, "Vom kooperativen Föderalismus zum 'Europa der Regionen,'" *Aus Politik und Zeitgeschichte*, B42/92, 9 Oct. 1992. See also Florian Gerster, "Die Europaministerkonferenz der deutschen Länder: Aufgaben-Themen-Selbstverständnis," *Integration*, 16(2) (Apr. 1993).

tion of the public's concern that their interests and regional identities not be lost in the process of integration.

Cultural and
societal goals

Public opinion had already shown some signs of flagging interest in the EC before 1989, but during the negotiation and ratification of Maastricht, growing anxiety and outright opposition came to a head, particularly in the 18 challenges to the Maastricht Treaty before the German Constitutional Court.[47]

A late-1992 major survey on German post-Cold War opinions has revealed an old pattern of conviction combined with reservations. European unification was viewed as the most important foreign policy issue. When asked how they would vote in a theoretical referendum on the Maastricht Treaty, 47 percent responded that they would vote "yes," with 29 percent opposed and some 23 percent undecided. Germans also have reservations about abandoning the deutsche mark; support for a common currency slipped from 48 to 43 percent in 1991.[48]

The Maastricht Treaty ratification demonstrated how central the deutsche mark was to German identity and culture on the part of both public opinion and experts; an example is the manifesto of sixty leading economists against Maastricht. Yet it reconfirmed support for the idea of Europe from the public and specialists,

whether economic—the response of the Dresdner Bank, the Commerzbank, and the Deutsche Bank—or political, such as the plea for Maastricht on the part of scholars.[49] German unification and European integration did not create opposition to the EC; they clarified it, at the same time that both processes evoked reaffirmation of support. Long-held positions have, then, hardened into advocacy of a "minimum community," on the one hand, and support for a maximum or federalist option, on the other.[50]

German proponents of the Maastricht Treaty refer to its promotion of coexisting identities at the regional, national and European levels, its capacity as a mosaic rather than a melting pot. But German officials also believe that they must give expression to Germany's national cultural heritage. Some commentators interpreted Kohl's December 1991 call for German to be the third EC working language as a sign of Germany's search for cultural dominance, but it should be seen more as an example of Germany's old cost-benefit calculation, made more urgent by the heightened public awareness of the EC's implications for daily life. German officials, therefore, emphasize fairness, accessibility, and rationality arguments in light of the

47. See Jürgen Wahl, "Guter Rat statt Stolperdraht," *Rheinischer Merkur*, 28 May 1993.

48. See Ronald D. Asmus, "Germany's Geopolitical Maturation," *RAND Issue Paper* (Santa Monica, CA: RAND, 1993).

49. See Rudolf Hrbek, "Kontroverse und Manifeste zum Vertrag von Maastricht: Zur Einführung," *Integration*, 15(4) (Nov. 1992).

50. See Wernhard Möschel, "Europäische Union-Modell Maastricht? Plädoyer für eine europäische Minimalgesellschaft" (Paper presented to the law faculty, University of Zurich, 17 Dec. 1992); Research Group on European Affairs, University of Mainz, "The Future of Europe: Alternatives-Strategies-Options" (Documents presented to the International Bertelsmann Forum, Petersberg, 3-5 Apr. 1992).

language's statistical importance, geographical scope, and bridging role to the north and the east, and the EC's claim to be a community for all of the people.[51]

The language question is both a practical matter affecting economic opportunity and part of a larger debate about German identity and the German role in Europe that surfaced in the 1980s but has climaxed with unification, the disintegration of the Soviet bloc, and initiatives toward European union. In their magnitude and complexity, immigration and asylum are new challenges whose resolution Germany has sought at a European level. Of those seeking asylum in the EC, 70 percent apply to Germany, with 440,000 applicants to Germany in 1992, five times the 1988 number. Germany has taken in 230,000 refugees from Yugoslavia, while France admitted only 2000 and the United Kingdom, 1300. At Maastricht, Germany's efforts for common policy in justice and home affairs fell short, except for commitment to joint action on visas and the creation of Europol, but the EC is at least committed to intergovernmental cooperation in these domains. The debate over revision of Germany's asylum law has underscored the nexus between national and EC levels.

The issue of congruence between domestic and EC rules is further confronted by Maastricht's provisions for Community citizens' participation in municipal elections. Turkish residents of Germany, including those born in the country, have no such rights. Regional upheaval is forcing Germany, and the EC as a whole, to define both the universal and the particular elements of cultural identity and serves as a test of whether the commitment to multiculturalism is serious.

Judging by the ferocity of the debate and the ugliness of attacks against foreigners and other minorities, the identity aspects of immigration will absorb Germans for a long time. In the short and medium term, Germany is addressing certain economic aspects of immigration through its initiatives in the EC on enlargement and the short-term, structural relationship to Eastern Europe.

Regional goals

Before 1989, Germany's *Ostpolitik* aimed ultimately at effecting change in the Soviet bloc, but it always involved an element of building stability—the question, politically, was how much—to legitimize the change. With fundamental upheaval a reality, after 1989 the priorities switched, for now stability is uppermost and change must be managed and incremental. For Germany, European integration and progress in Eastern Europe are locked in a symbiosis of stability: the clarifying effect of political union will provide the "anchor of stability" to deal with the immediate "risks and uncertainties" of East European countries and to stimulate the long-term political and economic stabilization that will permit their entry into the EC. Germany, unlike some of its friends, regards deepening (fur-

51. See Michael Burkert, "Deutsch als Amts- und Arbeitssprache in der Europäischen Gemeinschaft," in *Deutsch als Verkehrssprache in Europa*, ed. Joachim Born and Gerhard Stickel (Berlin: Walter de Gruyter, 1993).

ther integration) and widening (extending membership) as completely compatible. It was a fervent advocate of the Europe Agreements, has pushed for membership of certain Eastern European countries at the earliest possible time, and has called for the EC's speedy articulation of coherent and transparent conditions for entry.[52]

Germany has a special interest in Eastern Europe, but also a special advantage, not least in the close familiarity of eastern Germans with the region. Kinkel has been quick to point out that

in achieving political unification we derived a maximum gain from the end of the East-West conflict. On the basis of our central location, our size and our traditional relations with central and eastern Europe, we are predestined to derive the primary advantage from the fact that these countries have returned to Europe.

But he readily noted it could become a burden, for "the other side of the coin is that we are exposed, as no other Western country is, to the enormous problems confronting the young reforming countries from the Oder to Vladivostok."[53]

Even though the context has changed, the EC still serves a triple function for Germany with respect to East Central Europe: it multilateralizes the political and economic cost

of influence (there is a decline in German public support for speedy EC membership), spreads the burden and responsibility for failure, and reduces the potential for unilateralism.

For the same reasons, Germany has developed its relationship to the new independent states in an EC context, pushing for partnership and cooperation agreements that could lead to the former Soviet Union's inclusion in the European Economic Area but not EC membership. In both regions, Germany's contributions in humanitarian aid and export credits have clearly outstripped those of other member states, and it is developing treaty-based bilateral relationships with a range of countries of the former Soviet bloc. Nonetheless, with respect to long-term structural political and economic connections, it prefers the EC framework. It recognizes, however, that such a vast task will require broader international cooperation, leading to a partial resolution of the old tensions between the transatlantic and European dimensions of German foreign policy.

International goals

The potential for U.S.-EC differences has been heightened with the loss of a clearly defined enemy and by confusion as to international role and purpose. Divergence has been obvious in the negotiations involving the General Agreement on Tariffs and Trade, particularly over agriculture, and in the development of a new European security system, particularly over the nature and mix of organizational elements—the North Atlantic Treaty Organization (NATO), the

52. See Helmut Kohl's Bertelsmann Forum speech, "Zielvorstellungen und Chancen für die Zukunft Europas," *Bulletin* (Press- und Informationsamt der Bundesregierung, Bonn), 8 Apr. 1992. See also Pierre-Henri Laurent, "Widening Europe: The Dilemmas of Community Success," this issue of *The Annals* of the American Academy of Political and Social Science.

53. Kinkel, "Verantwortung."

Western European Union, the CSCE, the Common Foreign and Security Policy.

As in the past, in agriculture and in security, Germany's special relationship to the United States sometimes conflicts with its special relationship to France. At one level, Germany already chose France in the 1980s, through its active commitment to European integration across the board, including defense; but it never relinquished its attachment to the United States. Now it seems to have devised a way of recoupling its European and transatlantic identities.

More than any other EC members, it has been Germans, in the public and the private spheres, who have identified the need and the instruments for a U.S.-EC international partnership to act jointly or divide the labor in responding to all manner of global and regional challenges. The prerequisite is a revived transatlantic relationship that comes in a number of variants: a "close and confidence-based partnership" (Klaus Kinkel); a "strengthened and expanded alliance" (Helmut Kohl); a NATO-plus "partnership of responsibility" (Hans-Dietrich Genscher); a treaty-based U.S.-EC "internal market" of economic, political, scientific, cultural, and military cooperation (Hans Peter Stihl); and "transatlantic structures" (Edzard Reuter).[54]

54. See Kinkel, "Veratwortung"; Helmut Kohl, "Wir gewinnen mit Europa" (Speech to the Christian Democratic Union party convention, Düsseldorf, Oct. 1992); Hans-Dietrich Genscher, "Der Atlantik darf jetzt nicht breiter werden," *Welt am Sonntag*, 7 Feb. 1993; Hans Peter Stihl, president of the German Conference of Chambers of Industry and Commerce, "Ansprache anläßlich des Neujahrsempfangs

While necessary and catalytic, the new transatlantic international partnership is not sufficient, because of both the magnitude of the burden and the danger of exclusion. From a German perspective, it must be expanded to other members of the international system, especially Japan. The sea change of 1989 has provoked Germans to envision a new fusion of realism (managed competition) and responsibility (inclusive cooperation) internationally.

CONCLUSION AND PERSPECTIVE

German unification is forcing Germany to define openly its national identity at home and abroad. If Germany genuinely integrates its old minorities and its new and seriously engages in the unfolding international system, then the complexion of national inevitably will be different from the past because of altered circumstances. Yet, for Germany, the process and the practice of defining national interest have been well established since 1949, and much of it has occurred within or through the EC. In this sense, in the confines of the EC, Germany has acted as a normal power, that is, with the same rights and obligations as the other members. The burden of its historical perpetrations, however, has endowed it with a special responsibility for taming—not eliminating—power through commitment to the concept of community. Judging the new Germany's behavior in the past five years against

der American Chamber of Commerce in Germany" (Stuttgart, 27 Jan. 1983); Edzard Reuter, "Alle müssen an einem Strang ziehen," *Die Zeit*, 22 Jan. 1993.

the balanced pattern established before 1989, one would have to conclude that it has retained its basic approach to the EC while adjusting both content and style to the altered context.

At the end of the twentieth century, the German question probably will not be whether it possesses overabundant power in the EC but, rather, whether it can replicate at home and in the larger Europe the sense of community through diversity it has helped build in the EC.

Germany continues to be a partner in the EC and likely will remain so in the future. However, the nature of its partnership—magnanimous or mawkish, shrill or silent—will depend on domestic, EC, regional, and international developments: the rejuvenation of the political process at both the federal and *Länder* levels in terms of public engagement and active leadership, including opportunities for eastern German influence; the length and depth of economic recovery; the fate of democratization in Eastern Europe and the new independent states; the denouement of the Yugoslav conflict; and the likelihood and quality of U.S. international leadership. Above all, Germany's perspective will be shaped by the EC's self-definition, which should be clarified in the preparations for the 1996 intergovernmental conference. Germans bought into an idea when they joined the EC; the idea is still valid, but it must be resold with conviction.

ANNALS, *AAPSS*, **531**, January 1994

Great Britain and
the European Community

By STEPHEN GEORGE

ABSTRACT: Adaptation by the British governmental elite to membership in the European Community has been slow and has been hampered by domestic political constraints. This article examines the problems of adaptation under the Thatcher and Major governments. The political sovereignty dimension, the U.K. budget contribution, British public opinion, and EC farm policy were central issues that London was to bring to the front burner of Community activity. The overriding problem of Maastricht in recent years has divided both the populace and the elites.

Stephen George is reader in politics at the University of Sheffield, England. His publications include Politics and Policy in the European Community *(2d edition, 1991);* An Awkward Partner: Britain in the European Community *(1990);* Britain and European Integration since 1945 *(1991);* The United Kingdom and EC Membership Evaluated *(edited with Simon Bulmer and Andrew Scott, 1992); and* Britain and the European Community: The Politics of Semi-Detachment *(editor, 1992).*

B RITAIN'S late entry to the European Community (EC), in 1973, meant it joined an organization that had already developed its own internal culture and methods of working. In particular, a close alliance between France and Germany had emerged as the key political relationship in the EC. It was partly for fear of domination by this alliance that the smaller member states supported British entry throughout the 1960s. But it was clear that if Britain were to be an effective political actor in the EC, it would have to work in alliance with other member states, and probably with one or the other of the two dominant states on most issues.

It was not easy, though, for Britain to form alliances with the original members. First, the common agricultural policy and the common budgetary arrangements that had been concluded before British entry worked against Britain's interests, but they were supported by all the original six members. Second, British governments tended to see the EC as an economic enterprise, a common market, whereas for the original six there was always a political dimension to the project. Linked to this was a British reluctance to surrender sovereignty to central institutions.[1] Third, partly because of the restrictive official view of the nature of the EC, there was no attempt to sell the idea of European integration to the British public: membership was pre-

sented in pragmatic terms as an economic necessity.

All of the foregoing factors need to be borne in mind in order to understand the relationship between Britain and the rest of the EC under the Thatcher and Major governments. From 1979 to 1984, the very real problem of Britain's excessive contributions to the Community budget dominated, and soured, the relationship. When that was resolved, in 1984, the new start became bogged down in a difference of perspective on whether what was needed went beyond a purely economic program and on how much sovereignty should be surrendered.

Throughout the period of Margaret Thatcher's premiership, there was no real attempt to form a special relationship with either France or Germany to rival the Franco-German entente. When John Major became Prime Minister, in 1990, he tried to move Britain closer to Germany in particular and to the center of EC affairs, but he was hindered by domestic political constraints that reflected the lack of any positive commitment to the EC on the part of large sections of his own Conservative Party.

THE THATCHER
GOVERNMENTS, 1979-84

In the course of 1978, both the Labour Prime Minister, James Callaghan, and his Foreign Secretary, David Owen, drew attention to the fact that as Britain's transitional period of EC membership drew to a close, it faced a situation in which it would become the largest net contributor to the Community's budget, de-

---

1. France under President de Gaulle shared this reluctance, but, following de Gaulle's political demise in 1969, successive French governments became adept at presenting their case in a way that was *communautaire* and acceptable to their partners, a trick that the British were slow to learn.

spite being only seventh in the economic rank-ordering of member states. Shortly after taking office, the Conservative Chancellor of the Exchequer, Sir Geoffrey Howe, announced that the size of this problem was far greater than the Conservatives had realized while in opposition and that something would have to be done about it as a matter of urgency.

At her first European Council meeting, in Strasbourg in June 1979, Prime Minister Thatcher put Britain's case in a very reasonable way, and the Commission was asked to prepare a report on the problem for the next meeting, in Dublin in November. This report suggested that Britain should get a cash rebate of £350 million, together with increased EC expenditure in Britain. But Thatcher rejected these proposals and demanded a £1 billion rebate, a figure from which she was not subsequently to shift. Her attitude precipitated a long argument, during which both sides dug themselves into entrenched positions.

During the early 1980s, while the budgetary dispute dominated the agenda of the Community, there was growing concern about the inability of Europe to recover from the effects of the 1979 rise in the price of oil. Japan and the United States recovered quickly, but Europe was left facing high levels of unemployment and low levels of industrial investment. In this context, schemes began to be floated to revive European integration as a way of tackling the problems.

In 1981, the German and Italian Foreign Ministers, Hans-Dietrich Genscher and Emilio Colombo, produced a Genscher-Colombo Plan,[2] and in February 1984, the European Parliament adopted a draft treaty for a European Union.[3] Both schemes involved not just economic measures but also a strengthening of the central institutions of the EC. As Genscher explained to the European Parliament when presenting his plan,

The economic problems now confronting us go to the roots of our democracies and of the European Community. Nevertheless, we cannot focus our efforts solely on the economic issues. We must, instead, set our sights on the grand design of the political unification of Europe, for it is from that design that we shall draw the strength to act as one and take decisions, on economic matters and others, which will not simply paper over the cracks but provide forward-looking solutions.[4]

The British government could not understand the determination of some of their partners to link practical economic measures, which the British agreed needed to be taken, with strengthening the central institutions. However, the momentum generated by these initiatives put the British in a difficult position: a serious possibility emerged that the six original member states would dominate the discussion on the future of the Community, and so long as the budgetary dispute dragged on, Brit-

2. The text of the German-Italian document may be found in *Bulletin of the European Communities*, point 3.4.1 (Nov. 1981).

3. Juliet Lodge, ed., *European Union: The European Community in Search of a Future* (London: Macmillan, 1986).

4. *Official Journal of the European Communities: Debates of the European Parliament*, 19 Nov. 1981, no. 1-277/216.

ain would remain marginalized, unable to influence those discussions.

Thus both Britain and the rest of the EC had an incentive to get the budgetary issue resolved. They came near in 1983, but a series of unfortunate diplomatic blunders on both sides allowed the question to drag on until the Fontainebleau meeting of the European Council in June 1984.[5] Here Thatcher accepted a deal that involved concessions on both sides, although it was presented to the British people as a victory for the Prime Minister. At the same meeting, the British government showed a serious intention to insert itself into the debate on the future of the Community by producing a paper setting out a program for reform.[6]

Although the British paper had a minimalist and free-market orientation that was entirely in line with the economic doctrine of the Thatcher governments, it did address the issues that were of concern to the rest of the EC: the importance of getting the European economy moving again; of overcoming the growing technological gap with the United States and Japan; of making the Community more relevant to the lives of the people; of combating pollution; of giving the EC an independent role on the world stage; and of strengthening the European arm of the North Atlantic Treaty Organization.

5. For details of the search for a settlement, see Stephen George, *An Awkward Partner: Britain in the European Community* (Oxford: Oxford University Press, 1990), pp. 153-55.

6. *Europe—The Future*, reproduced in *Journal of Common Market Studies*, 23:74-81 (1984).

Thus the Fontainebleau European Council appeared to mark a watershed in Britain's relations with the EC. The budgetary issue was finally resolved, and Britain made a constructive contribution to the debate on the future.

The biggest gap between the British position and that of France and Germany concerned institutional reform. The British paper was minimalist on this issue, reasserting the importance of the national veto and proposing only that the member states look at ways of keeping the European Parliament better informed and of responding to its suggestions. To tackle this thorny issue, a special committee of personal representatives of the heads of state and government was set up at Fontainebleau. It came to be known as the Dooge Committee after its Chairman, James Dooge of Ireland.

THE THATCHER
GOVERNMENTS, 1984-90

Throughout its work, the Dooge Committee was divided into a majority group, who were either enthusiastic about institutional reforms or were at least prepared to accept them, and a minority group, consisting of Britain, Denmark, Greece, and sometimes Ireland, which opposed many of the proposed changes.

The majority on the committee argued that institutional reform was essential to the future of the EC because the 10 member states could achieve their practical goals only if they improved their decision-making procedures. They proposed that the veto be abandoned in the Council of Ministers in favor of majority voting, except in areas that were too sensitive to allow national interests to be overruled; that only the President of the Commission should be nominated by the governments of the member states and that the President should then be allowed to nominate the rest of the Commissioners; and that the decision-making powers of the European Parliament should be increased.[7]

On each of these proposals there was a minority position opposing the majority. The British, Danes, and Greeks argued that the national veto was implicitly part of the terms on which they accepted entry, and they opposed its removal, although the British did propose that it should be made more difficult to invoke. The British response to the proposal concerning the Commission was that the member states should continue to nominate all the Commissioners, but that the President be nominated first and then be consulted about the other nominations. On the powers of the European Parliament, the British wished to retain its purely consultative role.

The report of the Dooge Committee was received at the Milan meeting of the European Council in June 1985. It was this meeting that approved the Commission's white paper on the freeing of the internal market and set the target date of the end of 1992. The single market was an objective that the British government could support enthusiastically, because it coincided with its own economic philosophy. However, in Milan, the institutional issue produced an other disagreement between Britain and a majority of the other member states. A proposal to convene an intergovernmental conference (IGC) to consider changes to the founding treaties was opposed by Britain, Denmark, and Greece; but the Italian presidency called a vote on the issue, the first time that a vote had ever been taken at a European Council meeting, and the proposal was accepted by seven votes to three.[8]

Despite Thatcher's anger at the decision to set it up, Britain did participate in the work of the IGC. Sir Geoffrey Howe, who by this time had become Foreign Secretary, and David Williamson, the Prime Minister's personal adviser on EC affairs, persuaded her that the other member states were less committed to institutional reform in practice than they were in theory. In the IGC, Britain adopted a relatively low profile, an approach that was vindicated by an outcome that involved concessions on all sides but went less far in the direction of institutional change than suggested by the majority of the Dooge Committee.

Britain accepted that there should be a revision of the founding treaties: this was the Single European Act (SEA), which was agreed at the Luxembourg meeting of the European Council in December 1985. There were also concessions from the minimalists on the principle of majority voting in the Council of Ministers and on increasing the decision-making powers of the European Parliament. However, majority voting was restricted to matters directly connected

7. *Bulletin of the European Communities*, point 3.5.1 (Mar. 1985).

8. *Bulletin of the European Communities*, points 1.2.2 and 1.2.10 (June 1985).

to the creation of the single market, and even then certain issues of particular importance to Britain were excluded, such as the harmonization of indirect taxation, the free movement of people, and employees' rights. The increase in the powers of the European Parliament was limited to giving it an opportunity to propose amendments to legislation that came under the rules on majority voting.[9]

While it would be incorrect to describe the SEA as a victory for either the maximalists or the minimalists in the debate about institutional reform, the limited extent of the changes indicated the benefit to Britain of remaining involved in the negotiations. But there were more issues than just institutional reform on which the British position did not coincide with that of other important member states. Indeed, it was largely because of suspicion about the policies that would be followed if more decision making was centralized that Britain held out against strengthening the central institutions. The specific issues that were to cause problems were social policy and monetary union.

Social policy, in Community parlance, refers mainly to the rights of workers. The policy covers such issues as health and safety at work, benefit payments, and the consultation of workers. With the exception of measures concerned with health and safety at work, proposals to insert social policy into the majority-voting provisions of the SEA were vigorously resisted by the British government. The British government remained wedded to the free market and opposed to intervention, whereas the governments of other member states were prepared to see far more extensive intervention.

An illustration of the extent of the difference on this issue came during the British presidency of the Council of Ministers in the second half of 1986, when one of the centerpieces of the program was a proposal to reorient EC employment policy toward a package that stressed aid for small businesses and the self-employed, the encouragement of more flexible working practices, better training, and more help for the long-term unemployed.[10]

Little progress was made on this agenda during the presidency, and when Thatcher tried to insist that it be written into the communiqué of the London meeting of the European Council in December 1986, she was able to get her way only by agreeing that there should also be reference to the importance of EC-level discussions between employers and trade unions—"the social partners." Thatcher tried hard to avoid any such reference, as the corporatist implications of such a social dialogue ran counter to everything that she stood for in British politics; but she was opposed on this even by other conservative leaders such as Chancellor Helmut Kohl of Germany. As the *Financial Times* observed, "The debate emphasised the divide between the

9. Commission of the European Communities, "Single European Act," *Bulletin of the European Communities*, supp. 2 (1986).

10. George, *Awkward Partner*, pp. 187-89.

British Government's economic approach and that of the rest of the Community."[11]

The issue of social policy continued to fester, and it reemerged when Jacques Delors, the President of the European Commission, addressed the annual conference of the British Trades Union Congress in Bournemouth. He said:

It is impossible to build Europe on only deregulation. . . . 1992 is much more than the creation of an internal market abolishing barriers to free movement of goods, services and investment. . . . The internal market should be designed to benefit each and every citizen of the community. It is therefore necessary to improve workers' living and working conditions, and to provide for their health and safety at work.[12]

Delors went on to list three principles that the Commission believed were essential to the social dimension of 1992: that existing levels of social security provision should not be reduced; that health and safety standards should be improved; and that there should be Europe-wide collective bargaining, with every worker having the right to be covered by a collective agreement and with guarantees on the status of temporary workers. For this Delors received a standing ovation from the Trades Union Congress delegates but a sharp rebuke from Thatcher when she spoke to the College of Europe in Bruges in September.[13]

Thatcher's Bruges speech has gone down in Eurodemonology as a

11. Quentin Peel, "Mrs Thatcher Finds the Middle Ground," *Financial Times*, 4 Dec. 1986.
12. *Independent*, 9 Sept. 1988.
13. Margaret Thatcher, *Britain and Europe* (London: Conservative Political Centre, 1988).

vicious attack on the whole European project; in fact, it was simply a restatement of long-standing British objectives. It provoked such a strong reaction, however, because it involved an explicit repudiation of the social dimension that Delors had advocated so strongly and because it suggested that it was a socialist concept. This notion was undermined when leading European Christian Democrats came out in support of the social dimension.

In the end, though, it was Thatcher's opposition to monetary union that divided her so strongly from the rest of her government that she was forced to step down as prime minister.

In the run-up to the Hanover meeting of the European Council in June 1988, monetary union emerged as an important issue on the agenda of the EC. For the French and German governments, a single European currency was a logical and necessary corollary to the freeing of the internal market. They were arguing for the existing European Monetary System to be strengthened by the creation of a European central bank and by moves to establish the European currency unit as the common currency of the EC.

In a statement to the House of Commons in the week preceding Hanover, Thatcher rejected the arguments for monetary union and a European central bank. She said that there was no necessary connection between the freeing of the internal market and the creation of a single currency, and she argued that the corollary of a central bank was a European government, which she did not believe that her partners were any more prepared to accept than she was.[14]

At Hanover, there was an open disagreement on this issue, with Thatcher again appearing to be isolated. A committee was set up under the chairmanship of Jacques Delors to produce a report on monetary union. This appeared in April 1989 and proposed a three-stage timetable for progress to economic and monetary union.[15] Shortly afterward, the British Treasury produced an alternative plan that involved the European currency unit becoming an extra EC currency existing alongside national currencies.

This evolutionary approach was treated with suspicion by the other member states, who tended to see it as yet another British diversionary tactic. Their suspicion appeared to be confirmed by Thatcher when in reply to a question in the House of Commons she said that she did not believe that the European currency unit would be used by the British government.[16]

At the Rome meeting of the European Council in October 1990, Thatcher was again isolated on the adoption of a timetable for monetary union, and agreement was reached to convene two IGCs, one to consider monetary union and one to consider political union.

As it became increasingly obvious that the other member states were prepared to push ahead to a single currency with or without British participation, concern grew in business and financial circles that Britain would become a second-class member of the single market. In political circles the specter was raised of repeating the mistake made in the 1950s, when Britain could have been a founding member of the new European Communities but missed the opportunity and lost the chance to share fully in a period of rapid economic growth.

In November 1990, Sir Geoffrey Howe resigned from his position as Deputy Prime Minister, citing concern about Thatcher's handling of the issue of monetary union. Shortly afterward, he made a speech in the House of Commons explaining his resignation, in which he launched a strong attack on the Prime Minister's European policy.[17] A challenge to Thatcher's leadership followed from Michael Heseltine, who since his resignation from the Cabinet in January 1986 had cultivated the role of leader-in-waiting. The strength of his challenge owed much to the unpopularity of the government, and of the Prime Minister in particular, in the country. Conservative members of Parliament, who were the voters in the leadership election, were worried about losing the next general election and felt that perhaps the time had come for a change after more than 11 years of Thatcher. Such was the strength of Heseltine's challenge on the first ballot that Thatcher chose to resign rather than risk a win on the second ballot for the man whom she

14. Great Britain, *Hansard* (Commons), 6th ser., 23 June 1988, col. 1255.

15. Committee for the Study of Economic and Monetary Union, *Report on Economic and Monetary Union in Europe* (Luxembourg: Office of the Official Publications of the European Communities, 1989).

16. Great Britain, *Hansard* (Commons), 6th ser., 21 June 1990, col. 1111.

17. Great Britain, *Hansard* (Commons), 6th ser., 13 Nov. 1990, cols. 461-65.

least wanted to succeed her. Her own chosen heir was John Major.

THE MAJOR GOVERNMENT, 1990-92

Soon after Major came to office, he gave a new tone to British relations with the EC. In March 1991, he made a visit to Bonn, in an effort to mend Anglo-German relations, which had become strained in the latter months of Thatcher's premiership.[18] While there, he made a speech to the Christian Democratic Union, the party of Chancellor Kohl, in which he stated that he wished to see Britain "where we belong," at the very heart of Europe working with its partners with enthusiasm in building the future.[19]

This change of tone, however, did not mark any sudden or startling change of substance in British policy, as became evident in the two IGCs that took place in 1991. On monetary union there was greater flexibility and pragmatism in the British position, but on the issue of a social dimension there was no significant change, nor was there any newly found enthusiasm for increasing the powers of the central institutions.

The change of tone was significant, though, in allowing the British to negotiate effectively in the IGCs. It was always a misreading of the situation to see Britain as totally isolated in its positions, although Thatcher's aggressive approach to negotiations had often driven other like-minded governments to oppose her. Now the more reasonable and cooperative approach allowed the British to negotiate as normal partners and to attract support from other governments that had doubts about particular aspects of the Commission's program.

Even France came to be on the same side as Britain in the negotiations on political union, where agreement crystallized around a concept of the European union that must have been disappointing to the Commission because it set aside cooperation on foreign policy and external security, and cooperation on internal security and policing, as separate pillars of the union, in which the Commission had no privileged role and in which intergovernmentalism remained entrenched as the principle of voting.[20]

But the question of majority voting on social matters proved a difficult issue, and an agreement at the Maastricht meeting of the European Council in December 1991 proved possible only because the social chapter was dropped from the draft treaty and replaced with a protocol in which the other 11 member states—excluding Britain—committed themselves to progress on social issues using majority voting.

This was a considerable concession to the British, which was achieved only by active and cooperative diplomacy on their part. Less noticed were the concessions that Britain made in

18. On the incidents that caused a cooling of relations, see Stephen George, "Britain and the European Community," in *Contemporary Britain: An Annual Review 1991* (London: Blackwell, 1991), p. 77.

19. John Major, "The Evolution of Europe," *Conservative Party News*, 11 Mar. 1991, p. 13.

20. Council and Commission of the European Communities, *Treaty on European Union* (Luxembourg: Office of the Official Publications of the European Communities, 1992), Titles V and VI.

other directions, particularly in agreeing to an extension of the range of issues on which there would be majority voting in the Council of Ministers and agreeing to increase the powers of the European Parliament.

Monetary union, though, became the really difficult issue for the Major government. Britain did get a special protocol written into the treaty that would allow it to opt out of monetary union at a later stage, but this gave the impression that Britain was again the awkward partner in the Community. It also led to the risk that industrialists would think twice before investing in Britain so long as a question mark remained over whether the country would participate in any eventual monetary union.

Despite these difficulties, Major obviously felt that the opt-out clause was necessary to appease the Thatcherite wing of his party, which was still influential and was hostile to the whole concept of monetary union. In November 1991, Thatcher herself used the opportunity of a debate on the IGCs in the House of Commons to call for a referendum on monetary union before Britain agreed to participate.[21]

The campaign in Britain against the treaty was given a boost by its rejection in a referendum in Denmark on 2 June 1992. The British government's immediate response was to suspend the ratification debate on the treaty in Parliament; but when a parliamentary vote was taken on reintroducing the bill, at the beginning of November 1992, there was a real threat that the government would be defeated by rebel Conservative mem-

bers voting with the Labour Party, which had decided that its wish to inflict a defeat on the government outweighed its avowed commitment to European unity. To stave off defeat, the government had to promise the rebels that it would allow full debate of the bill, clause by clause, in the Commons as a whole and that it would not proceed to ratification until after a second Danish referendum. This put ratification back until the early summer of 1993, a great disappointment to those of Britain's partners in the EC who had taken John Major's side in the Maastricht negotiations in the hope that it would finally resolve the differences between Britain and the rest.

At the same time, Britain took over the presidency of the EC Council of Ministers in the second half of 1992. Here was an opportunity to assert the new approach to the EC in practical terms. Unfortunately, it did not prove to be a very successful presidency from that point of view. Nonetheless, it had several positive achievements to its name: the 1992 program was all but completed in time for the deadline of 31 December; an outline agreement was reached with the United States over trade in agricultural products, opening the way to an agreement in the Uruguay Round negotiations of the General Agreement on Tariffs and Trade (GATT); the Edinburgh session of the European Council that rounded off the presidency negotiated agreement on terms for Denmark that would allow a second referendum to be held there; agreement was reached on long-term budgetary reform; and there was agreement to proceed to negotiations

21. Great Britain, *Hansard* (Commons), 6th ser., 20 Nov. 1991, cols. 297-98.

on enlargement of the EC to take in those members of the European Free Trade Association that had applied for full membership.

Set against these achievements, there was a certain amount of ill feeling generated by the manner in which the British handled the presidency. Two issues in particular caused friction. Both concerned areas where there were long-standing differences of perspective between Britain and other member states: the GATT negotiations and monetary union.[22]

On the GATT negotiations, the agreement on agricultural trade, which had been delaying an overall agreement, was worked out by the Commissioner for Agriculture, Ray MacSharry. Friction between Britain and France occurred when the deal was discussed in the Council of Agriculture Ministers. The French Minister voiced France's reservations about an agreement that had met with widespread protests from French farmers; according to some reports, he was not alone in expressing unease. But John Gummer, the British Minister who was chairing the meeting, told the press that his summing-up supporting the agreement had been accepted unanimously, a version of events that did not match the recollection of others who had been present.

This dispute faded into insignificance, though, in comparison with the dispute with Germany that blew up over the events of September 1992, when the pound sterling was

22. The following points are drawn from Peter Ludlow, "The UK Presidency: A View from Brussels," *Journal of Common Market Studies*, 31(2):246-60 (June 1993).

forced to leave the Exchange Rate Mechanism of the European Monetary System. The decision to remove the currency from the Exchange Rate Mechanism was taken unilaterally by Britain after failure to get agreement to a temporary suspension of the system. The Chancellor of the Exchequer, Norman Lamont, publicly suggested that the crisis was precipitated by statements made by the President of the Bundesbank, Helmut Schlesinger, and that the Bundesbank had refused adequate support for the pound when it came under speculative pressure, a version of events that was rejected by the Bundesbank and the German government.

By the end of the presidency, then, there was ill feeling again between Britain and both France and Germany and disappointment in most of the other member states at Major's weak line with the Conservative rebels.

CONCLUSION

Throughout the period of British membership in the EC, there has been a slow learning process going on within the governmental elites. Adapting to the ways of working of an organization that had been set up without British participation, and that incorporated within it very different political traditions, was never going to be easy. The difficulty was compounded by the genuine problems that Britain had with its budgetary contributions; but these in turn were exacerbated by Margaret Thatcher's uncompromising approach to the negotiations, which was perhaps aimed more at impressing a domestic audience than at achieving a speedy agreement.

After the 1984 settlement of the budgetary issue, however, the continuation of the Thatcher approach became increasingly counterproductive.

John Major's government recognized that British objectives within the EC were unlikely to be achieved if Britain was not trusted by other member states and particularly if Britain was not centrally involved in negotiations on all the developments that might be proposed. It was this fear of isolation while important decisions were being made that precipitated the leadership challenge to Thatcher, from which Major emerged as the new Prime Minister. Unfortunately, Major did not feel able to challenge the Thatcherite component within his own party, which seriously weakened his attempt to restore Britain's position within the EC.

The value of the new approach was shown by the outcome of the IGCs.

The treaty that was signed at Maastricht gave much more to the intergovernmental view of the future European Union, the view that Britain had always championed, than it did to the federalist view, despite the claims to the contrary of many of its opponents. This piece of successful diplomacy was then undermined by the government's bowing to domestic pressures. Yet Britain was too enmeshed with the EC economically and politically to be able to stand on the sidelines.[23] There was no alternative—a phrase much beloved by Margaret Thatcher—to active British participation in the affairs of the EC, at the heart of Europe.

23. On the extent of British integration into the EC, see Simon Bulmer, Stephen George, and Andrew Scott, eds., *The United Kingdom and EC Membership Evaluated* (London: Pinter, 1992).

ANNALS, *AAPSS*, **531**, January 1994

The Council and the Commission
on the Brink of Maastricht

By HELEN WALLACE

ABSTRACT: This article surveys the roles of the Commission and the Council of the European Community (EC) in the period from early 1991 to spring 1993. It sets these in the context of the unusually crowded agenda of the EC and the debates around the drafting and signing of the Treaty on European Union. It argues that these two institutions that lie at the heart of decision making in the EC suffer from structural problems that remain to be addressed in future discussions of institutional reform.

Helen Wallace is director of the Sussex European Institute and was head of the European Programme at the Royal Institute of International Affairs from 1985 to 1992. Her recent publications include The European Community: The Challenge of Enlargement *(with Anna Michalski, 1992);* The Wider Western Europe *(editor, 1991); and "The Europe That Came in from the Cold,"* International Affairs *(October 1991).*

THIS article surveys the roles of and relationships between the Council[1] and the Commission of the European Community (EC) in the period that covers the debate about European union, as defined by what became known as "Maastricht." In a period of continuing uncertainty over the ratification of the Treaty on European Union (TEU; also known as the Maastricht Treaty),[2] or at least uncertainty as to whether the treaty negotiated in Maastricht in December 1991 will receive the assent of all 12 EC members, it is hard to define the subject matter sharply. To clarify, therefore, the article addresses three topics: first, the records of the Commission and the Council from 1991 to spring 1993[3]; second, the changes in the functions and positions of the two institutions envisaged under the TEU; and, third, their strengths and weaknesses as cornerstones of the EC system, with or without the move to European union.

As a preliminary, however, some explanation is needed of the rather unusual context that surrounds this particular period in the evolution of these two institutions. In the early 1990s, policymakers and politicians in the EC found themselves peculiarly overwhelmed by both events and uncertainty as to their own developing roles. The unification of Germany had changed, perhaps fundamentally, the character of the most important member state of the EC. There was a lengthening queue of would-be new members of the club, from all quarters of the continent. The end of the Cold War had generated an awesome range of tasks associated with post-Communist reconstruction and the redefinition of European security.

Yet the old agenda of the 12 West European members of the EC remained incomplete, with the single market still to be turned into a functioning reality and the debate over economic and monetary union (EMU) still taking shape. Meanwhile, as subsequent developments were to reveal, it was by no means clear that all 12 shared the same broad policy objectives or a definition of the shape of their collective enterprise. The Danish referendum of June 1992 and the difficulties of ratifying the TEU in the United Kingdom demonstrated that at least two member states were disgruntled participants in the process of creating the European Union. Moreover, public opinion evidence and the voting patterns in the French referendum of September 1992 revealed public dissatisfaction with the EC in many quarters of its territory. The old permissive consensus on which the EC had been able to ride could no longer be taken for granted.

Nor were the challenges restricted to the political and the geopolitical. Although remarkable progress continued to be made with defining rules for the single market, it became clear

---

1. The Council is the European Community organ in which ministers meet to negotiate, to legislate, and to take various decisions. In addition, there exists the European Council, that is, meetings of heads of state and government.

2. *Treaty on European Union* (Luxembourg: Office of the Official Publications of the European Communities, 1992).

3. For the previous period, see Helen Wallace, "The Council and the Commission after the Single European Act," in *The State of the European Community*, ed. L. Hurwitz and C. Lequesne (Boulder, CO: Lynne Rienner, 1991).

that this would be insufficient to sustain buoyant economies across the EC. As recession struck, the predicted debate about the winners and losers from economic integration began to gather force, and proposals for forms of industrial policy and contingent trade measures became louder. The questions about what kind of social corollaries might be both necessary and acceptable became more contentious. The neat logic of proceeding from market integration to monetary integration also came under fire, not least because of the dependency of the project on the confidence of financial markets and on the buoyancy of the German economy.

Thus the period that concerns us here was one of extraordinary contrasts—between Cold War "victory" and troubled malaise, between economic confidence and economic crisis, and between ambitious extensions of the integration model and defensive institutional retrenchment. These factors permeated EC activities and the climate in which they took place, and they had very direct impacts on the Commission and the Council, the Commission because of its task in generating policy proposals and the Council because of its responsibility for generating consent and focusing controversy.

1991-93: AN OVERCROWDED AGENDA

The agenda of issues facing EC decision makers over this period was vast. The remaining items on the list of measures to complete the single market included some persistently difficult items. In many "flanking" areas—social, environmental, and industrial—there were plenty of substantive dossiers to address. The removal of border controls on persons was proving tricky. A successor budgetary package had to be prepared to follow on the settlement of February 1988 called Delors I, with its familiar points of contention on agricultural reform and claims for resource transfers to promote cohesion. The Uruguay Round of negotiations on the General Agreement on Tariffs and Trade (GATT) remained persistently on the point of completion, but the EC's room for maneuver was blocked by the difficulty of winning French endorsement for the agricultural element.

Externally, the EC was locked into negotiations to create a European Economic Area (EEA) with the countries of the European Free Trade Association (EFTA). New Europe agreements were being framed to develop extended partnership with the countries of Central and Eastern Europe, and policies were required to contribute to the stabilization of the former Soviet Union. In many European countries beyond the EC, the debate continued on their expectations of the EC and yielded more applications for EC membership. The Yugoslav situation deteriorated rapidly and then flared into crisis, while the wider issue of how to reshape the framework of European security begged big questions about how the EC would develop. Meanwhile, the convening of the intergovernmental conferences (IGCs) to deal with EMU and with European political union (EPU) prompted EC leaders to address systemic questions about the reshaping of the EC in very broad terms.

This dense clustering of issues posed an unprecedented challenge to the key decision-making organs of the EC. Simultaneously, they were on test to pursue established areas of policy, many of which demanded policy adjustment, and to invent policy under dramatically changed conditions, notably as regards the rest of Europe. The Commission and the Council thus had to dig deep to find the human resources and political attention to respond. Routine processes needed to be maintained and tested on stubborn issues (value-added tax harmonization, agricultural policy reform, environmental safeguards—the list was long), but new issues had also to be assessed from first principles and policy shaped fast under the pressure of events.

The Commission

The Commission came to these tasks buoyantly after a period in which it had succeeded in inserting itself firmly at the center of EC decision making.[4] Jacques Delors was widely regarded as an outstandingly successful Commission President and a force to be reckoned with. The Commission's mastery of the Single Market Program had shown a capacity for targeted and shrewd policy development and was being impressively matched in the development of

4. See Peter Ludlow, "The Commission," in *The New European Community: Decisionmaking and Institutional Change,* ed. Robert O. Keohane and Stanley Hoffman (Boulder, CO: Westview Press, 1991).

tighter rules of competition. There were grounds for optimism that these assets could be drawn on in addressing other issues, issues that demanded both subtle propositions and persuasive argument.

The subsequent performance of the Commission, however, revealed a mixed pattern of achievement and frustration. As regards the core of the Single Market Program and the pursuit of enhanced competition, the Commission continued to show flair and determination in developing market rules and defining their application. In particular, those responsible for competition policy, both Leon Brittan, the Commissioner, and the responsible officials in Directorate General IV, set about proving that the Commission would be fierce in its application of its powers and quite willing to take on powerful national and corporate interests.

Similarly, to condense what was a much longer story, the Commission proved able for a second time to define the parameters and the main substance of a new budgetary package for the EC. The Delors II package, drafted, like its predecessor, within the Commission and again raising tricky issues on agricultural expenditure, cohesion, and own resources, emerged in final form in December 1992 in a shape that was close to the original draft. Though it took many months of hard negotiation and brinkmanship, in December 1992 John Major, leader of a country that was a substantial net contributor to the EC budget, found himself in Edinburgh—as Helmut Kohl had similarly in February 1988—presiding over an agreement that largely endorsed what the Commission had proposed.[5]

In some adjacent areas of policy, however, results were harder to identify. The controversial debate over the social dimension continued, with the Commission failing to persuade a vehemently resistant U.K. government to soften its stance but also struggling to win deep-rooted support from the rest of the member states much beyond the level of rhetoric. In the preparation of the EC· position for the Earth Summit in Rio de Janeiro, the Commission revealed itself to be internally divided between environmental concerns and the competing industrial and energy interests. Ray MacSharry vigorously pursued the cause of agricultural reform but still found himself boxed in by the continued reluctance of the French government to accept the implications of policy change, notably as regards the Uruguay Round, so much so that he dramatically resigned in midnegotiation with the U.S. administration. Here it should be recorded that on the GATT package as a whole, the failure to move the negotiation forward was not for want of great efforts by the Commission, which found itself squeezed between the often ill-judged provocations of the U.S. administration and the inflexibility of several EC governments, especially the French.

On the external front, the Commission, both Commissioners and officials, felt themselves to be on their mettle to demonstrate that they could rise to the challenge of Europe. At the outset of the period under review here, the Commission was engaged in developing two initiatives for the countries of Central and Eastern Europe ("PECO" in the emerging new Eurospeak acronym): the PHARE program of technical assistance, coordinated with the Group of 24 donor countries of the Organization for Economic Cooperation and Development, and a new form of Europe agreement of association for individual countries, as they became "ready" for this new status.

This is not the place to discuss the substance of these initiatives. On both, the Commission played a very important part in developing EC policy. In both cases, policy had to be invented more or less from scratch, and new teams of officials had to be marshaled where only small units had preceded. Everything from principles to detailed procedures had to be set in place. Quite new combinations of political assessment, economic evaluation, and technical judgments had to be brought to bear. Three features of this policy process within the Commission deserve note. First, it stretched the human resources of the Commission to the limits, especially given the lean staffing of the relevant services and the very limited number of officials with appropriate backgrounds who could be released from other duties. In particular, it rendered almost unmanageable the span of responsibilities of Directorate General I. Second, it required dense coordination across Directorate Generals and services, never the greatest strength of the Commission. Third, the content of the Europe

5. For this and other references to Edinburgh, see European Council, *Conclusions of the Presidency*, Edinburgh, 12 Dec. 1992.

agreements demanded a willingness to take on those vested interests within the EC that would have to give ground in order to give effective access to EC markets in agriculture and sensitive industrial sectors. Here the Commission, like the member governments, found itself hemmed in by the limitations imposed by powerful lobbies.

In parallel throughout the period, the Commission was engaged in what proved to be a very difficult negotiation with the EFTA governments over the EEA. Again the details go beyond the scope of this article, but the EEA concept had been devised by the Commission, partly in the hope of deflecting applications for full membership. In practice, the Commission kept trapping itself in arguments about the *acquis communautaire* and the orthodoxies of EC procedures, which contributed to delays and the dislocation of the whole negotiation on the issue of whether or not the European Court of Justice, with an extended EEA chamber, could determine EEA litigation cases. The court vetoed the Commission's proposed formula, and thus the EEA agreement was modified in ways that almost certainly contributed to the negative Swiss vote, rejecting EEA membership, in December 1992 and made some EFTA governments even more determined to press their applications for full membership.

The EEA and PECO cases are instructive. Both show the scope for the Commission to develop new ideas and to insert itself at the center of the EC policy process. But both also reveal the difficulties for an underresourced and overloaded Commission of sustaining a clear and focused strategy and of shifting away from EC traditions and established rules on difficult and controversial issues.

A broader political point also needs to be borne in mind. In dealing with all of these rest-of-Europe issues, the Commission was paying a price for the absence of an agreed European policy for the EC, that is, of a policy that really bound the EC as a whole to an approach that could incorporate both political and economic dimensions, let alone a shared security perspective. The Commission could not substitute here for what member governments had failed to elucidate. Yet the Commission also could not itself easily inject sensitive political judgments to fill the vacuum. Among the many criticisms that can be leveled at the hesitancies of EC responses to the Yugoslav crisis is the considerable contortion of the debate within the Commission in summer 1991 over whether and how the EC might apply economic sanctions to deter the escalation of the conflict.

As for the IGCs on EMU and EPU, the Commission had already made a pivotal contribution to the former by its role in drafting the Delors Report. The agenda on political union was much less clearly defined and had been comparably sifted, unlike the previous IGC that prepared the Single European Act. It proved in practice very difficult for the Commission to insert its own ideas into the negotiating text. In addition, there was a delicate issue of strategy for the Commission, faced with a contentious negotiation between EC governments.

In the event, the Commission did not make a big bid for enhanced powers for itself but, rather, concentrated on specific and narrower proposals. It laid much of the groundwork for clauses in the more technical areas of policy. On issues of macro reform, Commission papers were presented concerning the need for coherence in the management of external policies and on a different systematization of EC legislation, neither of which were much reflected in the final text. It was very active in the discussions over subsidiarity. But overall there was much less of the Commission's mark on the final text than had been the case for the Single European Act.

The Council and the European Council

The Council and the European Council were similarly weighed down by this tough agenda, likewise charged with a burden of legislative proposals and with devising outlines of new policies, especially as regards the rest of Europe and the IGCs.[6] Given the intense political sensitivities of the IGCs and the imposition of events that demanded responses, it was foreign ministers above all who found themselves in peculiarly intensive intra-EC bargaining, while struggling also to keep pace with developments on the wider international front. Heavy loads also fell on heads of state and government, given

6. For general coverage of the Council, see Enrique Gonzalez Sanchez, *Manual del negociador en la Comunidad Europea* (Madrid: Oficina de Información Diplomática, 1992); Wolfgang Wessels, "The European Council and the Council," in *New European Community*, ed. Keohane and Hoffman.

the number of genuinely difficult issues that demanded time in and around European Council sessions, and on finance ministers, given that their core subject was in contention in the EMU negotiations.

The most consistently demanding dossiers during the period under review related to the two IGCs. These dominated the Luxembourg and Dutch Council presidencies of 1991, all the more so because, especially in the case of EPU, the detailed agenda was so shapeless. The Luxembourgers had, after all, to concoct a single negotiating text from the 300 or so individual papers that were tabled. That they did so in the draft treaty text of June 1991 was no mean achievement, but it is hardly surprising that they should have had little attention or expertise to devote to other issues.

For the Dutch, too, the IGCs kept claiming primacy, though the unfolding Yugoslav crisis also kept forcing itself onto the agenda. Indeed, the problems of keeping pace with the range of unavoidable issues found even experienced Dutch ministers struggling to retain coherent and consistent positions in the Council. The ill-fated Dutch negotiating text tabled in the summer of 1991 for the IGC had neither been fully agreed in The Hague nor thoroughly prepared with partner governments. The story of its proposal and retraction illustrated the weakness of the infrastructures for managing Council business when such controversial and delicate issues were in contention.

In the event, the two presidencies of 1992 were similarly troubled by the awkwardness of events. Portuguese and British ministers in succession found themselves overtaken repeatedly by Yugoslavia, by the difficulties of settling the Uruguay Round package, by the problems of concluding the EEA treaty, then by the Danish referendum and the ratification problems of several member states, and in September by the turbulence surrounding the currency crisis. That January 1993 should have found a handicapped and, in the event, short-lived Danish government in the Council chair makes it hard to conclude that the presidency had enhanced its credibility for dealing with either regular EC business or taking on the tasks of the enhanced intergovernmental cooperation envisaged under the new pillars of European Union.

Away from the glare of attention of the more dramatic issues, business in the Council continued on a somewhat more even keel in the well-established areas of cooperation. But the uncertainties of the surrounding political climate and over when and whether the new TEU would be implemented made it hard for the Council to focus its attention. The Delors II package had to be handed up to the European Council. The follow-up to the internal market program did not get the sustained attention that the subject deserved.

But then the Council was going through a period of considerable instability in two senses. First, many member governments were severely distracted by domestic issues; and, second, the balance of relationships between member states was altering. The range of domestic distractions was wide: the burden of unification for the Germans, the collapse of the political establishment in Italy, the relentless pressures on Belgian unity, the declining popularity of tired socialist governments in France and Spain, an impending political embarrassment in Denmark, surprise electoral recovery followed by disturbing governmental confusion in Britain, a government only just maintained in Greece, and the collapse of the Irish government on a vote of confidence. This was not a period in which governments could be expected to be extrovert or to take risks with sensitive domestic interests. On policy, therefore, ministers in the Council tended toward caution and defensiveness, while on issues concerning the overall development of the EC governments, they worked hard to insert their own special pleadings, as both the main text of the TEU and its associated protocols and declarations reveal.

There was also a competition between ministers in the Council to claim ground in defining the issues, most vividly on the IGC agenda and the widening/deepening debate. Though the Franco-German relationship continued to set much of the tone, the relative positions of these two partners had altered, giving the French less leverage over the Germans. Italian skills of intermediation were crippled by domestic crisis. The British found themselves beleaguered within the IGC and during the currency crisis, thus again failing to position themselves in the mainstream of the Community debate. The Spanish proved persistently stubborn on issues of substance affecting direct Spanish interests—for example, Delors II, EEA—though thoroughly committed to advancing European union. On several issues—Turkey, Macedonia, support packages for the Greek economy—the Greek government kept finding itself put in the dock by other member governments. Impulses of individualism were more compelling than those of consensual harmony.

One important consequence of this political climate in the Council was that it turned Council debates in on themselves even more than usual. The combination of an overcrowded agenda with the other preoccupations of Council participants found ministers especially concerned to protect their positions and to do so behind the cover of closed Council sessions. When situations were tense—Maastricht, the Danish referendum, the currency crisis—reactions veered between the search for scapegoats, with the Commission in particular becoming the object of much criticism, and exercises in collective damage limitation, which accounts for the remarkable list of agreements at the Edinburgh European Council in December 1992.

WHAT DIFFERENCE WOULD
EUROPEAN UNION MAKE?

The TEU as agreed in Maastricht was built on a muddled compromise between those who favored strengthening of the EC into a form of more fully fledged union or integration and those who wanted to set a ceiling on integration by entrenching subsidiarity and reinforcing intergovernmentalism in crucial respects.[7] Both

sides claimed victory, and neither side was enthusiastic about the result. One of the curiosities of the IGC negotiations is how little detailed attention they paid to the workings of the Council and the Commission or to the relationships between these two principal organs of EC decision making.

Instead, it became a governing precept of the IGC that the broad balance of the relationship between Council and Commission should remain undisturbed. The Commission was not to become the focus of governance for the Union. The Council and, more explicitly, the European Council were to have plenty of scope for defining policies for the Union. The precarious interdependence of the two organs was to continue, and the competition for a different and more explicit set of institutional choices was deferred. After all, it was agreed that there would be another IGC in 1996. Such changes as were envisaged were at the edges of the hard-core issues about institutional development.

There were several reasons for this. First, there was no clearly agreed prescription for radical reform around which a consensus could be built. Second, the prospect of further and perhaps extensive enlargement of the EC was bearing on the negotiators without their having found or chosen to find political energy to direct toward the challenge of

---

7. For one practitioner's account of the negotiations, see Philippe de Schoutheete, "Ré-

flexions sur le Traité de Maastricht," *Annales de droit de Louvain*, 1/1993, pp. 75-90. For a broader survey, see Christian Engel and Wolfgang Wessels, eds., *From Luxembourg to Maastricht: Institutional Change in the European Community after the Single European Act* (Bonn: Europa Union Verlag, 1993).

how to handle it institutionally, except to say, "Not yet." Third, the undoubted grounds for reassessing the methods of functioning of both the Council and the Commission required a willingness to admit to structural weaknesses in both institutions, a willingness that most of those involved did not reveal. Fourth, the IGC ducked the question of how to compose the next Commission and instead temporized by insisting on the appointment of the next Commission for only two years.

Subsequently, the extreme caution induced by the Danish referendum led to extreme prudence on institutional issues, reflected in the measured text of the Commission's report to the Lisbon European Council on enlargement. Yet the Danish vote and the troubled debates in France and the United Kingdom, buttressed by disturbing public opinion evidence from still more countries, pushed the European Council into a speedy discussion of institutional adaptation of both Council and Commission.

The TEU provisions on the Commission strengthened the link between it and the European Parliament by requiring that the new President and Commissioners be subject to a vote of approval from the Parliament and that their term of office coincide with the Parliament's electoral cycle. This was a weaker proposal than that which had been canvassed for, allowing the Parliament to choose or to elect the President, but nonetheless would change to an extent the basis for the Commission's authority. Given the other extensions of the Parliament's powers, these provisions might reinforce

the vaguer association of these two institutions that derived from earlier treaty powers. Yet the IGC ducked the question of the size of the Commission, as the larger member states proved reluctant to see a reduction to one Commissioner per member state.

The Commission did not win a position linking the three pillars of the new TEU structure, a task that was assigned to the European Council. Indeed, the pillar structure itself, by grafting new arrangements alongside the EC proper, set a limit to the powers of the Commission in new fields. Yet the Commission was to be associated with Articles J and K, dealing, respectively, with the Common Foreign and Security Policy and with judicial and home affairs. There was an ambiguity in these dispositions that remains to be tested in practice.

As regards the Council, the main formal impacts of the TEU are to extend qualified majority voting, though not dramatically, and to allow the Parliament more legislative scope.[8] It could, however, also be argued that the decision to create a Committee of the Regions, albeit with a skeletal role, indicates a vacuum that the Council had not been able to fill. After all, it refers to a range of opinion within the member

8. On the experience of qualified majority voting, see Christian Engel and Christine Borram, *Von Konzens zur Mehrheitsentscheidung, EG—Entscheidungsverfahren und nationales Interessenpolitik nach den Einheitlichen Europäischen Acte* (Bonn: Europa Union Verlag, 1991); Christian Lequesne, "Quelques considérations sus la pratique du vote au sein du Conseil des ministres des Communautés européennes," *Centre des pouvoirs européens*, pp. 19-23 (Autumn 1991).

states that was clamoring for inclusion under the EC umbrella.

The European Council and the Council also won new fields of action. Most important, the European Council is to assume responsibilities in relation to the European Union as the board of directors legitimized by treaty to hold the three pillars together. The Council under Articles J and K has an extended domain, all the more important in that now, under treaty and with the Commission in a constrained role, the Council takes charge of these intergovernmental areas. Nonetheless, *passarelle* clauses and the prospect of another IGC in 1996 allow the possibility for these arrangements to be temporary.

Although, then, the relationships between and the tasks of Council and Commission are not overhauled by the treaty, there is a fluidity added with the new arrangements that invites testing and could well give rise to some frictions. These are further complicated by the treaty provisions on subsidiarity, which is now extended as an operating principle across the board. The insistence that proposals to extend the Union's sphere of action or to apply preexisting powers be subjected to a subsidiarity test or, indeed, to post hoc scrutiny can be variously interpreted. For some, it is at last the welcome arrival of a states'-rights clause, a normal feature of a federation or proto-federation. For others, it represents a device to freeze the level and scope of political integration within the treaty. Moreover, the lack of clarity as to the procedures according to which subsidiarity will be assessed suggests that the debate on this is far

from over. But if one looks beyond the treaty provisions to the political debate, it becomes clear that the addition of the notion of subsidiarity to the operating principles of the European Union reflects in part a lack of trust in the existing institutional arrangements.

In broad terms, therefore, the TEU substantially alters the context in which the Council and the Commission would subsequently operate but more narrowly fails to address a number of other specific issues about the effectiveness of each of them. Interestingly, in the period following the Danish referendum of June 1992 and the exposure of EC institutions to rather widespread criticism, both Commission and Council found themselves severely censured. The thrust of the criticism was that both were too insulated from wider opinion, too meddlesome, too remote from scrutiny, and too opaque for examination. In particular, the Commission's proclivity to be hyperactive in formulating legislative proposals and the Council's preference for legislating behind closed doors came under attack.

These criticisms caught EC decision makers at a vulnerable moment as they struggled to reestablish their own credibility and to facilitate the ratification of the Maastricht texts. The result was a series of exhortatory pronouncements from the Edinburgh European Council. These sought to add to the definition of subsidiarity; to make the Council more open and transparent, even with the occasional session to be held in public or at least to be televised; and to urge the Commission to be visibly more amenable to consultations and to using green-paper techniques of canvassing policy proposals.[9]

SOME UNDERLYING ISSUES OF INSTITUTIONAL EFFECTIVENESS

The provisions of the TEU notwithstanding, the question as to the effectiveness of the Council and the Commission and of their capacities to handle a large and difficult agenda remains on the table. In the record of the last three years, several factors stand out. First, there is a real problem of overload, which has nothing to do with subsidiarity and rather more to do with events. The Commission is underresourced to carry out tasks that clearly fall within its purview.[10] The Council is a cumbersome body that still lacks a sustained collective identity and has been overdependent on a presidency system that is stretched to and sometimes beyond the limit.

Second, there is a deficiency in both institutions as regards strategy. Both institutions easily become hyperactive, but both find it hard to provide an environment in which strategic policy decisions can be adopted or reassessed. The EEA, the Europe agreements, and the pressures for enlargement have all found both institutions struggling to formulate a strategic sense of direction.

Third, the problem of segmented decision making persists in both Council and Commission. The difficulties of linking agricultural reform

9. On these points, see the details in European Council, *Conclusions of the Presidency*.

10. See Les Metcalfe, "After 1992: Can the Commission Manage Europe?" *Australian Journal of Public Administration*, 51(1):117-30 (Mar. 1992).

to wider trade liberalization in the GATT or of enlarging market access to exports of sensitive goods from Central and Eastern Europe or of handling the fisheries' dossier for the EEA all reflect and are aggravated by the persistent divisions between specialist councils and by the competition between Directorates General in the Commission.

Fourth, there has persistently been an underinvestment in management capabilities and best management practice within EC institutions. An internal screening report was carried out inside the Commission in 1991 that identified a number of measures that might be taken; the measures included many echoes of the Spierenburg Report of 1978. Most of its proposals remain to be addressed, and the way in which the Commission responded to the rejigging of portfolios in early 1993 hardly leaves grounds for optimism as to progress in this field. Moreover, those who follow the day-to-day operations of the EC have long argued that the great burst of new legislation and regulation associated with the internal market requires a thoroughgoing overhaul of management capabilities and new regulatory devices.

Nor are these technical problems confined to the Commission. The Council also tends to lurch from dossier to dossier, despite the great skills of the Council Secretariat in dealing with the flow of business. Many eccentric ministerial whims are incorporated into Council decisions without enough thought for the consequences. The European Council, its role elevated under the TEU, still lacks systematic underpinning and relies too much on weary officials and ministers in the margins of the meeting of heads of state and government cobbling together drafts, often impromptu—the social protocol at Maastricht is a telling example, but not alone—that then find their way into the rule book.

If and when the Council and the Commission settle down to their redefined tasks under the TEU, as they face their still-large agenda and as they turn again to the question of preparing both for the next IGC and for enlargement, their members need to take a more sober and more willingly self-critical view of what needs to be done. The EC has a great capacity for defying logic and pulling rabbits out of hats against the odds. Decision makers on the whole want to make their actions credible and convincing. In that case, they need to take a more hardheaded approach to both drawing constitutional lines and to improving management practice.

ANNALS, *AAPSS*, **531**, January 1994

The European Parliament
and the Authority-Democracy Crises

By JULIET LODGE

ABSTRACT: Since its inception, the European Parliament has stimulated integration and the transition to a European Union based on liberal democratic principles. Its Draft Treaty establishing the European Union remains the benchmark for a new constitution. Institutional change and the alteration in the balance of power between the Commission, the Council of Ministers, and the European Parliament are useful indicators of the transition of the European Community (EC) to a federal union whose flexible parameters remain contested. The European Parliament, as the chief advocate of democracy, efficiency, accountability, and openness in the EC, continues to play a constituent role and to seek means of redressing the EC's democratic deficit, which exists not only in the legislative sphere but also on a horizontal and vertical plane within the union. New legislative practices and the Committee of Regions alone will not close the gap.

Juliet Lodge is professor of European politics, codirector of the European Community Research Unit at the University of Hull, and visiting professor at the Université Libre de Bruxelles, Belgium. The 1992 European Woman of the Year, she has published widely on European Community politics and international affairs. Her research focuses on European union, judicial cooperation, and foreign and security policies. Her books include Direct Elections to the European Parliament 1989 *and* The EC and the Challenge of the Future; *she is completing* The EC's Crisis of Political Authority.

THERE are curious parallels between the situation of the European Parliament in 1993 and that in 1978. On both occasions, the European Parliament was on the brink of a new era. In 1978, the first elections to Europe's transnational Parliament were due to be held. In 1993, the European Parliament prepared for the fourth set of direct elections on the eve of one of the most turbulent phases both in Europe's history and in the evolution of the European Community (EC) itself.

On both occasions, federalism was seen to be lurking in the closet. Unbidden and unwanted—certainly by the most centralized and unitary state of the EC, the United Kingdom—political developments based on democratic ideals espoused by members of the European Parliament (MEPs) provoked much soul-searching as to Europe's destiny, the meaning of European union, the purpose of the EC, and the future role of its Parliament.

THE IMPORTANCE OF EURO-ELECTIONS

A perennial fear of federalists and governments alike was that the moment the European Parliament was directly elected by universal suffrage in line with the long-evaded Rome Treaty obligation, its MEPs would seek fundamental reform of the EC's institutions. Some governments, who saw sovereignty as residing in the superior elected Parliament, equated direct elections with wholesale transfer of national sovereignty from the national to the supranational level.

At issue, however, was not the question of MEPs' challenging the authority of national parliaments. National governments had deliberately relegated the MEPs to negligible roles in monitoring, scrutinizing, and influencing EC legislation in order to preserve the legislative supremacy of the Council of Ministers. Rather, at issue was the question of the continuing supremacy of national government over parliaments at both the national but more especially the supranational level. This surfaced in the argument as to whether a democratically elected supranational Parliament could legitimately justify a claim to augment its minimal legislative powers through a redistribution of power among EC institutions to the Council's—and hence national governments'—disadvantage. Herein lay the federal specter.

The problem for MEPs was, therefore, how to devise a strategy to enable them to achieve that objective without so antagonizing national governments—who ultimately could veto institutional reform—as to jeopardize the whole enterprise.

Immediately prior to the Euro-elections in 1979, candidates and their predecessors—legislators nominated from national parliaments—had argued that an accretion of the European Parliament's powers was neither the logical nor the necessary outcome of direct elections. This somewhat disingenuous argument was designed to prevent governments from reneging on their commitment to hold the elections at all.

However, shortly after the newly elected MEPs had taken their seats up, a dual-pronged strategy was developed within the European Parliament to make it more effective. Two committees played pivotal roles. The first was the Political Affairs Committee, which insisted that greater effectiveness could be achieved if the European Parliament simply fully exploited its existing powers. The other was the ad hoc Institutional Affairs Committee, which took a thorough look at improving the functioning of the Parliament.

The Political Affairs Committee advocated a gradual, minimalist approach to institutional change. To that end, it helped the European Parliament to augment its influence by stealth. By successfully challenging the Council's adoption of a Commission proposal prior to receipt of the European Parliament's opinion, which was legally required, the legislation in question was struck down and Parliament acquired a power of delay. Used judiciously, this helped to ensure that henceforward the Commission and the Council paid heed to its views. This was a novel experience for the Council, which was accustomed to ignoring Parliament. The Commission was less cavalier, and gradually mutual consultation grew up. The Council, however, made only minor concessions to the European Parliament. Even so, the Political Affairs Committee continued to chip away at institutional relations in order to establish a corollary power to the power of censuring the whole Commission through the practice of engaging the Commission President in an investiture vote of confidence. This was subsequently to become the basis for the formal amendment in the Maastricht Treaty on European Union in 1991 to provide for the European Parliament's confirmation of the Commission President-elect.

The Institutional Affairs Committee, emboldened by the series of reports on institutional relations and possible reforms tabled within the European Parliament from the late 1970s to early 1980s onward,[1] adopted a different, maximalist approach. For it to stand any chance of success, it was imperative that any recommendations enjoy broad-based, all-party, cross-national support. Its architect was federalist Altiero Spinelli and his Crocodile Club.[2]

The Crocodile Club reasoned that the EC's member states would not be able to attain mutually beneficial goals unless they increased the EC's—and hence its institutions'—capacity to act and to realize "an ever closer union" as prescribed by the Rome Treaty. It is striking that this endeavor coincided with another attempt, initiated by the European Parliament, to counteract the growing problems of the EC's declining competitiveness in the international political economy: the Single Market Program, which had its origins in pressure from Philips, successive Commission reviews, and the 1983 Albert and Ball reports commissioned by the European Parliament.

1. See European Parliament, Committee on Institutional Affairs, *Selection of Texts Concerning Institutional Matters of the Community from 1950 to 1982* (Luxembourg: European Parliament, 1983).

2. R. Cardozo, "The Crocodile Initiative," in *European Union: The European Community in Search of a Future*, ed. Juliet Lodge (London: Macmillan, 1986).

THE EUROPEAN PARLIAMENT AND INSTITUTIONAL REFORM: THE EUT

There can be little doubt that the attempt to promote European union and institutional reform would not have come to anything had the governments themselves not ultimately been convinced of the need for change and for institutional reform. While they were not prepared to endorse fully the European Parliament's recommendations outlined in the Draft Treaty establishing the European Union (EUT) of 1984, they did take many of its points on board. Moreover, the EUT was to remain the benchmark against which all subsequent attempts to reform and revitalize the EC were to be measured.

The EUT

The EUT was certainly federal in inspiration, in its prescription of a federal, territorially based separation of authority and division and separation of executive, legislative, and judicial power. Its prescriptions of exclusive and concurrent legislative competence also reflected the idea of authority being shared between a central or federal level of government and its component parts.

Far more germane to the EC's problems, however, were its recommendations on the creation of a bicameral legislature and a system of decision making based on majority voting. Indeed, its advocacy of a principle of majority voting based on a minimum voting coalition comprising two-thirds of the population of the member states subsequently found an echo in the Maastricht Treaty's formula for the Common Foreign and Security Policy provisions whereby decisions could be taken by majority, providing 8 member states—out of 12—agreed.

The EUT's scope

The EUT consisted of a preamble and six parts: (1) the union; (2) the objectives, methods of action, and competences of the union; (3) institutional provisions; (4) policies of the union; (5) finances of the union; and (6) general and final provisions.

The preamble outlined the union's aims as being the revival and continuation of the democratic unification of Europe; the preservation of peace and liberty by an ever closer union; and the attainment of goals in accordance with the principle of subsidiarity. This was a concept that caused so much anguish during the Maastricht deliberations when the United Kingdom, alone of all governments, misinterpreted it to mean devolution from the supranational to the national level instead of the exercise of authority at the lowest possible level of government compatible with the fulfillment of the task at hand.

The EUT also referred to other principles that subsequently found expression in the Maastricht Treaty almost ten years later: union citizenship; respect for fundamental rights and freedoms; acceptance of the Community patrimony or *acquis communautaire*; expansion of the scope of integration to international relations and judicial cooperation; and financial equalization.

Notions of common action and cooperation are also clearly presented along with the rudiments of the union's laws and processes—the Acts of the Union. These found expression again during the sometimes acrimonious discussions of the Luxembourg "Non-Paper" and Dutch presidencies' proposals in the run-up to Maastricht over the desirability of defining a "hierarchy of norms" for the union.[3]

THE EUROPEAN PARLIAMENT: BUILDING EUROPEAN UNION

At a critical juncture in the EC's history, the European Parliament, in a very direct way, played an extremely important constitutional role. Though not always recognized in the Anglo-Saxon world, this role was crucial to the often extremely difficult negotiations of the mid-1980s that culminated after the infamous Milan European Council, at which the Italian presidency took the unprecedented step of deciding by majority vote that an intergovernmental conference (IGC) should indeed be called—against the wishes mainly of the United Kingdom and also of Denmark and Greece—to promote institutional reform and further integration. This led directly to the series of reports that formed the basis of the treaty amendments known as the Single European Act of 1985, which came into force in July 1987 after having been ratified by all the member states.

It is true that the European Parliament was not directly party to the deliberations on the Single Act, but its activities not only stimulated elite awareness but prepared the ground for the necessary psychological shift in attitudes among political elites and publics. Italy, for example, held a referendum on European union to coincide with the 1984 Euro-elections.[4]

A CONSTITUENT ROLE?

The question of the European Parliament's eventually assuming a constituent role for the EC was publicly broached. In this, MEPs were continuing the European Parliament's tradition of creating visions for the future. This time, not only were they pragmatic but, critically, they enjoyed the support of French President Mitterrand and EC Commission President Delors. The confluence of political leaders in the Council's presidency was also sympathetic.[5] This enabled the EC to break the deadlock that had strangled earlier attempts at reform as exemplified by the Genscher-Colombo Draft Treaty on European Union (1980) and the 1983 Solemn Declaration of European Union, which were considered alongside the EUT by the ad hoc Dooge Committee, entrusted by the

3. Juliet Lodge, "The Luxembourg 'Non-Paper' versus the Commission's Composite Working Paper," in *Beyond the Intergovernmental Conferences: European Union in the 1990s*, ed. W. Paterson (Edinburgh: Europa Institute, 1991).

4. Juliet Lodge, ed. *Direct Elections to the European Parliament 1984* (London: Macmillan, 1986).

5. The presidency of the Council of Ministers—and with it that of the European Council—rotates every six months. The European Council meets at least twice a year and, as a summit, consists of heads of state and/or government. Its sessions are always chaired by the person (and therefore the state) that holds the Council presidency.

governments with elaborating the reforms subsequently agreed in the Single Act.[6]

The European Parliament was not successful, however, in exercising the sought-after constituent role. Nor was it to be directly involved in deliberations on either the content or the implementation of the Single Act. Consequently, it had to resort in 1985 to its tried and tested minimalist strategy of seeking fully to exploit treaty provisions in order to win for itself a genuine legislative capacity.

Once again, it set itself the task of capitalizing on the new provisions, working responsibly with the Council of Ministers and the Commission. At the same time, it embarked on a maximalist approach to treaty reform by examining continuing weaknesses in the EC's institutional arrangements. It was not simply spurred by self-interest. Rather, MEPs were genuinely motivated by a concern that the EC should develop into a functioning democratic polity. This meant that the deficiencies they had isolated prior to the Single Act in the discussions on the EUT required renewed attention: democratic legitimacy; operationally effective, efficient, transparent, and responsive institutions; the role and participation of the member states; and a separation of powers.

In short, MEPs accepted neither in 1979 nor in 1985 the view that the prerequisites of a functioning liberal

6. R. Pryce, ed., *The Dynamics of European Union* (London: Croom Helm, 1987); Juliet Lodge, "Plurilateralism and the Single European Act," in *Plurilateral Negotiations*, ed. I. William Zartman (Baltimore, MD: Johns Hopkins University Press, 1993).

democratic supranational system had been satisfied merely, as had been argued in 1979, by dint of direct elections to a weak Parliament, albeit one whose legislative influence had been augmented by its own efforts and through the cooperation procedure introduced through the Single Act.

The logical consequence of the European Parliament's acting responsibly in implementing and fully exploiting its newly won powers under the Single Act was for it to work on the principle that anything not explicitly forbidden was permitted. This enabled it to challenge the Council of Ministers and to use the cooperation procedure, introduced by the Single Act, in a political manner.

THE COOPERATION PROCEDURE: THE FIRST STEP TOWARD REAL LEGISLATIVE POWER

The cooperation procedure set up a system of two readings that enabled the European Parliament to decide with the Council of Ministers on measures falling under 10 articles of the Rome Treaty. Many crucial issues coming under this provision related to legislation to realize the single market by 1992. However, what the Parliament needed to do was to check that the cooperation procedure really did give it legislative influence that could be wielded in the name of higher standards and the common good.

In 1988, it rejected a proposal on dangers in the workplace from benzene after the Commission had refused to accept its amendments to the draft proposal. These had been designed to introduce stricter values and to provide for consultation with the work force. As a result of the Parliament's rejection, the proposal could then be adopted only if the Council of Ministers unanimously approved it in a second reading. Since Denmark wanted tighter controls along the Parliament's lines, this was impossible. Consequently, Parliament's amendments were subsequently accommodated.

The Single Act also augmented the Parliament's powers in external relations and encouraged the Parliament to identify continuing weaknesses in institutional provisions with a view to seeking remedies at the time of the review of Title III, on political cooperation, of the Single Act scheduled for 1989-90. In particular, in 1988 the Parliament successfully challenged the terms of a protocol with Israel and prevented its implementation because of restrictions on Palestinian agricultural exports.

A CONSTITUENT ROLE BEYOND THE SINGLE ACT

As a series of governmental deliberations confronted the prospect of further reforms endorsed by another round of IGCs, the European Parliament again resorted to reports to examine the parameters and needs for further reform. The all-party tactic was employed. A broader vision of the EC as an international player was floated, and the European Parliament tried, again unsuccessfully, to secure for itself a direct role in the IGC deliberations. This time it did not present a fully elaborated treaty, complete with legal text, but confined itself to a series of reports on specific issues—such as subsidiarity—and a

series of constitutional reports known as the Martin Reports, after their rapporteur.[7]

The Martin Reports

One of the most important features of the Martin Reports is the degree of continuity of purpose they exemplify. European union, as identified by Spinelli, remains the goal. The method for attaining it, though not identical, starts from the same basic premise, namely, that European union can be realized only if the EC's institutions are given the necessary powers and financial resources to enable them to tackle pressing problems in a democratic, open—or transparent—and effective manner.

The tactics employed were to be similar: generating a wide debate among national and European parliamentarians sharing a conviction in the need to effect a functioning parliamentary democracy at both national and supranational levels. The Martin strategy differed, however, in relying less on a broad debate between informed elites who could act as multipliers. In that sense, it was less sensitive and less political, necessarily so given the delicate issues confronted and historical circumstances.

Key proposals from the Martin Reports

The proposals were wide-ranging but pragmatic. They reflected the development of Parliament's thinking over several years. While security policy was seen as acutely sensitive,

7. David Martin, *An Ever Closer Union* (London: Spokesman, 1991).

it must not be forgotten that Parliament had discussed this in the context of industrial policy during the 1970s, when the issue of the civilianization of defense industries was not on the agenda but when its deliberations had been spurred by concern over sensitive exports in the context of the Cold War and U.S. interference in EC exports. The main proposals of the Martin Reports related to institutional reform and to an expansion in the scope of EC competence in order to render it able to act effectively in the international arena. These were coupled with a concern to maximize democracy and to ensure that individual rights were respected. The key proposals are echoed in the subsequent Maastricht Treaty. They may be summarized as

— codecision for the European Parliament with the Council of Ministers;
— election by Parliament of the Commission President on a proposal from the European Council;
— Council of Ministers meetings in public;
— generalized majority voting in the Council of Ministers;
— extension of majority voting in the Council of Ministers to environmental and social policies;
— cooperation with national parliaments but no new mixed chamber comprising delegates from the European Parliament and national parliaments;
— limited right of legislative initiative by the European Parliament;
— increase in the Parliament's investigative powers through the establishment of committees of inquiry;
— reinforcement of Parliament control over EC finance;
— stricter enforcement of EC law through an increase in the Commission's powers and the power of the EC Court of Justice to fine member states not complying with EC rules;
— proper representation for the regions;
— economic and monetary union;
— EC tax visible to taxpayers;
— firm commitment to a Declaration of Fundamental Rights—a bill of rights—with recourse to the European Court of Justice if necessary;
— Common Foreign and Security Policy; and
— more EC involvement in social policy including vocational training.

EUROPEAN UNION IN THE 1990s

The Maastricht Treaty on European Union (TEU) was to expand the scope of European integration significantly. In some respects, it codified existing practices and developments that had arisen in the context of realizing the single market.

The TEU is divided into three pillars, known as the temple approach. This separated supranational, or EC-level, decision-making rules and competences from two intergovernmental pillars: one on foreign policy and the other on judicial cooperation. Both of the latter were subject to intergovernmental decision making: government autonomy was respected and national governmental supremacy remained unchallenged. Neither could function without significant inputs from supranational institutions, notably the Commission. In short, both pillars were likely to be subsequently incorporated into the *acquis communautaire* and become supranational competences in the future.

Moreover, it was clear that the functioning of the single market itself imposed new demands for supranational action in specific areas that had hitherto been seen as the preserve of national governments. The section on judicial and home affairs cooperation was a case in point. Labor-mobility rules under the Single Act's provisions on the four freedoms—freedom of movement of goods, persons, capital, and services, in order to realize the single market—meant that if internal frontiers were removed and the external frontier around the EC strengthened, there would be consequences for internal and external border controls of legal and illegal movement of persons and goods as well as customs formalities. This had implications for issues that had not formally been considered at all within an EC context or that had been considered only on an ad hoc intergovernmental basis through European Political Cooperation. Among such issues were immigration, refugees, asylum, police, and anticrime activities.

The realization of the single market impelled a need for, at a minimum, cooperation and, later on, a degree of coordination and harmonization or approximation of national provisions in order to prevent the proliferation of discriminatory practice based on national rules that could be unfairly invoked or exploited, for example, by outsiders. There had been a marked reluctance on the part of some states—the United Kingdom again included—to advance supranational cooperation in these areas with the result that five of the original six EC member states founded the Schengen group to take measures more quickly. This inner core not only drove progress forward but ensured that any measures they agreed on conformed to EC provisions. Indeed, the Commission was fully consulted over their provisions, many of which then formed the basis for subsequent EC-level action both through European Political Cooperation—and the Terrorism, Radicalism, Extremism and International Violence (TREVI) group—and through the EC proper.[8]

A further consequence was that the notion of an EC citizen would have to be clarified. The European Parliament was quick to link the idea of political rights and obligations— such as the right to contest and vote in direct elections—with the far more limited concept of citizenship deriving solely from a concept of economic —that is, labor-mobility—rights customarily inferred from the Rome Treaty and later the Single Act and single market.

The TEU widened the area of the EC institutions' competence and entrenched intergovernmentalism in a supranational treaty. This was a major break with past practice.

The Single European Act had paved the way for this development. It had done so by incorporating a special title—Title III—on political cooperation in a single document that

8. Juliet Lodge, *Internal Security and Judicial Cooperation Beyond Maastricht* (Hull: Hull University, European Community Research Unit, 1992).

primarily encompassed reforms to existing articles of the Rome Treaty. Title III was especially significant, however, because it broached the taboo subject of security. This had been taboo since the EC's inception because security issues were seen to be the sole preserve of member governments and security policy was seen as the proper preserve of the North Atlantic Treaty Organization but not the EC, which was conceived of as an economic organization only. Whereas the Single Act referred to the economic and political aspects of security, the TEU referred specifically to defense and the development of a Common Foreign and Security Policy (CFSP). Moreover, it explicitly granted the supranational institutions a role in decision making in this area. The Commission is to be fully associated with CFSP work, according to Article 9, though precisely how is unclear.

The European Parliament has a far more limited role. It is to be kept informed regularly by the Council presidency and Commission and may be consulted by the presidency on the main aspects and basic choices of the CFSP. It may question the Council, make recommendations to it, hold an annual debate on the CFSP, and exercise all its existing—and potentially far more important—rights in the external relations field. These include the right to approve measures with financial implications—for example, financial protocols attached to trade agreements—and enlargement and association agreements. Used imaginatively, of course, these rights amount to a veto power, as the

Parliament demonstrated when it insisted on an agreement with Israel being amended to the benefit of Palestinian exporters. Similarly, it stated that it would not approve EC enlargement to include Turkey until Turkey respected human rights. It also insisted that any enlargement would be held up pending institutional reform in general.

The TEU does expand its powers somewhat in this delicate foreign affairs area, where parliaments in Europe tend to have negligible roles. While it can discuss any foreign affairs issue it chooses, since it alone has the right to set its agenda, and while this is a potent means of publicizing matters, it must be remembered that the new TEU powers are discretionary and relatively untried. In the past, neither the Council of Ministers nor the Commission has yielded much to the European Parliament without a fight. For real progress to be made, it has always been essential for the European Parliament to have allies in both institutions.

One of the paradoxes of 1993 was that Denmark, which was largely responsible for holding up the implementation of the TEU after its negative referendum on the treaty in May 1992, took over the Council of Ministers presidency. One of the first measures that it introduced played straight into the Parliament's court. Condemning excessive secrecy and a lack of transparency, the Danish Council President made history in opening up at least one of the hitherto secret Council sessions to the public. This was supposed to assuage Danish fears of an overly centralized and bureaucratic rather than democratic EC, but it also bolstered the legitimacy of the Parliament's quest for generalized improvements in democratic practice and greater openness in decision making. Openness of this sort remains discretionary, and secrecy is the norm.

The problem was, however, that the governments were not generally prepared to relinquish Council secrecy and passed the buck to the Commission. While already one of the most open of all bureaucracies in Europe, the Commission took steps to increase the transparency of its procedures further.

INCREASING TRANSPARENCY

The Commission improved a number of existing practices to increase general awareness of Commission proposals and decisions. These included steps to seek wider-ranging advice from interested parties at the predecisional stages of proposal drafting. The Commission now earmarks in its annual work and legislative programs proposals on which such advice is to be sought and publishes green papers (consultative documents) prior to their formal elaboration. Access to databases is also to be improved. The coherence of proposals is also to be ameliorated by regrouping various EC measures in one text when they deal with the same policy area. This should not only help the private and public sectors, interest groups, and the public to become more familiar with Commission proposals but also encourage national parliaments—otherwise largely irrelevant to the progress of EC legislation—to be better informed. This, too, is something that the European Parliament has pressed hard for.

The refinements in Commission work practice are welcome from the European Parliament's point of view. However, since the Single Act came into force, there has been far more cooperation between the Commission and the Parliament of necessity. This is because the Single Act introduced, through the cooperation procedure, a legislative process that was tied to a specific timetable. Each institution was given deadlines by which to reach a decision. This not only expedited decision making—the primary goal—but forced the Commission, Council of Ministers, and Parliament to liaise and cooperate effectively with one another.

To make this manageable, the Commission and the Parliament worked together to set up a legislative program whose schedule is known to all and which, once the technology is properly functioning, should result in interactive computerized exchanges to enable each institution to see at a glance which officials have primary responsibility for whatever proposal is on the table.

INSTITUTIONAL PREREQUISITES OF EFFECTIVE ACTION

It is one thing for the European Parliament to have won more powers, whether of the legislative, scrutiny and control, or budgetary nature. It is quite another to make those powers effective. The necessary preconditions for effective Parliament action remain improved party discipline inside the Parliament and effective cooperation and coordination with the Commission and the Council of Ministers. The Commission-Parliament axis is still extremely important but one that cannot be fostered realistically at the expense of improved Parliament-Council of Ministers relations. For the Parliament to be in a position to act, it must carry the support of a majority, usually an absolute majority of 260 of its 518 members. This places a premium on party discipline and cross-party and cross-national support.

A further area for improvement concerns the role of national parliaments in the EC. Their role has traditionally been negligible. However, the European Parliament's tactics for promoting European union along maximalist lines have rested on the establishment and maintenance of parliamentary consensus both inside the European Parliament and inside the national parliaments. Closer liaison between the two would be mutually beneficial. Indeed, the European Parliament initiated the Assizes in 1990 whereby issues of common interest were discussed in a formal setting between members of national parliaments and MEPs.

The Assizes were seen by some commentators as a prelude to a new, third parliamentary chamber— a Euro-Senate. However, they were not institutionalized partly because the Council of Ministers, in a bicameral system, would be the obvious chamber to perform the role of a Senate and partly because dialogue between the two can be maintained on a constructive basis without additional elaborate institutional machinery.

EUROPEAN UNION:
A BALANCE SHEET

There can be little doubt that, while the TEU does not meet the European Parliament's criteria for a constitution that supplants the existing treaties, it has significantly augmented the potential scope of the European Union's popularly elected arm of the legislature.

Specifically, the European Parliament has acquired new powers and rights that either expand existing capabilities or imbue it with new opportunities. A first set of new EC competences involves the Parliament in

— the assent procedure, as used concerning citizens' rights to reside and move freely within the EC; setting up a cohesion fund for environmental issues and the trans-European networks (TENs) in transport infrastructure; giving the European Central Bank powers of prudential supervision; and amendments to protocol of the system of European central banks;

— the codecision procedure, as regards incentives to achieve quality in education, health and consumer protection, culture, and TENs' guidelines;

— the cooperation procedure, as used in multilateral surveillance under economic and monetary union, specification of definitions precluding EC liability for public debts, rules on coin issue, vocational training, im-

plementation of the TENs, development cooperation policy, and negotiations on working conditions and the labor market;
— the consultation procedure, which is used in matters concerning electoral rights, additions to citizens' rights, visa policy, future rules on excessive deficits, appointment of the European Central Bank Executive Board, the European Monetary Institute, single currency and member states' readiness, measures to support industrial policy, the European currency unit, external currency exchange rate agreements, supplementary action on economic and social cohesion, aspects of environmental policy, proposed nomination of the Commission President, classes of action brought before the Court of First Instance and that court's composition, appointment of the Court of Auditors, the method for fixing European Monetary Institute resources, and the calling of an IGC to revise the treaties;
— the deferred consultation procedure, as regards emergency visa rules; and
— the dismissal of the Ombudsman, done at the Parliament's request by the Court of Justice.

A second set of existing EC competences reinforces existing procedures:

— assent where no Parliament procedure applied previously;
— assent in place of consultation, thereby giving the Parliament a de facto veto;
— codecision in place of consultation;
— codecision in place of cooperation;
— cooperation in place of consultation; and
— consultation where no Parliament procedure applied previously.

A third set of provisions grants the Parliament involvement through new reporting procedures that attest to the Parliament's right to hold other institutions accountable. The following now have to report to or inform the Parliament: the European Council, the Council of Ministers, the Council President, the Commission, the Court of Auditors, the Ombudsman, and the European Monetary Institute/European Central Bank.

Additional new rights codify existing practices of the Parliament or give it new powers. They include a right of initiative, a formal right of inquiry, a formal right to receive petitions, a right to appoint or dismiss the Ombudsman, a right to challenge acts and failure to act by other institutions, a right to information before budget discharge, and rights relating to the appointment of the Commission President and the Commission.

Further rights relate specifically to the new European Union and include the right to be consulted and/or informed about the CFSP and on cooperation in the field of justice and home affairs. The latter includes asylum policy; immigration; conditions of residence for third-country nationals; combating illegal drugs and international fraud; judicial cooperation in customs and civil and criminal matters; and police cooperation in drug trafficking, terrorism, and international crime.

The Parliament was quick to test out its new investiture powers[9] at the beginning of 1993, when MEPs voted on whether or not to endorse the newly appointed Commission. MEPs condemned the weakness of the Commission's program,[10] and the Socialists threatened to sack the new Commission. In practice, however, close liaison between the Commission and the Parliament is the precondition of effective action. The two are mutually dependent: the Parliament requires the Commission's technical know-how, and the Commission needs the Parliament to legitimize and lend democratic support to it. This has become acutely sensitive following the transparency arguments in the wake of the first Danish referendum. The Parliament retains its interest in preserving a strong Commission able to act independently of national governments. Any weakening in the Commission's authority, as the Single Act and TEU seemed to presage, would undermine further integration.

DEMOCRATIC LEGITIMACY:
MORE THAN A QUESTION
OF SUBSIDIARITY

Democratic legitimacy is not just about Euro-elections, reforming the current electoral provisions to bring national provisions broadly into line under a system of proportional representation. Nor is it only a matter of improving the transparency, efficiency, accountability, and democratic nature of EC institutions.[11] Inadequate parliamentary control over the Commission and more especially the Council of Ministers, coupled with the absence of direct elections, originally lay at the heart of the democratic deficit. The residual weaknesses on both counts contribute to today's deficit. Ideas of representativeness, accountability, and democratic practice remain intertwined. The presumed hierarchical ordering of direct legitimacy (as acquired by the Parliament through direct elections) over derived legitimacy (as assumed by the Council of Ministers, many of whose members had been elected to national government) continues to bedevil the debate. The democratic deficit is not just a problem of horizontal distribution of power among EC institutions, however.

The vertical dimension is important, both as it affects relations internal to EC institutions and as it affects relations between supranational, national, regional, and local levels of government and administration. This has been most potently ex-

9. See arguments presented during the Single European Act deliberations in European Parliament, Committee on Institutional Affairs, "Working Document on the EP Proposals Submitted to the IGC on the Appointment and Powers of the Commission" (Fanti Report), PE 101.517/1, 28 Oct. 1985.

10. European Community, Commission, *The Commission's Programme 1993-4*, SEC(93) 58 final, 26 Jan. 1993; the reply on the investiture debate by Commission President Delors in ibid.

11. Juliet Lodge, "Democratic Legitimacy and the EC: Crossing the Rubicon," *International Journal of Public Administration* (in press).

pressed through the debate over the concept of subsidiarity, a formula designed to ensure that decisions are taken at the most appropriate and lowest level of government. This implies the existence of regional and local governments with real authority throughout the member states.

In brief, the EC suffers from an authority crisis and a legitimacy crisis. The suspicion persists that EC institutions are unable to act authoritatively and are not entirely appropriate for the exercise of functions and tasks bestowed on them by the treaties.

The authority of EC institutions is open to challenge, notably by jealous national political elites who can manipulate dissent and blame the supranational institutions for their own failings. Moreover, the paradoxical effect of the Maastricht Treaty revisions on the Parliament's powers is to make its actions more visible but not necessarily more tangible or intelligible. Further confusion as to the locus of popular authority may also arise given the introduction of a Committee of Regions, which has negligible powers. This compounds the problem of national parliaments' having a small role and even less influence in the EC. As a result, the problem of the EC's democratic legit-

imacy and the alleged persistence of the democratic deficit has not been fully rectified by the Maastricht Treaty. Its revision clauses are therefore important, and the next IGC, scheduled for 1996, must address these gaps. For the present, the legitimacy crisis still revolves around contested issues of the locus of authority and the pervasive view that EC institutions have somewhat inappropriate competences and powers. National governments can be overruled and bound by majority votes in the Council of Ministers.

The democratic legitimacy crisis can be remedied only through further treaty revisions to clarify the relative positions and powers of the institutions in line with an agreed view of what elements make up a functioning democratic polity, since this is clearly what is being built at the EC level. In short, there is a pressing need for European union to be clarified. The European Parliament's role in it remains contested, but it has perhaps the greatest responsibility— as the legatee of the Spinelli draft treaty establishing the European Union—to ensure that appropriate practices are enshrined in a representative, pluralist, liberal democratic, parliamentary system at the EC level.

ANNALS, *AAPSS*, **531**, January 1994

The Economics of the
Renewed Integration Movement

By STEPHEN F. OVERTURF

ABSTRACT: Beginning in 1978, the European Community embarked upon a process that would leave the member states 15 years later at a significantly higher level of economic integration. The establishment and institutional development of the European Monetary System would be perceived to be a success, leading to the Single European Act and the eventual adoption of many of those policies characteristic of a single internal market within the Community. This, in time, provided a base upon which an attempt at establishing economic and monetary union could be made. Although difficulties associated with a premature vision of the true nature of the European Monetary System would need to be described as a setback to the process, it is nevertheless clear from a broader perspective, and from the desire shown by other states to join the Community, that the economies of Western Europe are integrating.

Stephen F. Overturf is Ferguson Professor of International Economics at Whittier College. His interest in the economics, politics, and history of the European integration movement is evidenced by his membership in the European Community Studies Association, his selection by the Delegation of the Commission as a Team 92 member, and several articles and a book, The Economic Principles of European Integration, *concerning the development of the European Community.*

THE economies of Western Europe are integrating. Due to the nature and intensity of the discussion over the possible political integration of the states forming the European Community (EC), the fact is occasionally lost sight of that, especially since 1978, there has been, and in all likelihood will continue to be, significant movement toward the economic integration of these same states. Moreover, the movement is now beginning to include other Western and even Eastern European nations in the centripetal force of trade, factor, and policy integration.

EUROPEAN MONETARY SYSTEM

The year 1978 is a particularly appropriate one for the consideration of the economics of the renewed integration movement in the EC. It was in this year that the European Monetary System (EMS) was conceived and, as it were, sold to the rest of the Community by West German Chancellor Helmut Schmidt and French President Valéry Giscard d'Estaing. In no small measure, it was the perceived success of this endeavor that lent evidence to the possibilities of the Single European Act and to the Maastricht Treaty (which is also called the Treaty on European Union) that followed.

The initial economic rationale for the EMS was clear enough; it was to create a "zone of monetary stability" in Europe. The desired stability applied both to exchange rates and, perhaps more by implication, to the coincidence of inflation rates among members. European countries have always been more concerned with un-

stable exchange rates than, say, the United States, because their economies are both more open in terms of international trade and linked to one another through trade. Exchange rates matter in such a setting, and controversy over what constitutes an optimum currency area cannot obscure the fact that fluctuations can have a direct and significant impact on inflation rates and levels of income and employment in an interdependent Europe.[1]

The potential negative effects of such fluctuations, therefore, were well appreciated by Europe and had been during most of the 1970s, as the result of the turbulence related to the oil crises and the breakup of the Bretton Woods system of fixed exchange rates. The benign attitude of the United States toward fluctuating exchange rates certainly encouraged the EC to revisit an earlier attempt at reducing such fluctuations in Europe, referred to as the snake, that had largely failed by the midpoint of the decade.

It is interesting to note that the economic motivation was certainly predominant to the political, in spite of some very mild language to the contrary in the documents establishing the EMS. Underscoring this notion is the fact that the system was created, on 5 December 1978, by a

---

1. In some ways, the original contribution to optimum currency theory by McKinnon spoke most directly to the European case, where an optimum area is defined by the openness of countries and by the resulting constraints on the ability to adjust exchange rates as well as macroeconomic policy variables. See Ronald I. McKinnon, "Optimum Currency Areas," *American Economic Review*, 53(4):717 (Sept. 1963).

resolution of the European Council from an agreement of the EC central banks, rather than through the regular institutional channels of the Community.

The design of the EMS incorporated an echo of the snake in establishing that the exchange rates of the members would not fluctuate, except by agreed "realignments," outside of fixed bands, either 2.25 or 6.00 percent, of one currency with any other. This was the bilateral parity grid of the Exchange Rate Mechanism (ERM) of the system, and it was, and is, the heart of the EMS.

There was also the creation of a new unit of account, the ECU (European currency unit), that would take on some aspects of money but was not a true currency as it simply represented a market basket of participating countries' currencies. In addition, in order to assault the notion that it was always the deficit, and not the surplus, countries that had to adjust their policies and economies to any imbalance, a "divergence indicator" was created to introduce more symmetry into the adjustment process. Finally, financing facilities were created, and an institution, the European Monetary Cooperation Fund, was established, intended to develop into a true European monetary fund with its own resources to help facilitate exchange rate stability among the members.[2]

2. For more on the institutional design, development, and economic results of the EMS, see Hugo Kaufmann and Stephen Overturf, "Progress within the European Monetary System," in *The State of the European Community*, ed. Leon Hurwitz and Christian Lequesue (Boulder, CO: Lynne Rienner, 1991), pp. 183-205.

As the EMS developed over time, from the official beginning of the system on 13 March 1979, the parity grid of the ERM predominated over the other aspects of the design. After an initial period, characterized by relatively frequent realignments, the French commitment to what Americans might call conservative economic policies, intended to reduce inflation and foster growth by fiscal and monetary constraint, led to much greater stability. After 1987, the ERM became virtually a fixed-rate system, with no significant realignments until a major rending of the system in 1992.

The fact of the matter is that the ERM of the EMS, in which, incidentally, the United Kingdom did not participate until 1990, had become a mechanism by which to abet and foster lower inflation rates and, ideally, higher and more stable long-term growth rates among the members, in addition to the original vision of reducing fluctuations in exchange rates. The model was West Germany, and the ERM allowed the rest of the Community economically to attach itself to the strict philosophy that lies behind the strength of the deutsche mark (DM) and of the German economy. Instead of reducing asymmetry, the EMS was actually used to encourage an asymmetrical convergence to the price stability of the DM as the "nominal anchor" of the system. With the agreements at Basle-Nyborg (1987) allowing for easier access to financing among the states as well as placing an emphasis on the use of domestic interest rates to curb pressures to devalue, the system, as noted, became perceived as virtually fixed.

The debate over the value of the ERM in leading to this end is an important one. The generally accepted argument is that the system lent credibility to what were widely considered the less fiscally conservative members. This credibility in turn altered expectations, including especially expectations of those involved in wage bargaining, sufficiently to allow for greater ease among the governments to pursue deflationary policies, even at the cost of unemployment figures that were relatively high.[3]

Another view is that it was the coincidental appreciation for disinflationary policies by the states that lent the EMS credibility, rather than the reverse. The facts that the divergence indicator was virtually ignored and that the ECU and the European Monetary Cooperation Fund never developed institutionally (as opposed to the former being embraced by the private market), lend credence to this view.

Be that as it may, it is true that, once established and functioning, the system became viewed as a successful intergovernmental political institution within the nexus of the Community, and once one committed to it, it would be difficult for a state to

withdraw—or even devalue—without threatening one's participation and acceptance in other areas.[4] This notion suggests something of a neofunctionalist role for the EMS: a successful "visible symbol of Europe" that could provide not only a Community focus for macroeconomic policy decision making among the separate states but also a rallying point for further integration.

SINGLE EUROPEAN ACT

The economic rationale behind the Single European Act, signed in 1986, was the economic malaise of low growth rates and high unemployment often referred to as Eurosclerosis, a condition made worse by comparison to the healthier conditions of the United States and Japan. A greater level of interdependence through trade increasing the size of the market, a very old idea indeed, was seen as a potential cure, especially when combined with the promise of greater economies of scale. The facts were that there were still significant trade barriers in what was supposed to be a common market and that, after 1983, all of the states were more or less convinced that old-style Keynesian policies, especially those conceived to work in a state of autarky, were bankrupt. The famous and influential Cecchini Report suggested that some of the benefits of creating a true internal market with a freer flow of capital, labor, goods,

3. Three examples from a large literature include Jacques Melitz, "Monetary Discipline and Cooperation in the European Monetary System: A Synthesis," in *The European Monetary System*, ed. Francesco Giavazzi, Stefano Micosi, and Marcus Miller (New York: Cambridge University Press, 1988); Francesco Giavazzi and Alberto Giovannini, "The Role of the Exchange-Rate Regime in a Disinflation: Empirical Evidence on the European Monetary System," in ibid.; Susan M. Collins, "Inflation and the European Monetary System," in ibid.

4. For reflection on this point, and much else dealing with these concerns, see John T. Woolley, "Policy Credibility and European Monetary Institutions," in *Euro-Politics*, ed. Alberta M. Sbragia (Washington, DC: Brookings Institution, 1992).

and services would increase the Community's gross domestic product by 4.5 to 7.0 percent, increase employment between 4.5 and 7.0 percent, and lower consumer prices by 4.5 to 6.0 percent.[5]

The political rationale was that it was time for a new initiative leading to greater European integration. There is also controversy on this point, however, with the alternative suggestion that the internal market to be concluded by 1992 was little more than the result of intergovernmental bargaining based on a relatively specific assessment of the costs and benefits to the states entering into the agreement for the Single European Act.[6]

Indeed, it is interesting that a conscious choice was made not to move directly from the EMS to the common currency objective of economic and monetary union (EMU), which would seem to have been the natural route. A story is that Jacques Delors would have preferred to have taken this route but that he was convinced otherwise due to certain opposition from the central bankers in the EC, as well as the expressed opposition from Germany that such a movement would be premature before capital market liberalization and policy coordination.[7] The alternative notion of the single market provided for a nice mix of deregulation and market—including capital market—liberalization with greater institutional integration that, nevertheless, did not include too great a sacrifice of sovereignty at this stage.

It is possible, despite this controversy, to accept all of this and still suggest that it would have been most difficult to move on to the single market without the prior perceived success of the EMS.[8]

In any case, by the targeted end of 1992, most of what was conceived to constitute the single market had been in place, with the noted exceptions of well-harmonized tax rates, free access to public procurement, and the elimination of border controls over the movement of persons to all states within the Community. In fact, by 1988 it had become clear that the single market would be a success, and thought was turned to the next economic step to take. Work began on the planning of EMU.

5. Michael Calingaert, *The 1992 Challenge from Europe: Development of the European Community's Internal Market* (Washington, DC: National Planning Association, 1988), p. 66.

6. See, for example, Andrew Moravcsik, "Negotiating the Single European Act," in *The New European Community*, ed. Robert O. Keohane and Stanley Hoffmann (Boulder, CO: Westview Press, 1991). In this view, West Germany and France favored procedural reform, while the United Kingdom did not, versus the United Kingdom and Germany's favoring deregulation and more competitive markets, while France was lukewarm to this. For other views, see Pierre-Henri Laurent, "The European Technology Community, the Meeting of the Elites, and the Creation of the Internal Market," *Il Politico*, 3:161-81 (1987); Wayne Sandholtz and John Zysman, "Recasting the European Bargain," *World Politics*, 42:95-128 (Oct. 1989).

7. See also Robert O. Keohane and Stanley Hoffmann, "Institutional Change in Europe in the 1980s," in Keohane and Hoffmann, *New European Community*, p. 11.

8. Cameron suggests that "the EMS, or something like it, represented a necessary precondition for the free flow of goods, services, and capital within the Community." David R. Cameron, "The 1992 Initiative: Causes and Consequences," in *Euro-Politics*, ed. Sbragia, pp. 47-48.

ECONOMIC AND MONETARY UNION

Whether or not reality conforms to a neofunctionalist vision of linkages, or spillovers, creating institutional progress toward integration, it is certainly true that the economic rationale for movement toward EMU in 1988 followed along these lines. In particular, the single market was seen as in some ways incomplete, or "not fully achievable," without movement toward a single currency in the EC. Moreover, the single market that would come into place in 1992 was seen actually to be unstable when supplemented by only the existing EMS.

This instability is due to the removal of capital controls and the level of financial integration that was part of the single market, conditions that could not be seen to coexist with both fixed exchange rates and independent monetary policies. There is an accepted view that, between countries, there cannot simultaneously be free capital movements, independent macroeconomic—especially monetary—policies, and fixed exchange rates; given the rapid increase in capital mobility internationally, this view has been taken quite seriously in the debate over EMU in Europe. A natural conclusion is that if fixed rates are important for international trade, as they are taken to be in an open Europe dependent on trade, it only makes sense to coordinate policies, and, eventually, to rule out the threat of exchange rate fluctuation entirely by moving to a common currency created by a single central bank.

The political rationale behind such a move was, of course, that there is not a much more important symbol of sovereignty than a state's currency, and such a move would be a most important step on the road toward a United States of Europe. That is not to say that countries would be somehow fooled into greater political integration but rather that it makes perfectly logical, economic sense that they should be so integrated.

The institutional development of EMU began seriously, as noted, in 1988 with the Hanover European Council instructing a committee, later to be named after Delors, to study the steps necessary to such an end. The group was composed largely of central bankers, a probably necessary but nonetheless masterful stroke that ensured that the final decisions of the committee would have a good chance of being implemented. As it turned out, the final report of the committee, the Delors Report, set the agenda and determined to a large measure the structure of the Maastricht Treaty.[9]

Briefly, the report linked the success of the EMS with the adoption of the Single European Act but also suggested a need to move on to EMU based on (1) the EMS having not fulfilled its full potential, including the lack of establishment of the European Monetary Fund; and (2) the fact that the single market would "reduce the room for independent policy manoeuvre . . . in each member country"[10] (as outlined previously).

9. Committee for the Study of Economic and Monetary Union, *Report on Economic and Monetary Union in the European Community* (Luxembourg: Office of the Official Publications of the European Communities, 1989).

10. Ibid., p. 14.

The report recommended approaching EMU by stages, yielding irrevocably fixed exchange rates and then a common currency. Control and issue of the latter would be by a European System of Central Bankers, later dubbed "EuroFed" but modeled more on the Deutsche Bundesbank than on the United States Federal Reserve System. This was so because the bank would, as with the Bundesbank, be independent and committed to price stability. This last point is important in that it shows the strength of the prevalent attitude that price stability is critical to a well-ordered economy, one that can be more successful in achieving higher growth rates in the long run than those that attempt to manipulate monetary and, by extension, fiscal policies for shorter-term macroeconomic objectives. In fact, because the latter policies cannot work in the long run, they should not even be attempted, and the institutional structure of the central bank should be such—through independence and a price-stability mandate—as to ensure their avoidance. This was the lesson of Germany to the world in the 1980s.

The report spoke to economic as well as monetary union, with reference to the free flow of goods, services, and factors, as well as fiscal coordination with "binding rules" on budget deficits and deficit financing.

The report was accepted, sent with modifications to an intergovernmental conference—by this time supplemented with one on political union—in December of 1990, finally yielding the language and signing by governments of the Maastricht Treaty of December 1991.[11] Again, the work of the Delors Committee is evident in the nature of this treaty, which has EMU proceeding by stages toward the final one, which would commence sometime between January 1997 and January 1999. Strict criteria are set out to determine which countries are open to being included, criteria regarding budget deficits and national debt, inflation and exchange rate stability. The control of the external exchange rate, a point of great controversy, was settled conservatively in favor of the European System of Central Bankers, but with some powers retained by the Council of Ministers.[12] Finally, the binding rules in the fiscal arena are no longer part of Maastricht, but there are strict provisions regarding, for example, deficit financing.

Political union is also spoken to, although hardly as forcefully, in response to a felt need, especially in Germany, to redress a democratic deficit among the EC institutions if sovereignty would be shifted seriously to the Community.

The history, of course, is that Denmark, requiring a national referendum for ratification, found its people rejecting the treaty in June of 1992,

11. A report, Directorate General for Economic and Financial Affairs, *One Market, One Money* (Belgium: Commission of the European Communities, 1990), was issued with the intention of serving as the equivalent of the Cecchini Report for EMU.

12. On this point, see Horst Ungerer, "Political Aspects of European Monetary Integration" (Mimeo., based on a lecture at the European University Institute, Florence, 3 Nov. 1992), pp. 19-20. For the political dimension of economic integration in this area, see Ungerer's entire paper.

generally on grounds other than economic, including potential threats to the environment and fear of control by Germany and Brussels. The French voted yes, but by a very narrow margin in September of the same year.

Leading up to and following the French vote, enormous strains were put on the EMS in the foreign exchange market, causing the United Kingdom and Italy to leave the system and forcing devaluation of the currencies of Spain, Portugal, and Ireland. The problem had been that the somewhat weaker ERM countries had, according to the rules laid down earlier, kept interest rates high in order to defend against exchange market attack, this being especially necessary in light of the international strength of the DM. As the Bundesbank was maintaining very high German interest rates in fear of the expansive monetary and inflationary implications of reunification, the markets simply did not believe the economies would be able to continue to keep rates so high in the face of increasing recession and unemployment in Europe. The very international capital mobility and relaxation of capital controls that led to the justification for EMU were responsible here for splintering the EMS.

The Delors Report, it turns out, had been partly prophetic in noting that incompatible national policies would "quickly translate into exchange rate tensions,"[13] but it is probably closer to the mark to say that creating the semblance of a fixed exchange rate union from 1987 on was unwise, that such a quasi union had great internal risks of cracking, and that realignments should have been allowed earlier so as not to put too much stock into the ERM as it was constituted as a transition to EMU. As it is, the cracking of the system threatened the progress on monetary union.

Observations on the purely mechanistic functioning of the ERM during this 1992-93 period found fault in the extended span of time, five months, it took to establish the final set of still vulnerable but relatively stable exchange rates, suggesting it all could have been done with prior consultation in one day. Otherwise, there was general agreement that it was not so much the system that was at fault as it was the way in which it had come to be viewed by the participants.

The Bundesbank, for example, could now suggest that new curbs be placed on foreign exchange market interventions required of strong currency countries in support of weaker currencies in the ERM. This was offered not as a criticism of the basic system; rather, it was seen as a way to allow for and even encourage necessary devaluations. Although the idea of a preestablished curb itself negates to some extent the psychological impact on the markets of potential government interventions, it nevertheless underscores the notion that it was not perhaps so much high German interest rates that were at fault at the time as it was the prevalent perception of the system, a perception that did not allow for timely realignments. In fact, the German central bank had engaged in several

13. Committee for the Study of Economic and Monetary Union, *Report on Economic and Monetary Union*, p. 15.

unsuccessful confidential meetings in 1990 and 1991 to encourage just such a coordinated realignment of rates.

After this experience of forced devaluations and departures from the ERM, people began to question whether all of the members of the EC could converge to the strict requirements of the treaty for entry into EMU. Talk of a two-speed Europe with a core of hard-currency northern states establishing EMU between themselves, leaving others, by implication less committed EC members, behind, raised old questions of optimum currency areas and even potential political disintegration. It had become apparent that an early freezing of parities, enshrined in one of the Maastricht conditions that required two years of unchanged exchange rate parities in the ERM prior to joining EMU, had combined with a delicately balanced European monetary system to threaten the very aim of the treaty itself. The 1993 vote by the Danes approving the Maastricht Treaty does not remove this uncertainty.

Perhaps more to the point, however, was the underlying cause for such uncertainty. This was the fact that with capital and foreign exchange markets increasingly integrated, it would be very difficult in the long run, as long as states wished to maximize trade flows within a single market, to avoid moving on to a common currency. In this way, the tumult created with the pressure on the EMS, even though viewed as a setback, could in the longer term serve to enhance the eventual prospects for monetary union in Europe.

CONCLUSION

In spite of the difficulties created by a premature fixity of exchange rates within the EMS, it was clear by 1993 that the EC was significantly more integrated economically than it had been 15 years earlier. The experiences of the EMS, the generally successful planning and implementation of the single internal market, and the steps taken toward EMU all spoke to the increasing maturity of the Community as an economic, if not yet political, unit.

In fact, with the breakup of the former Soviet Union and the sense and reality of instability in Eastern Europe, it was to the EC that these states turned for leadership and with hopes for inclusion into a broad and strong common market based on free economies and democratic institutions. Membership of even the stronger of these states seems ruled out for many years, due to the large financial outlays their economies would require from an EC already concerned over income differentials between the 12 present members. The eastern states combine low incomes with large populations and extensive agriculture, a formula for expensive support—probably too expensive.

The point is not so much whether or when the Eastern European states will be accepted into the Community, however, as it is the intensity of their desire to join. They view the EC as a viable and strong economic unit, one to which they must aspire to belong in order to become fully part of Europe and fulfill their economic potential.

This image of the EC is even more forcefully drawn by reference to the western, European Free Trade Association states that are applying for full membership, as opposed to weaker ties with the Community through a European Economic Area. Although these states, including Austria, Finland, and Sweden and perhaps Switzerland and Norway, would gain little net benefit from full membership over that from a European Economic Area, they are still anxious to join. The EC is more open to their applications than it is to those from Hungary, Poland, the Czech Republic, and Slovakia, of course, because they are high-income states that will bring substantial additional revenues with them into the EC budget, thus helping to share some of the burden of intra-EC income differentials.[14]

The fact that these states are willing to consider sacrificing some of their present and future sovereignty to achieve a degree of union with the EC speaks strongly to the conclusion that, despite setbacks, the economies of Western Europe are integrating.

14. As a group, it is estimated that the European Free Trade Association would increase the Community's revenues by 14 percent. See "Will More Be Merrier?" *Economist,* 17 Oct. 1992, p. 75.

The Significance of EC-1992

By JACQUES PELKMANS

ABSTRACT: The tortuous ratification process of the Maastricht Treaty, the turmoil in European currency markets in the autumn of 1992, the lack of political leadership ever since the Maastricht negotiation, and the recession would seem to have created a sense of disillusion about the much heralded post-1992 period for the European Community (EC). Is the Community drifting back to Europessimism? Was the impact of EC-1992 a fata morgana? What, if anything, was accomplished by EC-1992? This article shows that EC-1992 has enormous significance for the EC. There are four reasons. The first and most fundamental one is found in the induced transformation of the process of European integration in many ways. Second, EC-1992 has fulfilled a locomotive function, pulling the Community out of stagnation, bickering, and deadlock to great economic policy and political and market dynamism. Third, EC-1992 has bolstered the Community's position in the world economy and diplomacy. Fourth, the successful pursuit of EC-1992 has enabled the EC to assume the leadership in the post-Communist pan-European turmoil; although the EC role is not satisfactory, without EC-1992 and its impact, a disastrous leadership gap would have shown up.

Jacques Pelkmans is a senior research fellow at the Centre for European Policy Studies in Brussels, Director of EUROSCOPE in Maastricht, and adjunct professor to the Department of Economics of the University of Maastricht. His specializations include the economics of European integration, trade policy, standards, and the Association of Southeast Asian Nations. He has taught at the European University Institute in Florence and the European Institute of Public Administration in Maastricht.

O N 31 December 1992, the European Community (EC) ended an amazing steeplechase of seven and a half years and 282 hurdles called the EC-1992 program (also called the Single Market Program). That is, it declared it had met the ambitious challenge successfully, even though some 20 hurdles were left, including a few problematic ones. EC-1992 has oscillated between the peaks of an often hilarious psychosis, called Europhoria (1988-89), and the lows of almost total neglect or disbelief, from the second half of 1985 until somewhere in 1987. The end of this period came in an atmosphere of dutiful but less exciting workmanship in order to complete the program. The wrapping-up exercises at the end of 1992 could barely conceal feelings of disillusion, however: EC-1992 had lost its glamour, and other priorities had taken over, such as the ratification of the Maastricht Treaty (also called the Treaty on European Union), the turmoil in the European Monetary System, enlargement, the relationship with Central and Eastern Europe, and the rifts with the United States on agriculture. Moreover, unemployment was on the way up again, and growth—the greatest dividend of EC-1992?—had almost disappeared. Was the Community drifting back to a Europessimism similar to that of 10 years before? Had the anticipated impact of EC-1992 been no more than a fata morgana? What, if anything, had been accomplished by running this exhausting steeplechase?

In this article, it will be shown that EC-1992 had and still has an enormous significance for the Community economically, politically, in terms of the substantive guiding principles of European integration, and as a locomotive pulling the EC out of stagnation, not to mention its impact on the Community's place in the world. The article will subsequently set out how complete the internal market is and what remains to be done. A brief indication of the impact of EC-1992 on the actual functioning of the internal market itself will be provided, too.

THE INFLUENCE OF EC-1992 ON THE COMMUNITY

EC-1992 has changed the Community almost beyond recognition. Besides the economic impact—to be discussed later—five important elements of change can be identified.

Deepening of the internal market

The foundation of EC-1992 was the white paper *Completing the Internal Market*,[1] embraced by the European Council in Milan in late June 1985. Its aim was, in building upon the consolidation achieved in the period from December 1982 to the spring of 1985, to complete the internal market by a legislative program of incredible ambition spread over two Commission periods. Completion cannot, of course, be exactly defined. It depends, to a degree, on economic and political preferences, as is clear when comparing the internal Canadian market, the internal U.S. market, and the internal market of the

1. EC Commission to the European Council, *Completing the Internal Market*, 14 June 1985, COM(85) 310.

ket, and the internal market of the EC as foreseen by the white paper at the end of the steeplechase.[2] What is viewed as a complete set of rules for an internal market will also differ over time and hence cannot be fixed in a white paper forever. Such standards of perfectionism were not uppermost in the minds of the drafters of the white paper, however.

The Commission conceived completion above all as a catching-up process. The EC was seen as being intolerably behind in merely implementing the main principles of establishing a fully fledged common market, embodied in the four freedoms of movement of goods, services, capital, and labor. Lord Cockfield, the responsible EC Commissioner in 1985, stressed this point time and again: by and large the Commission was not more ambitious than the Community had promised itself to be in the European Economic Community (EEC) Treaty. This tactical position is understandable for political reasons, but from an analytical point of view, it is misleading, if not wrong. The white paper not only represented a maximalist integrative interpretation of the EEC Treaty—which is conditional or fuzzy in many respects—in some key policy areas, but, in combination with the Single Euro-

pean Act,[3] went decisively beyond the treaty text in some respects.

The deepening of the internal market as proposed in the white paper, and indeed as has been almost entirely accomplished, is drastic. The internal market in 1993 is simply incomparable with that of 1984. Concretely, the white paper implied the disappearance of internal frontiers for goods and persons; a large-scale assault on technical barriers in agriculture (veterinary and plant-health measures and inspections) and industry (the latter based on a revolutionary new approach of minimum harmonization and reference to standards as well as a new global approach to certification and testing, both in turn leading to major upheavals in the European standards-writing bodies as well as bodies for conformity assessment); the prizing open and much closer supervision of public procurement, also in hitherto excluded and up-to-then highly sensitive areas; the elimination of numerous remnants of national trade protection; the legislation of various facilitation measures to conduct business on a truly European basis; the harmonization and, to a degree, unification of intellectual property rights; and, last but not least, the liberalization of the major service markets at the EC level: banking, insurance, securities, telecommuni-

2. For this comparison, see Jacques Pelkmans and Marc Vanheukelen, "The Internal Markets of North America: Fragmentation and Integration in the US and Canada," *Research on the "Cost of Non-Europe": Basic Findings* (Luxembourg: Office of the Official Publications of the European Communities, 1988), vol. 16.

3. The first rewrite of the EEC Treaty, negotiated in late 1985 and in force since July 1987. The text of the Single European Act is reprinted in *EC Bulletin*, supp. 2 (1986). The white paper and the Single Act should be seen as twins in the EC-1992 program; both were indispensable and each was the other's complement.

cation services, and all six modes of transport, but especially road and air. The details have meanwhile been spelled out in an avalanche of publications on EC-1992. Perhaps the mere scale and tremendous complexity of the exercise has made it exceedingly hard to appreciate the far-reaching nature of EC-1992.

There is, however, a simple yet telling illustration to help many readers understand. It is well-known that European business had pressed for years to remove the obstacles to internal free trade and the Europeanization of business in the common market. This lobbying culminated in the Dekker Plan, launched in early January 1985 when the first Delors Commission began its work. Wisse Dekker was then the president of Philips electronics company but also chairman of the influential Industrial Market watchdog committee of the European Round Table of Industrialists. Although the plan responded to the concerns of Philips, it doubtlessly expressed a view widely held by business, and its strategy and proposals were applauded in many circles of European industry as appropriate and timely though rather bold. The plan comprised the completion of the internal market with respect to four key areas[4] and a detailed calendar until 1990. The considered and well-presented strategy quickly assumed something of a public good character, bolstered by a relentless

---

4. Those areas are trade facilitation (reducing the costs of internal frontiers), opening public procurement, indirect tax harmonization, and the removal of technical barriers.

campaign of speeches by Dr. Dekker throughout the Community.

Nevertheless, despite the Dekker Plan's fame and boldness at the time, it is little realized that the white paper, published only five months later, is both more encompassing and radical. To use EC jargon, the latter implies even more "widening" and "deepening" of the internal market. A faithful execution of the Dekker Plan would not have altered the Community nearly as much as EC-1992 has done, as exemplified by the following:

1. The internal frontiers would not have been removed for goods, let alone for persons.

2. National exchange controls would not have been dismantled.

3. The major services markets would have been neither Europeanized, nor somewhat deregulated.

4. Stubborn remnants of national trade protection would not have been abolished.

New regulatory principles

The introduction of EC-1992 signaled the end of total harmonization. In numerous cases, EC regulation has been aimed at a mere minimal harmonization, concentrating on what the EC Court calls the essential requirements for safety, health, the environment, and the like. This focus is complemented by mutual recognition of the laws of the EC member states. In addition, new regulatory principles include the abolition of internal frontiers—this is neither mentioned nor implied by the EEC Treaty but follows only from Article 8A of the Single European Act—and subsidiarity, the notion that EC regulation and policy should be pursued only if it is more effective than tackling the issue at the national level.[5] Another new principle consisted in far-reaching horizontal cooperation between the member states, something long known in the United States but thus far little practiced in the Community, where the only relevant administrative interface for regulatory implementation was that between the EC and its member states. Finally, the combination of mutual recognition, the four freedoms, and absence of internal frontiers gave rise to regulatory competition between the member states and, to a modest degree, the regions.

Together, these new principles have thoroughly changed the nature of EC regulatory processes, facilitated decision making on many substantive issues, and helped to undermine the power of hitherto powerful sectoral lobbies.

Impact on decision making

In the eight years since the Single Act was negotiated, the EC institutions have become used to majority decisions and serious efforts to com-

5. Note that a functional application of subsidiarity leads to an advanced stage in establishing an internal market (for example, the four freedoms). In turn, this will enable a much wider application of subsidiarity. Thus the emergence of the principle of subsidiarity in the EC can be understood as a response to the initial success of EC-1992. Subsidiarity can be applied internationally as well but only when mobilities are not hindered too much by frontiers.

promise. Even in cases of unanimity, instances of playing out veto rights to complete deadlock have become rare. This emphasis on qualified majority and flexibility has had at least four beneficial consequences: a much higher speed of decision making than before 1985; far more decisions per year (greater effective decision making capacity); more scope for open policy debates with new options, alternatives, and policy innovation, prompted by the need for coalition building in the process of forming blocking minorities or passing majorities (by the Commission, active member states, and the Council presidency); and, finally, a higher quality of regulation since, without vetoes, it is hard to impose on others costly, cumulative provisions (to satisfy different member states) on artificial constructs (reflecting hard-won compromises).

The opening-up of the Euromarket to third countries

EC-1992 had the unexpected result of significantly liberalizing access to the EC market for third countries. This is not due to a policy switch in the liberal direction following the U.S.-led Fortress Europe campaign. The Fortress Europe campaign may have helped to bend the EC-1992 debate in a more liberal direction in a few policy areas in which the Community has some room for external policymaking, to wit, measures with reciprocity provisions, because of a lack of General Agreement on Tariffs and Trade rules. In most areas, however, the external dimension of EC-1992 is so liberal because the formation of the internal market does not easily tolerate inconsistencies between internal and external measures. Examples include the removal of technical barriers; the abolition of national quotas for cars, footwear, and textiles and clothing; financial capital; the market for telecommunications terminal equipment; and the moderate and purposefully delayed application of reciprocity in the case of financial services.

Foundation for EMU

EC-1992 has led to a highly significant spillover effect, namely, getting economic and monetary union (EMU) accepted as a treaty obligation. EMU is the hard core of the Maastricht Treaty on European Union, signed December 1991. It is true that Denmark and the United Kingdom have obtained opt-out clauses, but it remains to be seen whether they will actually invoke them in four or six years. The spillover effect was prompted by functional pressures that could have been foreseen, had one carefully reflected on the radical nature of completing an internal market.[6] This is not to say that such functional pressures cannot possibly be resisted; they can, at a cost. It is also not to deny that other political factors contributed to the acceptance of EMU; some clearly did, and the unification of Germany is one of them.

There is also another way in which EC-1992 promoted the acceptance of

monetary union. EC-1992 has come to approximate an economic union, thereby greatly facilitating the shift to monetary union. One critical difference between the first EC attempt to create a monetary union, in the early 1970s, and the current one is the *E* of EMU. On 9 February 1971, the Council adopted a resolution on the realization of an EMU in 1980, including a specification of the requirements of the first stage toward this realization.[7] Comparing today's first stage with the specification from 1971 brings to light a tremendous discrepancy in ambition: EC-1992, including cohesion,[8] goes far beyond the substance of the first stage formulated in 1971. What precisely an economic union is is hard to define with authority,[9] but that the specification of 1971 would fall short of it would appear to be uncontroversial. In contrast, EC-1992 has, in coming close to building an economic union, laid a solid foundation for a monetary union. This is important, as adjustment processes, private and pub-

6. See, for example, Jacques Pelkmans, "The Assignment of Public Functions in Economic Integration," *Journal of Common Market Studies*, 21(1-2) (Sept-Dec. 1982).

7. See *EC Bulletin*, no. 4 (1971).

8. The term "economic and social cohesion" refers especially to the efforts of preventing a North-South problem when completing the internal market. Its inclusion in the Single Act was critical for the act to be signed by all and agreed to by the members-to-be, Spain and Portugal. The famous "cohesion" decision of the Council in February 1988—doubling the Structural Funds for this purpose—was critical to the success of the EC-1992 program.

9. For different concepts of economic union, see Jacques Pelkmans, "Towards Economic Union," in *Setting EC Priorities 1991-92*, ed. Peter Ludlow (London: Brasseys, 1991). The Canadian literature on economic union is very interesting; see, for example Economic Council of Canada, *A Joint Venture: The Economics of Constitutional Options* (Ottawa: Economic Council of Canada, 1991).

lic, and competitive markets (across intra-EC borders), which are made possible in such an economic union, magnify the benefits and reduce the costs of having one single currency.

THE INTERNAL MARKET: IS THE JOB DONE?

There is an understandable inclination to follow the process of completing the internal market by reading the score charts of the white paper program. For a better comprehension, however, a much broader approach is desirable.

The inner dynamics of EC-1992

It is more appropriate to view EC-1992 as a process than as the ticking-off of a list of 282 white paper measures on a score chart. It is little realized that EC-1992 not only induced greater dynamism but was itself transformed over time by an inner dynamics of the process. The upshot was a steadily rising ambition of widening and deepening. In this sense, the white paper should be seen as a catalyst rather than as the technical guide to follow in the EC-1992 process. The inner dynamics have decisively moved EC-1992 far beyond the white paper.

Within the confines of this brief survey, the process view of EC-1992 can be substantiated only by summarizing eight elements of EC-1992 that were not included in the list of 282 proposals.[10]

1. Some important components had been adopted before the white paper was published—for example, the common customs document, in late 1984, and the new approach to technical harmonization and standards, in May 1985.

2. Later additions to the program were often not included in the white paper list, the most prominent example being the endeavor, launched in 1988, to complete the internal energy market.

3. Other nontrivial elements were never explicitly mentioned in the list or the score chart, yet were inevitable consequences of the completion exercise. An example is the abolition of hundreds of national import quotas for cars, footwear, and textiles and clothing.

4. A widening of the white paper approach to EC-1992 was gradually realized in key service sectors, such as civil aviation and telecommunication services. With respect to air transport, the white paper still insists on doing no more than adopting the Second Memorandum of 1984, although this would have been a far cry from the realization of a single market for civil aviation services. Only after an arduous process of changing the mind-set of the national trunk carriers and "their" transport ministers did it become politically feasible to propose and, indeed, adopt a second and a third package, realizing a single market. Telecommunication services are not even mentioned in the white paper—though telecommunication equipment is—and a somewhat

---

10. Elaboration and an explanation of the driving forces behind these elements are beyond the scope of the present article. An elaboration will be provided in Jacques Pelkmans and Jeanne-Mey Sun, *How "1992" Changed European Integration* (London: Brasseys, forthcoming).

artificial notion of realizing a common information market does not refer to telecommunication services either. It is only with the Green Paper on Telecommunications of 1987 that a single market in this area became part and parcel of the EC-1992 process.[11]

5. It should also be realized that the white paper itself could not be complete because some necessary decisions were of an intergovernmental nature and hence not in the domain of Community law. Thus the agreement about the white paper did not automatically imply an acceptance of such measures. Worse still, intergovernmental decisions are by definition unanimous and—by virtue of their being outside EC powers—relatively sensitive. Examples include the Community patent, certain aspects of the border controls on persons and export controls on goods of military-strategic importance. Despite the formidable obstacles, including some of a constitutional nature, great progress has been made in all these areas.

6. EC-1992 has also been widened and deepened by changes in competition policy. The widening refers especially to the policy's application to service markets, where a fascinating interaction between a crowbar approach to judicial review—test cases forced by the EC Commission, the European Parliament, or, at times, member states concerning fundamental issues of interpretation—and the Council as a hesitant legislator

has generated a much larger scope for the single market in services, particularly in telecommunication services, transport in general, and air transport in some respects. The deepening consists of a tighter control of state aid to industry and services—with greater vigilance vis-à-vis state-owned companies—and the adoption of the Merger Regulation, which was on the white paper list.

7. Flanking measures have added another dimension to EC-1992. Of those mentioned in the Single Act, economic and social cohesion and research and technology policy are the most important. Since 1988, the social dimension of EC-1992 has come to the fore, although it is mentioned neither in the Single Act[12] nor in the white paper; however, its actual significance is almost entirely political, hardly economic or social as will be argued later in this article. It nevertheless represents an interesting instance of spillover with long-run potential. Another flanking policy, which is additional, is the attention to truly European infrastructure. Under the influence of relentless lobbying and useful proposals by the European Round Table of Industrialists as well as the great success of EC-1992, member states reduced their stubborn and dysfunctional resistance to a systematic attack of the missing links in the EEC-European Free Trade Association area. By 1990, a more strategic approach prompted the idea of transeuropean networks

11. One can therefore consider it as a later addition to the white paper proposals, although it never was included in the score charts, or, alternatively, as a widening of the white paper concept of a single market for services in general.

12. The Single Act merely provides a legal basis for occupational health and safety regulation at the EC level; it also encourages a social dialogue between what in Europe are called the social partners, without attributing any formal powers.

(TENs), again suggested first by the European Round Table of Industrialists. The strategic nature of TENs follows from the nature of the underlying policy question, What are the transport and communication conditions needed to enable EC business to exploit the future single market fully for purposes of competitiveness and growth? For the next decade or so, TENs in roads, inland waterways, rail (rapid trains), air traffic controls (where archaic splintering generates tremendous costs for air transport), and telecommunications represent the EC response to this question. In the Maastricht Treaty, modest EC competences for TENs are included.

8. Broader still is the idea that EC-1992 also comprises the greatest possible openness to the world economy as well as the stability of exchange rates.[13]

When asking the question, Is the job done? it is proper to first define what the job is—in other words, how narrow or broad one's view of EC-1992 is. There is little doubt that the Community's ambition has greatly increased during the years 1985-92. During the last two or three years, the EC has pursued the widest notion of EC-1992, as described previously. The score-chart measurement, on the other hand, is based on the narrowest approach to EC-1992, namely, the white paper list of 282 measures. In

13. This cannot be elaborated here. For the rationale, see, for example, Jacques Pelkmans and Alan Winters, *Europe's Domestic Market* (London: Routledge, 1988), chap. 3. See also the articles and EC declarations in Finn Laursen, ed., *Europe 1992: World Partner?* (Maastricht: European Institute of Public Administration, 1991).

continuously increasing its ambitions, the Community has become more vulnerable to criticism for failing to live up to the ever higher expectations. Sober analysis reveals that such criticism was often premature— many politically difficult proposals succeeded in the end—or highly selective. Furthermore, the nature of the process of EC-1992 was often not well understood, and the inner dynamics were largely neglected.

Indeed, what should be explained is not that some issues were deadlocked and that there is still unfinished business to be tackled. That this occurred can hardly be surprising. What ought to be explained is that both the initial aims and a great deal of the higher ambitions were successfully pursued. What political or public choice theory would confidently have predicted such an outcome, given a period of seven and a half years, two successive Commissions and 15 Council presidencies, at least one—often two—elections in every member state, an election for the European Parliament, and the mere requirement of taking 282 complex legislative decisions as well as many other ones outside the white paper always with 12 member states?

The preceding list of obstacles is not all, as the following reminders of difficulty suggest: a number of EC-1992 proposals required unanimity; the program comprised more than a dozen policy areas with powerful, vested, national interests as well as deeply ingrained protectionist traditions; and the acrimonious budget quarrels in the 1980-84 period drastically reduced the likelihood that member states would agree to large additional budget outlays for the purpose of cohesion. As if this overkill of hindrances for EC-1992 is not enough, the initial history of the Single Act was littered with the following seemingly fatal problems. In June 1985, Prime Minister Thatcher declared that the United Kingdom would not participate in the autumn negotiations to rewrite the EEC Treaty; Denmark and Greece also refused at first. In December 1985, all 10 of the EC members signed, but subsequently, the ratification process was threatened by two referenda, in Ireland and Denmark; ultimately, these both supported ratification. Finally, the initial debate on the merits of the Single Act among prominent Community lawyers led it to be vilified not only as useless for the completion of the program but even as a step backward.[14]

A faithful reconstruction of the starting position and the many hindrances of EC-1992 underscores the intellectual interest in explaining the success, not the relatively few failures, of EC-1992.

*The white paper
score chart*

Nevertheless, the white paper score chart remained important as a

device to measure progress in the hard core of EC-1992. By 31 December 1992, the Council had adopted 260 proposals, and on 2 it had reached a common position.[15] Thus the score was almost 95 percent of the consolidated white paper list when the steeplechase was over. Of the remaining 20, 7 were unanimously declared as being of low priority. The 13 leftovers consist of 2 plant-health measures, 1 draft directive in food law, 1 in banking, 1 difficult case in company law, 4 regulations in trademark law and 1 in biotechnology protection, 1 directive facilitating tax consolidation for multinational corporations in the EC, and 2 marginal tax directives. The 4 regulations in trademark law are held up not by the substance itself but by the highly politicized matter of the seat of the EC Trademark Bureau and the number of languages to be employed. It is clear that these last few measures do not throw any doubt on the completion of the internal market, as narrowly conceived.

The matter is different for implementation, for which score charts have been kept since 1989. In December 1992, already 216 measures were legally in force, of which 177 should have been incorporated into the laws of the member states. The average incorporation rate among the member states was 79 percent, which is unsatisfactory. More serious is that, since not every member state incorporates exactly the same directives

14. Without pretending to do full justice to this misleading but influential debate, I will note here that an important reason for the asserted retrogression was Article 100A, introduced by the Single Act, containing a possibility for derogations from harmonization decisions; the debate was wrong-footed because too few authors had understood the great significance of Article 8A of the Single Act, on abolishing internal frontiers.

15. On a common Council position, the European Parliament gives a second reading before formally adopting the legislation; complications might arise if the Parliament rejected the common position.

at any moment in time, the number of directives having been incorporated in all 12 member states by December 1992 was no more than 79! A truly single market requires the number to be equal to 282 minus those, such as regulations, that need no national implementation.

In January 1993, more measures went into force. More important, a widely shared view is that, since that date, Article 8A of the Single Act, defining an internal market "without internal frontiers," will have direct effect and hence override many other provisions. In addition, the costs of late implementation to member states will also rise, following the EC Court's ruling on 19 November 1991 in the *Francovich and Bonifaci* case, holding that member states are required to compensate individuals for damages caused by violations of Community law—such as implementation after the deadline—for which member states are responsible.

DEEPENING AND WIDENING OF EC-1992 TODAY

The widest concept of EC-1992 is so ambitious and arose so late in the program that there is a shopping list of unfinished business. Completing the internal market in this sense may take a good deal of the 1990s. In a strategic and much richer view of the single market, it is seen as the greatest asset of the Community, which should be so designed that it can be exploited to maximum benefit for sustainable growth, employment, competitiveness, and innovation. It is no longer a priority to tick off a checklist of measures, irrespective of their weight; what matters is the proper

functioning of this single market, much more an economic and entrepreneurial than a legal and institutional notion.

The strategy turns on seven items, only one of which—infrastructure—is expressly facilitated by the Maastricht Treaty. Necessary though insufficient are the adoption of the few draft proposals of the white paper list remaining on the table and a structural approach to what the Commission mislabels the "management" of the internal market. The misnomer is the consequence of a legal-administrative conception of the internal market, viewed as a set of rules and obligations in a fairly decentralized system of two-layered government. Thus the management of the internal market has nothing to do with interventionism, managed trade, centralized bureaucratic blueprints for sectors, or European champions; rather, it refers to a machinery at the EC member states' interface, ensuring timely incorporation into national law, proper enforcement, a more EC-oriented approach for national courts, adequate and easy legal redress, as well as rapid complaint and infringement procedures and adequate sanctions. The intellectual basis for this management is the Sutherland Report.[16]

The other five elements deserve some elaboration.

The external dimension

The external dimension of EC-1992, especially the white paper list,

16. See Peter Sutherland et al., *The Internal Market after 1992* (Luxembourg: Office of the Official Publications of the European Com-

has proved to be liberal. Service sectors and public procurement have been opened up, although the United States claims that in, for example, telecommunication services, the shift is not radical enough. An even more radical liberalization took place in traditional sectors such as footwear and textiles and clothing, as well as in the car sector, where national quotas were abolished and—in footwear and cars—not replaced by EC-wide quotas. In textiles and clothing, EC quotas already existed under the Multi-Fiber Agreement, but the Uruguay Round of the General Agreement on Tariffs and Trade is expected to dismantle this agreement over a period of 10 years. One should expect this more open single market to induce the needed adjustment out of comparative disadvantage segments which hitherto dragged down growth and profitability. It is in the long-run strategic interest of the Community not to compensate for this liberalization with excessive antidumping harassment or voluntary export restraints imposed on successful exporters to Europe. Closing in does not help competitiveness.

In factor markets, the external dimension shows a mixed picture. The freedom of movement for financial capital is *erga omnes*; that is, it also applies vis-à-vis the world capital market. In intellectual property rights, EC regulation will, of course, have to prevail. But in labor markets,

the very opposite of the approach to capital applies. The Community is inching toward a common immigration policy, but national competences and extreme sensitivities about nonpolitical asylum, which has drastically increased since the late 1980s, render its realization very uncertain. Today, national immigration laws are restrictive, and the loophole of nonpolitical asylum is gradually closing. The matter is also tied up with the elimination of intra-EC border controls for persons, which hinges on sufficient confidence in the effectiveness of common external border controls. It is especially the United Kingdom, a group of islands, that wages a war of principle here and is likely to be dragged before the EC Court. Although there are economic arguments in favor of more liberal immigration—rejuvenation of the labor force; greater flexibility in the labor markets; importation of scarce skills—social tensions, housing problems, and fundamental issues of assimilation into society prevent such a functional strategy from being implemented. Even foreign policy and security interests of the Community have thus far not led to liberal immigration but rather to greater emphasis on financial aid to Eastern Europe and privileged market access. The accusation, however, is that the EC does too little on all fronts: aid is very low per capita, direct investments do not figure very large, market access is too conditional for some key export sectors, and the immigration gates are basically closed.

Network markets

The Europeanization of network markets such as telecommunica-

munities, 1992). A nontechnical exposition of the problems and some early suggestions can be found in Jacques Pelkmans and Peter Sutherland, "Unfinished Business: The Credibility of '1992,'" in Centre for European Policy Studies, *Governing Europe* (Brussels: Center for European Policy Studies, 1990), vol. 1.

tions, broadcasting, gas and electricity, air transport, and, to a lesser degree, rail and mail is perhaps the least expected result of EC-1992. The demonstration effect of deregulation elsewhere and the impact of new technologies—especially in undermining natural-monopoly arguments—have greatly stimulated the higher ambitions of EC-1992 in these areas. The vested interests—also thought to be protected by Article 90 of the EEC Treaty—in the member states were long believed to be untouchable. It is especially in these fields where the completion of the internal markets will continue through the decade. Basic decisions on air transport have been taken, but full application commences only in 1997. Also, in European scheduled—that is, noncharter—air transport, intercontinental travel outweighs domestic services, unlike in the United States, and the former is restricted worldwide by a network of old bilaterals. In telecommunication services, value-added services have been liberalized. Following two landmark Court rulings on Article 90 of the EEC Treaty, in, respectively, 1991 and 1992, the Council politically accepted in the spring of 1993 that the main cash cow—voice telephony and fax— would be liberalized by 1998. In telecommunications equipment markets where Europe is forced to uphold its waning competitiveness, drastic measures were already initiated before 1993.[17]

The internal energy market is a controversial issue. The pressure of new technologies is absent here and the case for deregulation is more problematic. Nevertheless, the high costs of energy input for energy-intensive output—for example, in the production of aluminum, steel, paper, bulk chemicals—reduce the competitiveness of several key industries in Europe at a time when market shares are under pressure. The cases of mail and rail are mixed up with social and regional considerations that prevent selective, cream-skimming competition. Indirect and intermodal competition may accomplish a more service-oriented attitude, however, if infrastructure and stricter state-aid rules can be realized.

The network markets are more and more viewed as critical for an effective exploitation of the single market's potential. Their liberalization at the European level is expected to unleash great entrepreneurial initiative and growth. Its public complements are an appropriate competition policy and advanced European infrastructure.

Competition policy

As noted, EC competition policy has been widened and deepened. The proper functioning of the single market critically depends on the adequacy of this policy. Especially the widening to services and network markets is extremely demanding.

---

17. The terminal equipment market was fully liberalized (also open to third countries, without a reciprocity clause); a European mobile telephony market and standards were initiated; a new telecommunications standard institute was founded embarking on a huge European standardization program; the network holders were separated from their other business units; and open network provision, with the concomitant competition policy, was introduced.

These domains tend to be regulated to some degree, and, with deregulation, competition policy tends to assume a quasi-regulatory character to prevent abuse of monopolistic positions.

The deepening relates to mergers—relatively unproblematic—and tighter controls of state-owned companies, the Achilles' heel of the policy. Continued or reinvigorated privatization in Italy and France in 1993 may well prove to be more effective in reducing the problems for competition than the controversial controls themselves. Leading public monopolies in France—in gas and electricity—have already launched a counteroffensive, and, in 1993, France won its case before the EC Court against the sharpened control imposed by the EC Commission.

Pan-European infrastructure

The infrastructure in the EC has been tailor-made for national purposes. Interconnections have often been designed as an afterthought, too little, with missing links; too late; expensive, as, for example, those between national telecommunications networks; or of lower quality. Today, two breakthroughs may have strategic value. First, the infrastructural needs of the single market are now defined in European terms and with an entrepreneurial view to key continental services such as rapid trains and advanced communications. This should fundamentally improve the functioning of the European economy and the competitiveness of EC business while expanding the quality and

range of services. Second, the forty-year division of Europe into east and west and the tremendous infrastructural needs of the area formerly organized by the Council for Mutual Economic Assistance have led to plans for pan-European infrastructure. In the medium to long run, this should greatly help the emerging pan-European market west of the former Soviet Union to yield high productivity and greater competition.

The social dimension of EC-1992

The significance of the social dimension for EC-1992 is little understood. The greatest problem is that there is a tendency in social affairs to confuse rhetoric with reality. Although the rhetoric might suggest otherwise, virtually nobody is in favor of a genuine social dimension of EC-1992 regulation. What would such a social dimension imply? In analogy with the internal markets for products, services, capital, and technology, it must consist of the appropriate combination of the free movement of labor, EC regulation, and mutual recognition that allows a relatively undistorted functioning of a Community labor market.

Obviously, this is simply not in the books. On all three scores there is at best only a beginning. The free movement of labor exists legally already; it has existed since 1968. As should be well understood, this is an extremely restricted freedom, as one needs a job before being able to enjoy the freedom. Given the enormous fragmentation between national labor markets—languages, diploma recognition, information—this requirement simply means that labor mobility will never go beyond a trickle. As was considered normal in other markets, EC-1992 might have been expected to include harmonization and various forms of facilitation. The harmonization program emerged only very late—after the Social Charter of 1989—and is so minimalistic as to have virtually no economic meaning for the emergence of a Community labor market.[18] Also, mutual recognition, which could greatly boost the economic significance of the free movement of labor, is prevented as soon as it is feared to assume economic significance. Thus a person from member state A is not eligible for social security in B unless he or she has worked in B for a minimum period (often half a year). Indeed, jobless persons have obtained the right to move only since the EC-1992 program, but they must have enough means to support themselves; an active effort on the local labor market elsewhere in the EC cannot be sustained very long. In one case, a special directive has been enacted to prevent regulatory competition in social provisions between the member states that might arise,[19] despite the lack of mutual recognition.

All in all, and the great success of EC-1992 in other types of markets notwithstanding, there is no such thing as a Community internal market for labor. Unlike what the slogan "EC-1992 is only for business" suggests, the failure of realizing a single market for labor is not due to business but to (national!) labor unions and ministers of social affairs. Not only has harmonization of labor market rules never been attempted seriously, but the related social security and health insurance systems have all remained national. Practical obstacles and inconsistencies are formidable, as is well-known from the never ending soap opera of cross-border migrant workers. The inference is obvious: the member states, the labor unions, and organized European industry do not desire the social dimension, although the first two players assert the opposite in vague terms.

This digression is meant as a clarification, not necessarily as a criticism. This curious combination of lip service paid to the social dimension, the explicit political commitment to avoid a Thatcherite downward spiral of national social standards,[20] and the wholesale refusal to facilitate the emergence of a single labor market was in the interest of all players and no doubt in the short-term interest of the Community. It made EC-1992 socially acceptable. An economically consistent application of the EC-1992 idea, applied to this field in analogy

18. Examples include a draft directive—with numerous exceptions—to limit the workweek to 48 hours (!), adopted in the spring of 1993, and a directive, adopted in 1992, preventing pregnant women from working night shifts. Both led to long debates in the Social Council, although, of course, they have little if any impact on how labor markets in Europe operate.

19. Namely, if workers from A work in B but remain workers of the contracted firm in

A, A's labor law cannot be applied in B, except when the workers' stay is very short. Such a regulatory competition would amount to what has been dubbed social dumping.

20. The Hannover Summit in 1988 explicitly endorsed high social standards.

to goods, services, and capital, would never have worked. This genuine social dimension might take a generation or more before it comes about, if indeed it will, since social security entitlements would inevitably have to be involved and precisely on that point the Maastricht Treaty denies the EC any power.

SIGNIFICANCE OF EC-1992 FOR BUSINESS

The Cecchini Report and the ensuing debate[21] have clarified the insight into the economics of EC-1992. Attention was paid to the report's macroeconomic simulations giving a real additional growth of around 6 percent, a net creation of 1.8 million jobs, and lower inflation. Today it is possible to trace the actual EC-1992 effect from mid-1987 to mid-1990, the magnitude probably being in the range of 1.0-1.3 percent annually. Since the outbreak of the Gulf war, other macroeconomic shocks have blurred the picture too much to identify a continued impact with confidence.

Direct macroeconomic effects were never among the original reasons for launching EC-1992, however. What mattered was the cost-competitiveness of EC business, its badly needed restructuring, and a competitive response preparing it to better withstand market penetration by the Japanese and others as well as gearing up for globalization. A few notes on corporate strategies and reactions can be summarized:

21. See, for example, "The Economies of 1992," *European Economy*, no. 35 (Mar. 1988); Alexander Italianer, " '1992'—Hype or Hope?" *Economic Papers* (EC Commission), no. 77 (1990).

1. It is evident from many questionnaire surveys as well as from empirical analysis that many companies, and sometimes entire sectors, have responded forcefully or have been forced to react, say, because of restructuring. It seems that there is a correlation between the expected EC-1992 effect per sector and the intensity of the response. It is almost impossible, however, to measure the numerous horizontal EC-1992 effects on business in areas such as public procurement, European standardization, and quality assurance—one has to make do with qualitative analysis and description.

2. Competition in the Euromarket has increased. It has increased in many goods markets but above all in service markets. The increase may take many forms and is by no means measured only in terms of price. With respect to the proper functioning of the internal market, what is crucial is that potential competition from anywhere in the Euromarket has become a prominent factor in corporate strategies.

3. What observable trends there are point in a similar direction. Merger and acquisition(M&A) activities rose fast after 1986—and faster still than in the United States—and prominent in M&A were intra-EC cross-border activities, precisely the category that had never blossomed because of barriers, reduced or removed by EC-1992. There have been numerous rationalizations, often because of scale effects or because the original rationale for a plant—a non-tariff barrier—fell away. The Europeanization of wholesale and retail—at both the sourcing and the output

sides—accelerated through M&A, direct investment, and purchasing syndicates. One also observes a renewed rise in the intra-EC share of total EC exports.

4. The ultimate measuring rod is the resulting competitiveness of EC industry and services, both in Europe and in the world market. EC-1992 has had two functions in this respect: first, removing hindrances and distortions so that the internal market could be better used and so that unnecessary costs—waste resulting from fragmentation—would no longer reduce competitiveness; second, fostering intra-EC competition, which in turn forces restructuring, revitalization, innovation, and better quality. Far too much has been expected from the first function. For all the enthusiasm that the Cecchini Report's simulations injected into European business, it was little noticed—though clearly and repeatedly emphasized in the report—that the great gains resulted from the second function much more than from the first. The adjustment to the second function of EC-1992 for business is far from accomplished. Also in this sense, EC-1992 will be with us for the rest of the decade. As long as the single market stays open, however, there is no reason to suppose that this adjustment will not run its full course. It will yield a leaner and more entrepreneurial European business.

CONCLUSION

It is hard to overstate the significance of EC-1992 for the European Community. However, EC-1992 never was designed to be a job-creating machine, delivering the harvest before the next election. To assess EC-1992 on its direct and short- to medium-run impact on growth and jobs amounts to a failure to understand its nature and pervasive influence. Nevertheless, positive effects on growth and jobs can be traced. Given the supply-side characteristics of the program, however, actual macroeconomic benefits will be almost entirely indirect and long run, hence identifiable only with a large measure of uncertainty.

The significance of EC-1992 lies first of all in the transformation of the process of European integration. The first main section of this article identifies the drastic deepening and widening of the internal market, new regulatory principles, its impact on the decision-making process, the opening-up of the Euromarket in some product sectors and services, and the gradual emergence of the economic union, being the foundation for a beneficial monetary union.

Second, EC-1992 has pulled the Community out of an atmosphere of disillusion, bickering (about the EC budget!), deadlock on nitty-gritty matters, and lack of political and economic dynamism. By 1987, it had proved to be the locomotive of a reinvigorated Community. By 1988, it had induced radical ideas such as a social Europe and monetary union to reach the very top of the political agenda. By 1990, the political leaders were gearing up for a much more radical rewrite of the EEC Treaty than barely five years before.

Third, the resilience of the Community and the renewed realization that the single market is its greatest asset rehabilitated the EC in the world economy and, to a degree, in world politics. The Fortress Europe campaign, after an initial spell of amazement and disbelief about so much misunderstanding outside the EC, helped greatly to boost the EC's confidence and determination. It began to export EC-1992 principles to the Uruguay negotiations on services, public procurement, and technical barriers, thereby embarrassing the United States with its more circumspect positions in these areas. It began to roll back a large number of national and EC grey-area measures, among others, vis-à-vis Japan and some newly industrializing countries. It became a major target for foreign direct investment from European Free Trade Association countries, Japan, the United States, and Canada.

Fourth, by a fortunate sequence of history, EC-1992 started four years before the Iron Curtain fell. In the mid-1980s—let alone in, say, 1982— the EC would not otherwise have been able, politically or economically, to assume leadership in the post-Communist pan-European turmoil.

No doubt, one may criticize, at times even question, the Community's leadership in foreign policy (which, in fairness, the EC was only half-heartedly assigned to pursue by the Treaty of Maastricht), the delays in opening up the Euromarket for Eastern Europe in agriculture, steel, coal, and clothing, as well as financial aid. Without EC-1992, however, there would have been a disastrous leadership gap.

In the wider view of EC-1992, as analyzed previously, activities of liberalization and market integration will continue until the end of the decade. What remains, even when the impact is appreciated, is a puzzle for all those historians, political scientists, lawyers, and economists trying to understand public policy. The puzzle is twofold: how could such an ambitious program emerge and even increase its ambitions significantly over time; and, once firmly on the political agenda, how could it actually accomplish such high scores of success in a configuration of no fewer than 12 states, against so many vested interests, and over such a long period?

ANNALS, *AAPSS*, **531**, January 1994

West European Cooperation
in Foreign and Security Policy

By REINHARDT RUMMEL

ABSTRACT: The development of a collective foreign and security policy for Western Europe was shaped by both the international environment and the policy of West European regional integration. Although initially put on the back burner, a common European defense has been defined as a goal within the Treaty on European Union. Unification in the three areas—economic (European Community), diplomatic (European Political Cooperation), and military (Western European Union)—has advanced differently but, as a whole, has reached a stage where comprehensive union is possible. Western Europe is currently in a transitional period and is still feeling the pains associated with being thrust into the position of a world power after years of comfortable existence under the umbrella of one of the two antagonistic superpowers. In the beginning of the 1990s, a much more assertive role than in the 1970s and the 1980s is being expected of Western Europe by the international community.

Reinhardt Rummel is a European foreign policy analyst based at the Stiftung Wissenschaft und Politik at Ebenhausen, Germany. He edited and contributed to Evolution of an International Actor: Western Europe's New Assertiveness *(1990);* Integration and Security in Western Europe: Inside the European Pillar *(1991); and* Toward Political Union—Planning a Common Foreign and Security Policy in the European Community *(1992).*

THE history of the Community[1] has been an interplay of union building and problem solving. The connectedness of integrational and functional activities is particularly rich in the field of foreign and security policy. Preparing the Twelve to conduct external relations in a coordinated manner contributed to European unification in general, while, at the same time, joint policies of EC member states helped them to cope better with external challenges. Thus organizing cooperation among the Twelve must be regarded as a way to adapt to changes in international relations and to optimize Western Europe's influence in world affairs. The skills of this approach are in particular demand in an era of secular change in international relations.

The dissolution of the Soviet empire at the beginning of the 1990s pushed the world into a process of undoing most of the postwar order and of redefining the challenges and structures of the future international system. Western Europe has been part of this process both as one of the most affected regions and as an actor in a formulative role. Questions of a fundamental nature are being raised: Will the EC and its member states be able to cope with this new strain?

1. Throughout this article, the notion "Community" is meant to encompass both the European Community (EC), based on the Rome Treaty, and the European Political Cooperation (EPC) regarding foreign policy cooperation between the 12 EC member states. The expression "European Union" adds the Western European Union (WEU) to the Community and refers to the union established by the Maastricht Treaty. The term "Western Europe" is used to describe all of these multilateral bodies plus the nation-states in this region.

Will the integration process come to a halt and even regress, or will it rather be remotivated? Certainly, the Community has not been an alliance like the North Atlantic Treaty Organization (NATO), which is now grappling with the loss of its enemy and the quest for new tasks, but has the EC not been an integral part of the Atlantic value system, a cornerstone of the Western anti-Communist bulwark? With the Communist dragon slain, can Brussels continue on with business as usual while societies in Europe, East and West, are rediscovering national values?

It seems that the very core of regional integration is at stake and, with it, the concepts and strategies of unification, especially regarding the sector of foreign and security policy. Are Robert Schuman's and Jean Monnet's ideas no longer useful? Their ideas were useful in the immediate postwar situation. They helped to tie former West European enemies into ever closer cooperation and perhaps can now serve as a guide for East European countries as well. EC nations have reached the point of no return: a war between them can be excluded. WEU, once an instrument of military control over Germany and Italy, is now the vehicle for the European pillar in NATO and the catalyst for the gradual development of a common West European defense policy. Today, the West Europeans can cohabitate without their longtime pacifier, the United States of America; yet it is reassuring to have Washington around to balance both the successors of the former superpower Soviet Union and an emerging dominant Germany on the Continent.

To the extent that the West European integration effort has been successful, it was driven by an economic rationale rather than any other calculus. The need for further economic and monetary integration subsists because international competitiveness demands it. This does not imply a need to collaborate closely in foreign and security policy, as the past has demonstrated; the economically giant EC remained, with regard to foreign policy, a dwarf. The Community has been able to afford such asymmetrical development. It has been prospering over the last few decades within the protective provisions of an antagonistic world constellation. Whatever the need for solidarity in external crises, the Atlantic Alliance was there to provide it. With the Cold War over, Western Europe as an international actor is exposed to the "real world" and put to the test in a fluid and demanding context. The combination of the EC, EPC, and WEU will have to prove how much of an international stature it represents as of today and whether this West European entity can move on to achieve the status of a world power.[2]

UNION BUILDING IN
A SENSITIVE SECTOR

Integration in the foreign policy and security sector is both older and

2. For an in-depth reassessment of the process of integration in Europe, see Michael Kreile, ed., *Die Integration Europas* (Opladen: Westdeutscher Verlag, 1992). For the post-Cold War era changes, see David Armstrong and Erik Goldstein, eds., *The End of the Cold War* (London: F. Cass, 1990), particularly the contributions of Ieuan John and Pierre-Henri Laurent.

younger than integration in the economic field. It is older because early plans for integration in Western Europe such as the European Coal and Steel Community, the European Defense Community (EDC), and the European Political Community were largely inspired by strategic considerations. Coal and steel were regarded as key resources for the reconstitution of military power, which, in the concept of early European integrationists, needed to be checked by joint administration. The agreement on EDC as signed by the six governments in the early 1950s was more ambitious than any attempt at union building in the field of foreign and security policy thereafter, including the Fouchet Plans of the early 1960s and the Maastricht Treaty (also known as the Treaty on European Union) of the early 1990s. When it failed to be ratified by the French Assemblée Nationale, EDC was abandoned by the other Europeans and caused a major change in the concept of integration: a shift from the sensitive sector of security to the more pragmatic field of economics, from a defense-first to a defense-last approach in European union building.

This conceptual shift still holds today. After, over the course of time, all major policy areas have been included in the communitarian or cooperative activities of the Twelve, common defense is for the first time mentioned as a goal in the Treaty on European Union. It will take some time until it becomes clearer whether a defense union can be reached or not. A few recent measures such as the operational endowment of WEU and the establishment of the Franco-

German Euro-Corps can be interpreted as further steps in favor of a defense union. Unresolved perennial problems, such as the dual assignment of military forces to WEU and NATO, European representation on the U.N. Security Council, and the function and command of nuclear forces, are discouraging any serious plans for such a union, however.[3]

Whether this mixed record will tilt in one direction or the other in the near future is an open question. The issues of defense do not rank as high on the agenda as they used to during periods of territorial threat in Western Europe. Collective security, now in the foreground of national and international interests, does not require unison action but rather can be served by ad hoc coalition building. The squeeze on military budgets is forcing governments into burden-sharing arrangements. Given these conditions, the construction of a defense union will still be a sensitive enterprise, but it should allow for more pragmatic access to the issue than in the past. On the other hand, the upcoming enlargement of the Community by a number of neutral countries is likely to draw the process away from common defense and reinforce the currently existing trend toward renationalization of military policy.[4] In this context, the traditional integrationist argument that a European union without a defense component would be incomplete remains as tautological as it was in the past.

To state that the prospects for a security and defense union are uncertain does not deny that the EC and its member states have tried hard in the last three decades to enhance cooperation in foreign and security policy and to make external use of Western Europe's economic potential. Since the EC's inception, its external relations have spread far beyond trade and foreign aid into worldwide economic diplomacy.[5] The EC's Commission, based on the institutional system of the Rome Treaty, has been the driving force behind most initiatives in this field. Starting in 1970, EPC has been complementing the EC's economic foreign policy by coordinating diplomatic activities of the foreign ministries of the member states. These intergovernmental activities have remained outside the Rome Treaty and developed their own consultative network within which the Commission was rather a tolerated guest than a key player. Progress with EPC has been made by providing some legal basis for it, by developing its procedures, and by acquiring necessary instruments for action.

When, after nearly two decades of pragmatic development, EPC was finally codified in the 1987 Single European Act (SEA), this was only half of a breakthrough. Foreign policy co-

3. For the discussion of the pros and cons of security integration, see Mathias Jopp, Reinhardt Rummel, and Peter Schmidt, eds., *Integration and Security in Western Europe: Inside the European Pillar* (Boulder, CO: Westview Press, 1991).

4. See Peter Schmidt, ed., *In the Midst of Change: On the Development of West European Security and Defence Cooperation* (Baden-Baden: Nomos Verlagsgesellschaft, 1992).

5. For a comprehensive analysis of the EC's external relations, see Roy H. Ginsberg, *Foreign Policy Actions of the European Community: The Politics of Scale* (Boulder, CO: Lynne Rienner, 1989).

operation between the Twelve was henceforth based on a ratified multilateral treaty and helped to end the uncertainties of the so far purely political commitment among foreign ministers to concert their international activities. Yet the wording chosen in the SEA is generally that of a "commitment to endeavor," not of legal obligation. The intrinsic nature of the EPC provisions remains overwhelmingly political and their implementation remains hostage to the political discretion of each of the member states and the Commission. In this regard, the Maastricht Treaty does not constitute a progression either: foreign and security policy are not part of the jurisdiction of the European Court of Justice.

Over time, however, the margins for this discretionary power have been increasingly defined and narrowed by a set of procedural ground rules and common positions. The ground rules established in three reports (Luxembourg, 1970; Copenhagen, 1973; London, 1981) were endorsed by ministers but were neither elevated to treaty rank nor submitted for parliamentary approval. Yet, on a practical plane, they constitute a morally binding nonlegal foundation for EPC (*Coutumier*). Likewise, over the years, EPC has accumulated political positions that constitute the common basis and collective heritage of the Twelve on key international issues (*Relevés*) from which it is hard to break away. The obligatory effect of established rules and positions is the core of the dynamics of EPC-style integration and represents the equivalent to the EC system of treaty-driven integration. Via intergovern-

mental cooperation, EPC has created an *aquis politique* of its own, just as the EC has established its *aquis communautaire*.[6]

As EPC did not initially have any central institution at its disposal, the half-yearly rotating presidency was in charge of ensuring communication between member states, organizing meetings, preparing position papers, and keeping contact with EC institutions, especially the Council and the European Parliament. This presidential burden continues to be quite heavy, despite the establishment of an EPC secretariat, located in Brussels since 1987. Things may ease more substantially for the presidency once large sections of EPC's substructure are concentrated at the site of the EC, as stipulated by the Maastricht Treaty: most of the working groups and the Political Committee are supposed to convene in Brussels, while foreign ministers' meetings will be merged with Council of Ministers meetings. Only the European Council will be held in the presidency's country. Centralizing and institutionalizing EPC and merging it with the EC, even though only partly, amounts to a significant deviation from the 1970s and 1980s, when EPC was functioning like a merry-go-round, rotating from capital to capital while keeping its distance from the EC center.

A potentially giant step was made with the introduction of qualified majority voting in the Common Foreign and Security Policy of the Maastricht

6. For an insider's history of EPC, see Simon J. Nuttall, *European Political Cooperation* (New York: Oxford University Press, Clarendon Press, 1992).

Treaty. Although this principle will apply only in pre-established areas of common actions, it could revolutionize the EPC decision-making system, which, so far, is built on consensus rule. Certainly, it had been obvious to the member governments early on that bringing everyone on board for each move in external relations could paralyze EPC or at least slow down joint foreign policy action. The other risk was that, in a given practical situation, EPC countries would rather go it alone than be willing to wait until all member states had found a common line. Or they would feel that the common denominator was either too weak or too strong and required a unilateral addition. Other member states, large as well as small, were tempted to instrumentalize the consensus rule and tried to block decisions within EPC. EPC has experimented with ways to circumvent the problem by introducing abstention clauses, methods of persuasion, and techniques of more or less gentle coercion. But national interest and sovereignty in foreign and security policy have proven to be strong; thus integration efforts have hit at deep-rooted boundaries.[7]

To pass from internal consensus building to external action, EPC needed instruments and assets. These were found either with the individual member states or within the EC. It took EPC several years to develop tools of its own, such as the group-to-group meetings, the institutionalized dialogue, and the Gymnich formula. Leverage such as economic assistance, sanctions, and military support still needs to be borrowed from national, EC, WEU, or NATO sources. These sources are international actors in their own right, following their own policy in areas overlapping with those of EPC. Taken together, Western Europe constitutes a collective international actor and conducts a composed foreign and security policy that integrates elements that are national, intergovernmental, and communitarian in nature. The interaction of these components is a West European answer to both integrationist aspirations and operational efficiency. It is more the outcome of various lines of uncoordinated development than the realization of a grand design—unless optimizing international influence is regarded as such a design.[8] So far this composition does not represent full unification, nor does it enable reliable cohesive and forceful action. Flexibility and adaptiveness are its main characteristics. To most West Europeans, this complex structure appears natural; the outside world, on the other hand, is rather puzzled by it.

7. For a view into the inner dynamics of EPC, see Philippe de Schoutheete, *La coopération politique européenne* (Brussels: Editions Labor, 1986).

8. The theory of international relations is not very rich on the explanation of collective foreign policy. For one of the rare attempts, see Joseph Weiler and Wolfgang Wessels, "EPC and the Challenge of Theory," in *European Political Cooperation in the 1980s*, ed. A. Pijpers, E. Regelsberger, and W. Wessels (Boston: Martinus Nijhoff, 1988), pp. 229-58. Optimizing international influence can also mean avoiding loss; see Janice Gross Stein, "International Cooperation and Loss Avoidance: Framing the Problem," *International Journal*, 47(2):202-34 (Spring 1992).

DEVELOPING AN
INTERNATIONAL PROFILE

While it was difficult to elaborate a sophisticated inner fabric of a new international personality, it was even more difficult to introduce this new player into world affairs and to provide it with a strong identity. Perceived from the outside, it was obvious toward the end of the 1970s that the EC was defining increasing sections of Western Europe's trade and foreign aid policy, whereas EPC—and even more so WEU—appeared to deal with a more limited set of issues and at a much lower degree of commitment, especially compared to that of individual member states and to NATO. Yet the more member countries that the EC and EPC took on, the wider was the panoply of views to be harmonized—a problem in the case of Greece since 1981—and the richer the diplomatic connections became—an asset in the case of Spain and Portugal since 1986. For WEU, membership was extended twice, too. The first time was when Spain and Portugal joined in 1990. The second time was in 1992, when, in preparation for the ratification of the Maastricht Treaty, Greece became a full member, Denmark and Ireland became observers, and Turkey, Norway, and Iceland—the three European members of the Atlantic Alliance that are not members of the Community—accepted associate status.[9]

The range of external concerns and the scope of the EC's, EPC's, and WEU's actions have grown with each of these enlargements. Recently, within a very short time frame, WEU caught up with the external reach of EC and EPC and embarked on a broad range of international missions, from naval observation tasks in the Adriatic[10] to a dialogue with the East European defense establishment.[11] EPC took much more time, until it gradually reached a point where virtually all items of foreign and security policy could be found on its agenda. In the 1970s, consultation between EPC member states was confined to a selection of foreign policy items. Significant progress was made when the 1981 London Report allowed official discussion of "political aspects of security" in EPC. Issues like the deployment of American intermediate-range nuclear missiles on West European soil and President

9. Meetings of the Council and the working groups of WEU are now attended by 15 countries. The integration of the Independent European Program Group in WEU and WEU's adoption of some of Eurogroup's activities result partly from these enlargements.

10. In the Yugoslav crisis, WEU has played a modest role, first, following a decision by the Council in July 1992, dispatching warships, under WEU control, for surveillance of navigation, then extending this role to enforcement of the embargo. Later, through its members, it provided the United Nations with 5000 troops for the protection of humanitarian relief convoys in Bosnia-Herzegovina (UNPROFOR 2), the cost of this operation being borne by individual WEU member countries. By April 1993, when the enforcement of the no-fly zone was established in Bosnia-Herzegovina, NATO had become the United Nations' major military help.

11. Following the June 1992 Petersberg Council of Ministers, the member countries of WEU and eight countries of Central Europe created a Forum of Consultation, which will meet regularly in Brussels at both ministerial and ambassadorial levels. At Petersberg, WEU also decided to establish a gradual and phased dialogue with the Maghreb countries.

Reagan's Strategic Defense Initiative became part of the consultation. Finally, the SEA stressed the connection of economic and diplomatic aspects of Western Europe's external relations that enabled a more comprehensive approach to international politics.

Together with this widening scope, Western Europe projected the image of differentiated access to world affairs: it showed more interest in some regions of the world than in others, was especially concerned with principles of international behavior, and was particularly devoted to worldwide crisis management. The regional choices can be studied nicely by analyzing the record of EPC's activities.[12] From 1970 to 1975, the first items on the agenda were dedicated to problems in the immediate geographical neighborhood: the Mediterranean and the Middle East, Eastern Europe, and the Soviet Union. Beginning in 1976, questions arose with regard to southern Africa. It was not long before major Asian issues emerged in West European foreign policy cooperation. Latin America was the absolute latecomer to the EPC agenda, first gaining EPC notice early in the 1980s. This pattern of regional choices is confirmed in the

12. For a collection of official EPC documents, see Press and Information Office of the Federal Republic of Germany, ed., *European Political Cooperation* (Bonn: Press and Information Office of the Federal Republic of Germany, various volumes since 1975); European Policy Unit at the European University Institute and Institut für Europäische Politik, eds., *European Political Cooperation Documentation Bulletin* (Luxembourg: Office of the Official Publications of the European Communities, semiannual collections since 1985).

"Report on the Likely Development of the Common Foreign and Security Policy with a View to Identify Areas Open to Joint Action" (the June 1992 Lisbon Report), a document that identifies a limited number of geographical regions as being of prime interest for the European Union: Central and Eastern Europe, including Russia, the former Soviet republics, the Balkans and former Yugoslavia; the Maghreb; and the Middle East.

Western Europe's tradition of cooperative relations with its southern neighbors is more than simply a reflection of former colonial ties. The EC's economic cooperation agreements with the southern Mediterranean rim countries and the EPC's political dialogue with the Arab League were meant to contribute to a stabilization of a region that delivers critical quantities of crude oil to Western Europe. Cooperative relations with the Gulf Cooperation Council underlined this prime objective. France, the United Kingdom, Germany, and Italy have all held particularly close trade connections—including military equipment—with oil-rich countries in the Middle East, but they never achieved the strategic rank of the United States or the USSR. Rather, the Europeans ran repeatedly into trouble with Washington because they tried to increase their impact on the conflicts of the region by taking positions of their own, especially during the Iranian revolution, the Iraq-Iran war, the Israeli-Arab conflict, the Libyan affair, and Saddam Hussein's adventure in Kuwait.

The pattern also existed in Western Europe's relations with Eastern

Europe, except that Brussels was more selective in its contacts with eastern counterparts and that the NATO alliance disciplined Washington's European allies more than in relations with the South. During the 1970s and 1980s, the eastern part of the European continent remained the only white spot on the world map that neither the EC nor EPC had discovered. The EC had always rejected the desire of the Council of Mutual Economic Assistance (CMEA) to establish contractual relations. When Brussels finally agreed in 1990, the CMEA, just like the Warsaw Treaty Organization, subsequently dissolved. Likewise, EPC never opened a political dialogue with Eastern Europe. Western Europe's collective relations with the East were concentrated on deliberations in the Conference on Security and Cooperation in Europe (CSCE), where it primarily worked at reducing the confrontative nature of East-West relations. While most of the West Europeans, together with the Neutral and Nonaligned states, were trying to keep up the cooperative process despite the Soviet invasion of Afghanistan, the crackdown on the liberation movement in Poland, the deployment of Soviet SS 20s, and the downing of KAL 007, the U.S. government rather wanted to interrupt relations with the East or at least use the CSCE process as a forum to accuse the Soviet regime.

The Lisbon Report also specifies a number of horizontal domains within which the European Union is asked to define its stakes: strengthening democratic principles and institu-

tions; respect for human and minority rights; and fighting against arms proliferation, terrorism, and the traffic in illicit drugs. This catalogue of objectives is only slightly different from the one that the West Europeans have tried to live up to during most of the last decade, when the principles of independence, self-determination, and noninterference were high on the agenda. From Afghanistan to Lebanon, from Iran to South Africa, and from Poland to Central America, the West Europeans had engaged in defending these principles. More often than not, they limited their engagement to public declarations. In some cases, they offered advice; in others, they applied pressure or supported intervention. In each of these cases, it was hard to avoid ambivalence and double standards. For example, why should the Kurds in Iraq be protected by U.N.-mandated U.S. air control but not those in Iran or Turkey? Today, it has become even more difficult for the Europeans to send clear messages and to defend international norms: since the end of the bipolar world, the plea for self-determination and sovereignty of states must be conditioned, and minority rights and humanitarian help need to be aggressively implemented. Case by case, from Kuwait to Somalia to Bosnia, the West Europeans have been learning their lessons.

In addition to specific geographic regions and to horizontal domains, the third area of particular concern for the Common Foreign and Security Policy is international conflict and crisis management. The Lisbon

Report emphasizes the ambition of the European Union to counter international problems early on and to make sure that it takes the initiative and does not limit itself to reactive policy. In fact, Europe's collective foreign policy has never acquired an image of actively shaping events or exerting international leadership in a crisis situation.[13] Most of the time, the United States took the lead and the Europeans followed with some time lag and some distinction from Washington's position. This has been particularly obvious in such events as the Iranian hostage crisis in 1980 and during the Libyan involvement in international terrorism in the mid-1980s. Specific crisis procedures introduced as part of EPC with the London Report took almost a decade until they started to work properly: during the Polish crisis of 1981-82, the mechanism failed spectacularly, while Iraq's invasion of Kuwait in 1990 received prompt attention. In all but one of the major international conflicts of the last decade, the Community as a whole was affected, the exception being Argentina's invasion of the Falklands in 1982, when the United Kingdom was the only victim. Thanks to the EC and EPC, London's fellow Europeans demonstrated a remarkable solidarity. In summary, despite a partly good record in crisis management, the Community was very poor on conflict prevention, as

the Yugoslav war has most recently demonstrated.

AN INTERNATIONAL HEAVYWEIGHT IN THE MAKING

Incrementally, Western Europe has grown into the club of principal actors in the world. Taken together, the internal fabric and the external profile of the Community make for a new and influential player in world affairs. Like any other power on the world stage, it has its particular strengths and weaknesses. Although this actor now combines economic, diplomatic, and military components in a coordinated institutional setting, its international impact remains relatively modest. The Community—just like the EC 15 years ago—continues to show two faces, the image of potential and the picture of reality.[14]

The potential of the Community has grown with the Southern enlargement and will increase again when most countries of the European Free Trade Association become members in the mid-1990s. More important than the prospect of the combined resources of 16 or more member states is the reformative change in Western Europe and the openness of the international order. In a fundamental way, the foreign and security policy of the European Union can follow its internal shaping factors and can change major parameters of the

13. For a case study regarding this issue, see Christopher Hill, "EPC's Performance in Crises," in *Toward Political Union—Planning a Common Foreign and Security Policy in the European Community*, ed. Reinhardt Rummel (Boulder, CO: Westview Press, 1992), pp. 135-46.

14. See Michael B. Dolan and James A. Caporaso, "The External Relations of the European Community," *The Annals* of the American Academy of Political and Social Science, 440:135-55 (Nov. 1978).

world order.[15] With a partial U.S. withdrawal from Europe, the Community and its member states need to fill the gap pertaining to the transformation of Eastern Europe as well as the ethnic war in the former Yugoslavia. The West Europeans who used to rely on the United States as their senior partner are now asked to carry the main responsibility for stability on the Continent.[16] This role includes the resolution of conflict, the strengthening of democracy and market economy, the balancing of power, and the enforcement of basic norms. The demands on Western Europe are those of a superpower.

Just as a person's traits come to the fore in extreme situations, the war in the former Yugoslavia has revealed the qualities of Western Europe as an international power. The Community partly volunteered for a mediator's role, but it was also somehow pushed into such a position by U.S. reluctance and by the desire of the conflicting parties. Western Europe grew into a leading crisis-management position, developed a peace process, and exerted its influence by combining all its sticks and carrots. It became clear early in the process that a resolution of the conflict demanded more than the West Europe-

ans were able to offer. It was first of all the lack of preventive diplomacy that reduced the influence of the Community, not the lack of economic or military leverage, which had in early conflicts apparently limited the West European impact. For the time being, an early, comprehensive, and forceful West European response to major challenges seems to be excluded due to structural reasons: the Community itself lacks a central authority with political clout, and the member states—and this holds also for the future European Union—are distinctly diverging over vital interests. This leaves Western Europe with the choice of either accepting a merely modest degree of international influence or trying to rally friends and allies for a common cause. The West Europeans have proven such co-optive power in the Yugoslavia case. The next test case— a secular endeavor—is the peaceful modernization of Russia.

The main characteristic of the future world "concert of powers" is likely to be universal multilateralism.[17] The international system will need a few actors such as the permanent members of the U.N. Security Council or the Group of Seven (the economic summit meeting of the heads of state and government of the seven most important industrialized states plus the EC Commission President) to take the initiative in coping with major regional conflicts as well as with global challenges such as nuclear proliferation, mass migration,

15. A survey in all 12 Community countries draws the conclusion that the potential differences between them are rising rather than decreasing. See Alexis Jacquemin and David Wright, eds., *The European Challenges Post-1992: Shaping Factors, Shaping Actors* (Brookfield, VT: Edgar Elgar, 1993).

16. For the process of rebalancing transatlantic relations, see James B. Steinberg, *"An Ever Closer Union"—European Integration and Its Implications for the Future of U.S.-European Relations* (Santa Monica, CA: RAND, 1993).

17. For more reflection on the subject, see Richard Rosecrance, "A New Concert of Powers," *Foreign Affairs*, 71(2):64-82 (Spring 1992).

and environmental devastation. Given the size of the issues, the high expectations raised to find solutions, and the limited resources of individual nations, no single actor is prepared to go it alone. Western Europe is certainly a heavyweight within such a group of initiators; it has potential, but it needs partners to make its potential available.

ANNALS, *AAPSS*, **531**, January 1994

Widening Europe:
The Dilemmas of Community Success

By PIERRE-HENRI LAURENT

ABSTRACT: The historical process of enlarging the Community of Six to double that number in 1986 was based on the increasing economic dynamism and success of the European Community. With the end of communism, the number knocking at the door has increased, with the countries of the European Free Trade Association leading the way. The legion of issues that are to emerge with the fourth broadening exercise—and subsequent Mediterranean and Eastern European ones—will necessitate substantial institutional changes at a 1996 meeting, but there are questions whether the new entrants will eventually conform to the integration goals of the Single European Act and the Maastricht Treaty.

Pierre-Henri Laurent is professor of history at Tufts University. He was chair of the European Community Studies Association (1992-93) and Fulbright/EC Research Scholar (1993). He was the editor of the November 1978 issue of The Annals, *which focused on the European Community. He has contributed to* Technological Challenges and Opportunities of a United Europe; The End of the Cold War; Making the New Europe: European Unity and the Second World War; *and* The External Relations of the European Community: The International Response to 1992.

THE single most important agenda items for the European Community (EC) for the rest of this decade will be related to enlargement. With the completion of the Single Market Program and the route cleared for the Treaty on European Union (TEU; also known as the Maastricht Treaty), the 12 member states have committed themselves to at least one major test of integrating four states of the European Free Trade Association (EFTA) into their organization. Recent post-Cold War decisions have left the door ajar for further expansion, to include other EFTA members, Mediterranean states, and some Eastern European states formerly belonging to the Council for Mutual Economic Assistance.

A glance back at the evolution of the broadening of the Community provides a necessary and enlightening backdrop for examining and analyzing the most contemporary and future expansions. If the EC faced some difficult and trying circumstances in the first three enlargements, it now moves to absorb states with vastly diverse histories, economies and political cultures. If the impact of the earlier processes was a primary determinant of the EC development from 1969 to 1989, then more widening in the new era will alter the EC character and institutions even more.

FROM SIX TO TWELVE

The Treaty of Rome, which gave birth to the Community in 1957, included a provision—Article 237—for an expanded membership. The architects were obviously thinking about the United Kingdom primarily but hoped that others would seek a place alongside the Federal Republic, France, Italy, and the three Benelux nations. The conditions for joining were deceptively simple: the applicant state had to be European, democratic, and willing to accept the responsibilities and duties of what became known as the *acquis communautaire*. This denoted the necessity of new members to abide by all the past rules and laws that bound the original members from the treaty beginnings through the day of entry for the new member. The original Six had also provided alternative means by which states could affiliate or associate themselves on the basis of reciprocity of rights and obligations, but full membership was delineated as the most appealing category for those attracted to the Community.

Shortly after the Six officially began to operate, France and its new government under Charles de Gaulle announced its opposition to any British entry. The United Kingdom had turned down opportunities to engage in the diplomacy that led to the European Coal and Steel Community and European Economic Community in the 1950s. Yet there was an eagerness on the part of the other five that continued strongly into and through the 1960s.[1]

1. For British thinking, see Robert Lieber, *British Politics and European Unity: Parties, Elites and Pressure Groups* (Berkeley: University of California Press, 1970); for the Continental perspective, see Robert Marjolin, "What Type of Europe?" in *Jean Monnet and the Path to European Unity*, ed. Douglas Brinkley and Clifford Hackett (New York: St. Martin Press, 1991).

When the United Kingdom led the setting up of EFTA, with its minimalist free trade ideas, it was a response of disagreement and challenge to the Six that especially aggravated the French Fifth Republic. London bound together with the three Scandinavians—Denmark, Sweden, and Norway—plus Austria, Switzerland, and Portugal to become the Outer Seven to the Inner Six of the EC.[2] The British in effect forged their own economic club in 1960, which, as opposed to the Community, did not envision a common external tariff but centered on easing internal tariffs by mutual agreements. The essential difference between the two organizations was the question of surrendering sovereignty to a common authority, which the Six clearly committed themselves to do over time.[3]

This British resistance to the EC was short-lived. By 1961, the MacMillan government had applied for entry, pressed in that direction by both U.S. foreign policy and the European economic successes, primarily those of the European Coal and Steel Community. The inducements offered by the United States in the Kennedy Round of the General Agreement on Tariffs and Trade (GATT), when combined with the accelerated real earnings and growth of the Common Market states, led the British conservatives to seek membership even though the Labour Party, British farm interests, and Commonwealth advocates opposed the idea. There was, however, little question that an influential portion of the British public and private elite believed that the ultimate success of the Six would result in a large and rich market that might exclude the United Kingdom. They therefore led the British movement to seek admission and were the guiding forces behind the extensive negotiations of 1961-62.[4]

When de Gaulle vetoed the British entry in January 1963, his opposition was based more on questions of nuclear security and U.S.-U.K. relations than on economic issues. London had been demanding many concessions to cushion its entry, and this was repeated in the 1967 application under the Labour government of Wilson. Another French veto did not, however, quell the British ardor in the later 1960s, for now the dimensions of the EC achievements were more apparent and undebatable. When the Luxembourg compromise, forced on the Six by de Gaulle, appeared to deny further federalist goals, the British viewed membership with greater and more positive interest. The U.K. disinclination to yield large amounts of national powers to a regional authority appeared to be protected in an organization with limits to its supranationality.[5]

2. Iceland (1970), Finland (1986), and Liechtenstein (1991) joined EFTA after associate-status years.

3. John Pinder, *The European Community: The Building of a Union* (New York: Oxford University Press, 1991), pp. 43-59; John Newhouse, *De Gaulle and the Anglo-Saxons* (New York: Viking, 1980), passim.

4. Derek W. Urwin, *The Community of Europe: A History of European Integration since 1945* (London: Longman, 1991), pp. 116-29, 139-45.

5. Julius W. Friend, *The Linchpin: French-German Relations 1950-1990* (New York: Praeger, 1991), pp. 26-50, 53-94. See also Haig Simonian, *The Privileged Partnership: Franco-German Relations in the European Commu-*

The door opened wide for London when de Gaulle resigned in 1969 and the Pompidou government faced a more assertive and powerful Brandt ministry in Germany. The French strategy was to seek an internal counterweight to Berlin and its new clout. With British membership in the EC, France gained a partner that would hold back any further concessions on sovereignty, particularly in the political domain. For the British, their economic woes of the early 1970s propelled them to enter, as did again the thriving and therefore alluring economic progress and prosperity of the Six.[6]

The third British application, of 1971, was set forth in what became a historically significant context. The Franco-German agreement about the United Kingdom and enlargement was meshed with a commitment that the EC further fortify their institutions at the same time. Chancellor Willy Brandt and President Georges Pompidou said that deepening the institutional structure through monetary integration should run parallel to widening the Community membership. Thus deepening and widening as justifiable and viable simultaneous processes entered into EC thinking and history, if not reality.[7]

The first enlargement negotiations included Ireland, Denmark, and Norway alongside the British. All four governments were convinced that the greater market opportunities that the EC would provide in the future necessitated their quick entry. But weighty sectors of the Norwegian, British, and Danish populations were at best lukewarm and hesitant as the diplomacy was completed in 1972. A 1973 Norwegian popular vote rejected entry; even though London, Dublin, and Copenhagen gave their approval, the actual difficulties of the enlargement process for them and the Six were to emerge after accession. Nevertheless, the negotiations contained telling examples of critical dispute areas, with agriculture leading the way and fisheries and energy being prominent in Norway's case. Both dispute areas signaled the potential longer-range problems of actual coordination, harmonization, and integration.

Prior to the official expansion to nine members on 1 January 1973, the EC and the remainder EFTA states negotiated a special-relations agreement. The EC was fashioning a stepping-stone to later enlargements that would include the remaining EFTA states. The 1972 agreement, a predecessor to the European Economic Area of 1992, was a means of giving limited preferential treatment to EFTA states, containing any trade conflict, and allowing the outside to see the inside benefits of the EC while actually letting them gain very few.

All subsequent EC augmentation would be touched by the decision to apply the EC creation rules to its first expansion. The Six were to grant ap-

nity, 1969-84 (New York: Oxford University Press, 1985), esp. chaps. 4, 10, and 12.

6. Herman Van der Wee, _Prosperity and Upheaval: The World Economy, 1945-1980_ (Berkeley: University of California Press, 1983), pp. 358-79.

7. The stated EC objective was to pursue both tracks, but in fact enlargement took precedence and the monetary goals were lost in the economic downturns, oil crises, and Europessimism of the 1970s.

plicants a timetable for adaptation, that is, periods of time after entry when safeguard measures and escape clauses protected their economies as they moved into full integrated status. These periods of adjustment meant that all enlargements were to be more difficult than they appeared on the surface, particularly in the post-entry adherence to the *acquis*. It should not be forgotten that it took 12 years for the British to move from their initial application to their actual entry, 6 years in the Greek case, and 9 years in the Iberian case. It then took a minimum of 10, 8, and 6 years, respectively, to move from accession to full integration for each of these first-phase entrants. Enlargement, defined as joining and truly adhering to the integrated conditions of the member states, has been a painfully slow and internally combative process.

The contrasts between the first new members and the subsequent two enlargements were striking. In the 1980s, three Southern states— Greece, Spain, and Portugal—applied and entered the Common Market. These were nations characterized by their relatively lesser developed industrial and capitalist economies and weaker democratic government experiences. They were also more feeble in their attitudes about the goal of genuine European unity. These nations had been mostly outside the liberal industrialized and parliamentary framework of Western Europe in the years after World War II. Greece, in 1967-74, had lived under a military junta, and the Iberian states were under authoritarian rule until the mid-1970s. The fear of Eu-

rocommunism mixed with the Western European joy that dictatorial forms of government had collapsed in these Southern states. This resulted in a strong EC tendency to think of enlargement as a means of reinforcing democratic governance and free-market stability. These periphery states were seen by the EC as possible security risks in the Cold War era; the objective was to keep them non-Communist and in the democratic and capitalist camp. The post-accession woes, particularly in the Greek case under the Papandreou government, were again to be more troublesome than actual entry negotiations, with the last enlargements, comprising Spain and Portugal, to be, in fact, the easiest.

The two Iberian nations joined the queue quickly after the end of the Franco and Salazar regimes. The EC in reality procrastinated on commencing negotiations in order to have more stable Southern economies and governments, given the general turmoil around 1979. Within the negotiations, the Spanish and Portuguese not only proved to be adept and strong diplomats but benefited from major British assistance—again seeking nonfederalist allies—a booming Spanish economy, and the resolution of the British budget rebate controversy. The two Southern states would have joined earlier, but the French and Italian wariness on the farm sector problems and Prime Minister Thatcher's insistence that her contributions be lowered before either enlargement or completion of the internal market project was initiated combined to block negotiations until 1984. Once again, the interplay of political and economic factors dictated the widening process.[8]

INTEGRATION
AND ENLARGEMENT
AFTER THE COLD WAR

In each enlargement, the three major EC bodies increased their power via some streamlining and/or transformation of the operational procedures and structures. In 1973 and after, the EC became a more independent financial entity, and by 1986, the broadening of majority voting had emanated from the Iberian accession and the process outlined in the Single European Act. It is understandable that after 1989 those who aggressively advocated widening also perceived that new members would necessitate institutional changes. Once Soviet imperial control of the East ended, many EC states were to react favorably to this enlargement-change thesis, but for different reasons. Germany, with its integrationist and federalist aims and its renewed eastern interests, saw greater union and its own central EC role increased through enlargement. Great Britain had a pro-expansion orientation based on gaining partners to both control Germany and France and limit any further federalist achievements. Much more restrained about widening were the French and Italians, who were enthusiastic about getting past the 1992 project and TEU before any enlargement talks. They felt strongly that enlargement would be a major test of solidarity that could succeed only if monetary integration was accepted and collective commitments made on a common foreign policy and a Community defense policy.[9]

The EC decision was to deepen in 1991-92 before widening later. The ideas of Jacques Delors about monetary and financial integration became the core of the Maastricht Treaty, which was to take precedence over enlargement. The problem was that the new geopolitics and economies of those and subsequent years did not allow the process to evolve that way. By the time the internal market completion was over at the end of 1992, the Twelve were being pressed to push enlargement talks with four EFTA states without fully reaching an agreement as to whether

8. For the second and third enlargements, see Helen Wallace, *Widening and Deepening: The European Community and the New European Agenda* (London: Royal Institute of International Affairs, 1989), for both her look back and the agenda before the clouds of 1990-93 appeared. See also the Wallace argument, on the "overcrowded agenda," in her "Council and the Commission on the Brink of Maastricht," this issue of *The Annals* of the American Academy of Political and Social Science; on the new Germany and the EC, see Lily Gardner Feldman, "Germany and the EC: Realism and Responsibility," ibid. For the post-1989 period, see Peter Merkl, *German Unification in the European Context* (University Park: Pennsylvania State University Press, 1993), pp. 303-52.

9. Karen E. Donfried, "EC Enlargement," in *Europe and the United States: Competition in the 1990s*, U.S., Cong., House, Committee on Foreign Affairs, 102d Cong., 2d sess., June 1992, pp. 127-40. One example of awareness about the new conditions and their implications is that expressed by Valéry Giscard d'Estaing in his speech printed in *Le Figaro*, 30 July 1990. Reflecting the fear of many, he said, "If we want a close union, it must be built [first] for the Twelve. If we opt [now] for Greater Europe, one must comprehend that union will be limited and will constitute a reedition of the League of Nations for Europe."

they would systematize enlargement then or find ad hoc answers for a larger Community and its problems as they came along.

The outcome would be a fourth enlargement of the EC, an enlargement that was to be one of its greatest challenges. Two distinct historical phases were planned. First would be the actual negotiations of the Twelve with the new applicants; these started in February 1993 with Austria, Finland, and Sweden and in April 1993 with Norway. Second, assuming all four EFTA states' citizens approved in a public referendum, there would be a treaty-revising intergovernmental conference (IGC) scheduled for 1996, which would be forced to devise a new constitutional structure for the new EC of 16. This convention was to construct a design for a Europe of the future, meaning an overall structure that delineated the Community for the subsequent enlargements, too. This IGC would have the advantage of making Cyprus and Malta and possibly the Visegrad Four of Eastern Europe— Poland, Hungary, and the Czech and the Slovak Republics—well aware of the specific responsibilities and duties of membership well before negotiations. There would be a downside, however, in that preplanning and a firm structure before negotiations with more diverse applicants might pose rigidities in the diplomatic process for the Sixteen and the following candidates, too.

The forward planning for broadening, in the Commission and outside in European think tanks, had barely begun when actual bargaining started in early 1993. The EC shifted gears

swiftly, hastening to enlarge before it could devise, in advance, rules for an EC of 16 or more. The 1996 convention would be the first moment when the Twelve plus four could participate in laying down rules of EC operation that would apply to themselves and all other powers after 1996.[10]

The reasons for this milestone change in actual EC procedure and policy were contained in the fast-moving events after 1989 and the EC responses to them. Later critics were to claim "too much, too fast" for the EC decisions. The central conditioning factors were the collapse of communism in Eastern Europe in 1989-90, the fall of the Soviet Union in 1991, and the Western economic downswing and recession beginning in 1991. By early 1992, the Bosnian conflict and Western Europe's disunity about it had added to the problem.

The Twelve would come to view the remaining EFTA states as understandably attractive, given their economic vitality and strength. Their potentially significant role for the EC was increased, given the emergence of newly independent states and free-market economies in *Mitteleuropa*. The newcomers had excellent credentials and were collectively the EC's biggest trading partners. It was not simply the urge-to-merge enthusiasm of the new four but the potential short- and medium-term EC gains that these real nations would give to economic recovery and growth, and

10. Interviews with several Commission staff in early 1993 indicated that the Commissioners could not get the national governments to set additional and more precise conditions regarding enlargement, given their Maastricht worries.

the longer-term benefits in terms of making Europe more of a globally competitive trading power. This new wave of applicants was among the most stable, vital, and dynamic economies in the West and therefore would be net contributors to future EC budgets. They could share the EC burden, particularly in aid to the lesser-developed and poorer South and maybe also the East in due time.

What was clearly downgraded in the EC assessment were the multiple dilemmas of this widening. The potential for tensions based on a new regional imbalance of North-South components in a larger Community were put aside. An EC with 5 large and 11 small and medium-sized states presented another distributional conflict. The stresses between old and new, North and South, net recipients and major donors would be increased, with the potential disempowering of bigger states on one side and the less endowed status of poor, Southern nations on the other.[11]

From the perspective of the four EFTA states, the end of communism and the parallel completion in the West of a single European market meant joining now was not only preferable but mandatory. When the success of Project 1992 was virtually

guaranteed in 1989-90, Austria, Sweden, Finland, and Norway were, in part, intimidated into pressing their application because trade with the EC after 1992 would be increasingly difficult. The parallel between the first and fourth enlargements, with the perceived need to jump on the EC bandwagon, given its economic drawing power, was not missed in any European capital. The pull was so potent that even the promise of a better status, the halfway house offer of the EC called the European Economic Area, would not deter the four from pushing their applications. Their ambition to join was accelerated by their recognition that the newly independent Eastern states would find their recently gained associated status with the Twelve less bright and meaningful than full membership. The EC and EFTA leaders therefore met in 1992 when Brussels realized they needed the economic help that enlargement would bring and when the free traders saw they could accept Community conditions, without great risk, before the entry of other applicants already in line and before the former Soviet-bloc nations. The turning points were two for the EFTA applicants. First, there were the significant concessions granted the United Kingdom in the Maastricht Treaty negotiations that lessened both any additional federalist content and EC competence in noneconomic areas. Second were the equally significant exclusions from Maastricht granted to Denmark at the December 1992 Edinburgh Summit. London and Copenhagen were allowed to opt out of the single-bank and single-currency process and the

11. Werner Weidenfeld and Josef Janning, "The Future of Europe: Alternatives, Strategies, Options" (Paper delivered at the International Bertelsmann Forum, Bonn, 3-4 Apr. 1992). See also Axel Krause, *La Renaissance: Voyage a l'interieur de l'Europe* (Paris: Seuil, 1992), particularly chap. 9. For the specifics in one case, see "The Challenge of Enlargement: Commission Opinion on Austria's Application for Membership," Commission of the European Communities, *Bulletin of the European Communities*, supp. (Apr. 1992).

defense-integration schemes and, in the U.K. case, the social charter. Together, these EC compromises told the EFTA Four that they might enter without fear of losing major national interests. Some analysts saw a historic trade-off at this point of EC history, with the Twelve accepting slower and perhaps less integration for the more immediate benefits and solidarity-formation advantages of enlargement.[12]

The relative rush of the EC to broaden was both the result of member states' sagging economies and recessions urging them to find external solutions and a programmatic political response to internal disarray. The breakdown of the Community's "coherence exercise" on several critical issues in 1992, particularly Maastricht itself but including the European Monetary System, farm reform, General Agreement on Tariffs and Trade talks, and even EC disunity and paralysis on the Bosnian crisis, combined to produce a compromise on enlargement. The Twelve decided that negotiations with the EFTA Four would begin as the Single Market Program ended and before Maastricht was a fact. No major overarching principles, let alone reform ideas about a larger Community, would be devised until the constitutional reform to be discussed at the 1996 IGC. This EC consensus was uneasy, but there was accord regarding a relaxed perspective about broadening and even a permissive policy toward enlargement. Driven by economic and

financial considerations and internal Community political necessities, Brussels and the member states fell back on the coping answer rather than the planning response.[13]

Unaddressed was the central and indisputable fact about the 1993 newcomers. Austria, Sweden, Finland, and Norway represented states whose vision would most likely be at odds with the centralized federal union designed by the original architects. This EFTA proclivity was based on their reluctance about cessions of sovereignty, especially outside the economic area. In the sense that they leaned to intergovernmentalism at the maximum, the newest candidates joined London, Copenhagen, and perhaps Athens, which formed the backbone of the EC status quo group. There was, in enlargement, a distinct possibility that the aspirant states would resist the powers of the central EC organs, form a bloc to hold back more financial and monetary integration, and make more precarious any extension of the unity movement into the military, social, and foreign policy spheres.

All of the foregoing does not imply that the fourth enlargement is bereft of substantive negotiation issues. The central economic one concerns that ancient troublemaker in prior negotiations, agriculture, and the crucial noneconomic one, neutrality. The far-reaching reforms of the Common Agricultural Policy, agreed to by the Twelve in June 1992, do make agreement, primarily with the Norwegians and Finns, much more difficult. The farm interests in these two

12. Bob Hagerty and Charles Goldsmith, "Efforts to Expand Could Instead Turn Out to Be Its Downfall," *Wall Street Journal Europe*, 6 Apr. 1993.

13. "Prospects for the Next Enlargement," *International Herald Tribune*, 6 Jan. 1993.

nations, along with the fishing sectors of Norway, would no doubt resist the new principles that over time systematically diminish agricultural subsidies by the state. Doubtlessly, the avoidance of enlargement bargaining breakdown would hinge again on transitional stages of exemptions for the new entrants that could extend well into the twenty-first century. There is, however, certainty for the applicants in their eventual need to accept the Community *acquis*, that is, the reformed rules of the Common Agricultural Policy.[14]

Neutrality for Austria, Sweden, and Finland could still cause controversy. It would appear, however, to be overrated as a meaningful conflict factor in negotiations, for post-Cold War geopolitics, with its absence of a major power threat, would make it easier for these three states to make some commitments. This would not mean that they would be sympathetic and align in the formation of a common defense policy, but that they would not actively work against the North Atlantic Treaty Organization or the Western European Union. The end result, however, would be to further cleave the EC into advocates of the Maastricht-mandated formation of the Common Foreign and Security Policy and those who will not sign on to such a policy.[15]

14. Hagerty and Goldsmith, "Efforts to Expand." There are those who believe the EFTA Four will seek to avoid these reforms with the aid of France, given the Paris contention that the Common Agricultural Policy reforms need further discussions and adjustments.

15. It must be noted that issues concerning neutrality status have already taken a toll in that Switzerland has hesitated at the EC gate due to foreign and defense policy problems and

All this acknowledges the existence of diplomatic quarrels but, in the end, the making of the Sixteen. It may not be on the original schedule of 1994 and may actually run into 1996 before legislative approval is gained, but it will happen. The EC will be made richer, economically more stable, and globally more competitive. It will also make the EC a more solid anchor in material terms for the widening that will encompass the former Communist states later on. Most important, the EFTA Four will strengthen the EC through, for instance, their successful microeconomic policies, with inflation rates that are in line with requirements of economic and monetary union, and forward-looking and progressive environmental policies that are sometimes in advance of those of the EC states themselves.

CANDIDATES FOR EC
MEMBERSHIP AFTER
THE FOURTH ENLARGEMENT

Two of the most significant developments of the last half century—the emergence and growth of the EC and the 1989-90 peaceful revolutions that swept Eastern Europe—are about to meet. There is abundant evidence that even before 1989 some states of the Council for Mutual Economic Assistance were veering away from Communist thinking and policies, given the more and more visible and definitive impact of EC economic attainments. In the 1990s, EC expansion to the East to include Slav states has become accepted as historically

the confederal states' antipathy to "an ever closer union."

inevitable by most Western Europeans.[16] The timing is the only controversial point, but it is assumed that the process might coincide with the first decade of the next century, if the economic transformation to capitalism is basically succeeding. In the forward planning of the present EC, both economic and political/security factors have already made their way into projections about further widening. The end of Soviet domination meant new free-market and democratic states in Central and Eastern Europe in part because of the nearby, visible, and impressive economic accomplishments of the EC. The rather immediate aspiration of membership became the major long-term external goal of Poland, Hungary, and the then Czechoslovakia. Their pact at Visegrad in February 1991 bound them in terms of EC entry, making membership the nexus of their economic and political modernization.

The EC, for its part, had granted associational status to Poland and Hungary even before the Berlin Wall fell in November 1989. Some in the EC hoped that the offer of membership would suffice in 1990 and 1991, in that this would be a force that would intensify democratic and eco-

16. Switzerland and Liechtenstein will most likely follow the EFTA Four into the EC, and Iceland, too, if the Norwegians get adequate fishery protections in their negotiations. Malta will join without any stumbling blocks, but Cyprus, given the Greek-Turkish ethnic strife, will remain outside the EC for the foreseeable future. Turkey will have the same fate, given the Greek attitude and the religious and human rights problems. The other Balkan and Baltic states, let alone the states of the Commonwealth of Independent States, are longer-term possibilities, meaning three decades or more, if at all.

nomic reform and stability. Brussels upgraded these sectoral arrangements, committing the Twelve to early removal of customs duties; increased freedom of worker, capital, and services movement; scientific and technological aid; social reform assistance; and even more political dialogue.

But trade and cooperation accords, the promotion of freer and mutual trade, most-favored-nation status, and quota-restriction removal on top of large Western investment and aid packages have not been sufficient for the impatient and needy ex-Communist states. The Twelve have tried several ways of holding out against Eastern Europe's expressions for membership, and by mid-1993, the criticisms from the East had turned to anger. The question of the EC's raising false hopes and the Eastern anxiety about "the timetable of the twenty-first century" as "too little, too late" were ending in more interregional European conflict. The EC hesitancy, based on the poorness of the new states and their slow movement to privatization, was deepened by the troublesome westward migration movements and the threatening low-cost producer capabilities of the East. The EC worries were also based on the costs in budget transfers that an Eastern enlargement would require before 2010. One study that used the now-ubiquitous "best-case scenario" projected an amount 25 times the amount now moved annually in aid to the southern five of the Twelve.[17]

17. See Marc Maresceau, "The European Community, Eastern Europe and the USSR," in *The External Relations of the European*

Beyond the endless economic questions that an Eastern enlargement would entail—and it most certainly would retard the integration process—there are political and security challenges that would vault to the forefront for the EC states. The EC balance of power would become a giant question mark, with a French-led EC dread about a German-dominated *Mitteleuropa* at the top of the list. There is little doubt that both an EFTA-based and Visegrad-based EC expansion would empower Bonn. The uniting of Germany in 1989-90, with the absorption of the former German Democratic Republic, raised the still-unsettled domination and superpower questions for all of Germany's EC associates. For many of them, the response about a European Germany and not a German Europe will have less relevance and creditability if the projected Northern and Eastern mergers with the EC take place. And beyond the German question would be the Commonwealth of Independent States issue if the EC "moved east." Once the Community spreads into Slav regions, the entire Eurasian relationship of states, including primarily the Russian Federation, will make that enlargement in political, security, and economic terms a primary interest of every state in the world.

THE ISSUES
AT THE 1996 IGC

The paramount problems of making a revised set of rules for the bigger Community will be left to the 1996 intergovernmental conference. Given the fact that the EC institutions were built for six members and are heavily weighted down with twelve, the IGC task will be formidable. With more joining, the necessity to overhaul the Community is imperative. Integrating the next waves will take some careful maneuvering and creativity. Since a bigger EC must also be manageable and efficient, the IGC will have the job of constructing new mechanisms and rules. In fact, that process has already begun because the problems are clear. The prospects are that the newest members will tip the balance and, with the United Kingdom and some small states, redefine entry rules in the direction of a two- or three-track Europe. The June 1992 Lisbon Summit made it possible for the EFTA applicants to commence negotiations without any extensive internal EC dialogue that would revise entry conditions. Lisbon intentionally eased the route for the four, putting real reform off till 1996.[18]

The Community in 1996 will not have the luxury of its past procrastination. If nothing else, the line of applicants then will demand new ideas in negotiations. The increased cultural, linguistic, and political heterogeneity will severely exacerbate differences, lessen efficiency, and even jeopardize the governability of the EC. The panoply of problems will range from the issue of languages to

---

Community: The International Response to 1992, ed. John Redmond (New York: St. Martin's Press, 1992), pp. 93-119; "Eastern Europe: The Old World's New World," *Economist*, 13-19 Mar. 1993.

18. "The European Community: Altered States," *Economist*, 11 July 1992. See also Charles Goldsmith, "EC Considers Its Options before Difficult Convention," *Wall Street Journal Europe*, 6 Apr. 1993.

questions of Commission, Parliament (EP), and Council of Ministers size, voting rights, and powers. Exploring these examples in some depth only validates the notion that the IGC role in determining Europe's future will be decisive.[19]

If unchanged, the provisions concerning languages alone could bring the EC to a near halt. The Twelve have 2 working languages, English and French, and 9 official languages, meaning that for translation and interpretation purposes there are 72 obligatory language pairs: Portuguese-Greek, Danish-Spanish, and so on. Bringing in the languages of the next four member states would mean 13 total languages and 156 possible pairs, resulting in an enormous expense for translation and interpretation, endless delays, drawn-out meetings, an unbearable bureaucracy, and potentially an unbelievable legal chasm based on debates over linguistic precision and correctness. The language factor becomes even more absurd if the enlargement to the South and East is considered, since this would mean 21 languages and 420 pairs.

The apparent sensible solution on languages would be to establish a language limit in the current negoti-

19. In the spring of 1993, the present author gained greater insight into the upcoming IGC issues in extensive interviews with members of the Commission task force for the present enlargement and at the following organizations: the Center for Economic Policy Studies and the Trans-European Policy Studies Association in Brussels, the European Policy Forum and the Royal Institute of International Affairs in London, and the Institute of European and International Affairs in Luxembourg. The following points touch only lightly on the multiple problems.

ations and institutionalize it in the 1996 conference, with a cap on the number of official languages. This would mean that the absolute respect for language identity could not continue with the new members. A negotiated solution could create regional languages such as Scandinavian, which would embrace three and possibly four members, and could even include present members—for example, a Dutch-Luxembourgois agreement to accept German or a Spanish-Portuguese accord on an Iberian language. The latter possibility is slight since it would require present members to give up an original treaty principle that they fought hard to get.

Obviously of greater impact will be the decision-making turmoil that could reign in the EC of 16 or more. It is evident that change will be needed in all four institutions, with the crucial ones being the Commission, the EP, and the Council of Ministers. In the Commission case, adaptation will mean rethinking the present 17-member group, which would become 21. The bigger states would sense more and more that their populations are underrepresented, and therefore they would insist that even four more Commissioners are unacceptable. Subsequent enlargement involving Cyprus, Malta, and the Visegrad states would require addressing the Commission members' numbers game definitively at the 1996 convention. Most experts are convinced that the Commissioner numbers and member states must be delinked by that time. Scenarios for ameliorated decision making include an EP elected Commission President who appoints a dozen Commissioners with careful attention to regional balance and specific topical expertise. This process would then be tied to empowering the EP, for these Commissioners would be responsible to and report to the Parliament, as do American cabinet members, and would also be dismissed individually for cause by the EP.

One strong suspicion is that small to medium-sized new members would more easily outnumber and possibly outvote—given the Maastricht-mandated broadening of weighted-majority voting—the larger states in all EC bodies. The result would be the likelihood that large member states' private decisions outside the conference room would circumvent both collective bargaining and EC decisions themselves. This is most applicable to the efficiency of operating the European Council with four or eight additional members, for voting on taxes, environment, and energy, for example, still needs unanimity. Gridlock could result easily through either avenue, so even the weighted-voting concept demands reform. If one continues the notion that nations should receive voting strength equal to their size—now gauged on a 2-to-10 scale—it will be relatively easy for a small-state bloc to halt many EC decisions.

Size again is at the core of the presidency problem in the European Council. The idea of the six-month rotating term may not survive as is, for it would mean eight years or more between presidencies for any member. This would negate any expertise formation or learning through frequent or continuous performance. Furthermore, the troika system of leadership that has evolved for al-

most 20 years would be placed into question, since the past, present, and future presidents would pose questionable possibilities of either impotence or regional imbalance. Since the rotation goes by alphabetical order, the first troika problem would be in a Liechtenstein, Luxembourg, and Malta combination and the second might be Poland, Portugal, and the Slovak Republic.

Some expert studies project a decision-making alteration in the establishment of a directorate comprising permanent members—only the large members?—and elected-by-rotation term members. This is a concept applied with some success in the U.N. Security Council and is certainly appealing to those of the federal bent in that it might be employed to benefit these goals. Since this is evident to all, the directorate schema might be ditched by a confederal bloc. By the time of the IGC, this group of eight or nine states may want to press its alternatives, such as a regional presidency with one country acting for a group—one Scandinavian state for those three, one Benelux nation for those three, one Eastern state for those four, and so forth—or multiple presidencies, one for each policy area, such as defense or monetary affairs. Each of these latter two notions suffers from power denial and/or power diffusion, but they tend to gain confederalist approval.

The EP will have to grow as the EC expands, but new constraints will be needed to avoid moving from the present 518 members to double that number at century's end. EP growth would transpire naturally in that in 1994, enlargement of the EP as a result of German unification and population increases—the latter revealed by census data—will mean 567 Europarliamentarians. Another census adjustment plus the accession of the next four members and any other Mediterranean or Eastern new members will easily yield up a thousand legislators. The new EP deficiency would no longer be primarily the relative absence of democratic power but the distinct chance the institution could not function at all.

The Community convention in 1996 will face many of these thorny controversies and others as well. Some EC observers already asserted in 1993 that the only rational resolutions to these enlargement complications reside in acknowledging and planning for a multi-tracked Europe. They believe that the growing sentiment in the Twelve, fortified in the Sixteen, will be for membership chosen or rejected in certain domains of the Community. This "European house with many rooms" would have the advantage of voluntary belonging in desired areas, say monetary, and exclusion from others—for instance, foreign policy. It would result in collectives of eager and willing states racing quickly to supranational authority and institutions, while others would refrain from some sector membership yet not obstruct the programs of others.

The peril of the Europe à la carte approach, of choosing membership in one domain and rejecting it in another, is the absence of overall European unity, for never would there be a Europe speaking with one voice. This would have to be true for the short run, but one suggested compromise receiving much attention is a flexibility-now, commitment-later rule. This would mean the acceptance at the 1996 meeting by all members—old and forthcoming—of selective sectoral commitments, but clear-cut timetables that require full acceptance of common monetary, defense, social, and foreign policies by all members eventually. In sum, adjustment periods would be allowed, but new members could not stay out of the evolving comprehensive transnational structure of the EC permanently. The dangers involved in allowing too many exceptions to the existing *acquis* or the ability to opt out of portions of the overall Community for periods of time are an established EC fact. The previously mentioned Maastricht and Edinburgh grants to London and Copenhagen have become overnight precedents that will be tested at the 1996 IGC. Three of the four present applicants have indicated that they will want to cut their own deals, choosing only those parts of European unification that they find appealing and opting out of those they see as objectionable. If these exceptions are allowed in the present negotiations with the EFTA Four or in the *loi cadre* or framework for later enlargements, the EC will seal its fate as a nonsupranational set of loosely connected economic units with confederal institutions. The construction of a true trans-state political grouping of consequence would terminate before 2000.

CONCLUSION

If the Community is to be a vibrant and dynamic regional and global power at the end of the century, there must be decisions about enlargement in the 1990s that continue the construction of a true union.[20] The recent past and present European conditions would not predict a very good chance for this European venture. The EC economies, with their rising national debts, still-mounting unemployment, chaotic foreign exchange markets, and only negligible growth rates, have been so weak that in mid-1993 only Luxembourg could meet the Maastricht criteria set for membership within the single currency union. Since the TEU states standards of low interest rates, budget deficits, inflation, and government debt, it prescribes conditions for the medium term that are far from those of the widespread recession of today.

The outlines of renationalization, both within the EC borders and even more so on its frontiers, can be discerned in the post-1989 era; furthermore, they appear to be gaining in strength. This reemergence of European nationalism has been in every case at the expense of the EC, in the same way that the economic no-growth circumstances have undercut and weakened the integration process.[21] It is with expanded EC membership that the significance of resurgent national feelings comes into play, for building a united Europe demands firm actions of a collective nature that move beyond the nation-state. There are many forces that compete with integration and unity, but the nationalist urge is the strongest. The prospects of implementing the TEU, making a reality of the single bank and single currency and the shared foreign and defense policies, have been significantly crippled by the recent economic decline and other EC difficulties, namely, the long-delayed Uruguay Round trade talks and two years of EC diplomatic failure to confront and resolve the Balkan crisis. Many believe the EC tug of war has already been tilted in the direction where widening is a force that opposes authentic and full integration. If the federalist impulse is alive and well, it must make a comeback in post-Maastricht Europe, mainly in the construction of the bigger Europe. To many observers, 1993-96 is the juncture where the momentum of the union movement must move from a stalled, on-hold status to the *relance* stage. It is

20. Wolfgang Danspeckgruber, "European Integration after 1992: Completed Integration or Commencing Nationalization?" (Paper delivered at the Third Biennial Conference of the European Community Studies Association, Washington, DC, 28 May 1993); Neil Nugent, "The Community Integration Process Post-Maastricht" (Paper delivered at the Third Biennial Conference of the European Community Studies Association, Washington, DC, 28 May 1993).

21. Alan Milward, *The European Rescue of the Nation-State* (Berkeley: University of California Press, 1992), pp. 1-20, 435-46. This work, along with his earlier book on the origins of the integration movement, is the most important book on the EC published in the last decade. If Milward is correct, that the EC's historic evolution has been an integral part of the reassertion of the nation-state and that without integration the Western states might not have kept the support of their citizens, then the allegiance paid to Community institutions in member states is only secondary. As he asserts, "Whenever the Community member states have had to implement their surrenders of sovereignty, they have produced an arrangement which left almost all political power with the nation-state." Milward, *European Rescue of the Nation-State*, pp. 445-46.

apparent now that the union movement will either be relaunched again or it will be put aside en route to and at the IGC meeting.

If the 1990s are to reproduce the integration success of the 1980s, the EC will have to move from its present economic malaise and political disarray with a bold leadership that urges and gets decisions for a new Europe and not a Europe of nations. If Western Europe is to be redivided into camps or blocs where conflict, confrontation, and competition once again prevail, as they did before World War II, rather than the convergence, conciliation, and cooperation ideas of recent decades, the great and historic European integration process may be over before the new century gets under way.

ANNALS, *AAPSS*, **531**, January 1994

From Failure to Fortune?
European Electronics in
a Changing World Economy

By JOHN ZYSMAN and MICHAEL BORRUS

ABSTRACT: European industrial policy for high technology must be reformulated. First, past support of producers over users has undermined producers by not creating a sophisticated market, the single most powerful industrial policy tool. Second, global trade and investment are regionalizing. Policies aimed at rejuvenating sectors such as electronics must consider that regionalization will make access to technology and markets increasingly asymmetrical. The concepts of supply base and architecture of supply clarify this understanding. Europe must not just refocus domestic support but also secure access to the supply bases of the other two regions, America and Asia.

John Zysman and Michael Borrus are codirectors of the Berkeley Roundtable on the International Economy at the University of California at Berkeley, where they also teach. John Zysman is professor of political science. Michael Borrus is lecturer in the Joint Program in Technology Management of the Engineering and Business schools. They have recently coauthored The Highest Stakes: The Economic Foundations of the Next Security System. *John Zysman's other recent works include* Manufacturing Matters *and* Politics and Productivity. *Michael Borrus is the author of* Competing for Control.

AS the balance of industrial power in the world shifted during the 1980s, Europe began to reshape itself, to reconsider its position in the world economy and how to improve it. Throughout the decade, European governments and the European Commission sought to help their corporations establish or improve their position in global markets. Programs for promoting industries aimed not only to revitalize the European economy but also to help recast the political and industrial bargain that underpins the European Community.

The policies of the European national governments and the European Commission focused in particular on developing and promoting the electronics industry during the 1980s.[1] European policies in this article refer to the policies of both the Community, in the form of the initiative that created and emerged from DGXIII (General Directorate XIII), and the national governments. The two sets of policies cannot be easily separated and certainly cannot be differentiated in these pages.

The reasons for this focus are as numerous as they are obvious. The electronics industry generates transformative technologies that touch a broad range of economic activities; its development is central to the competitive position of firms in most industries.[2] The industry now approaches automobiles in output and employment, and it continues to grow rapidly. The electronics sector has also come to symbolize the foundation of advanced industry in the late twentieth century.[3] The sector's importance, both real and symbolic, makes it an excellent lens through which to view Europe's past and present industrial strategies, its successes and failures, and the challenges ahead.

The European policies—both those of the governments and those of the Commission—developed in the 1980s for the electronics sector, whatever their political benefits, did not lead to industrial success.[4] In the most visible sectors, European electronics firms remain weak. Indeed, there have been several dramatic competitive collapses, including the downsizing of Philips, the several crises at Bull, and the purchase of ICL by Fujitsu.

---

1. Wayne Sandholtz, *High-Tech Europe: The Politics of International Cooperation* (Berkeley: University of California Press, 1991). See also earlier works: Wayne Sandholtz and John Zysman, "Recasting the European Bargain," *World Politics*, 42:95-128 (Oct. 1989); Pierre-Henri Laurent, "The European Technology Community, the Meeting of the Elites, and the Creation of the Internal Market," in *Il difficile cammino dell'Europa unita*, ed. S. Beretta (Milan: Casa Giuffre, 1989), 125-34.

2. On transformative industry, see Stephen Cohen and John Zysman, *Manufacturing Matters: The Myth of the Post-Industrial Economy* (New York: Basic Books, 1987); Laura D'Andrea Tyson, *Who's Bashing Whom: Trade Conflict in High-Technology Industries* (Washington, DC: Institute for International Economics, 1992).

3. Michel Catinat, "L'informatique et les automatismes" (Paper delivered at "Le Devinir Industriel de La France: Cooperer," Seminaire International, Paris, 7-9 Sept. 1992), p. 11.

4. "The Report of the Information and Communications Technologies Review Board" (June 1992). This review board, chaired by Wisse Dekker of Philips, was invited by the European Commission to review the progress of the major programs in information and communications technologies.

Three Commission and national-government policy choices plagued the European electronics industry in the 1980s. First, government funding of large, national firms tended to push those firms into established and highly competitive market segments; indeed, this was often the intent of the policy.[5] Most spending supported the existing producers along identifiable technological trajectories and for usually unimaginative competitive strategies. Little wonder the firms found it hard to establish defensible market positions; their governments pushed them into strategically difficult situations. Second, favoring producers over low prices and easy access for industrial users discouraged widespread diffusion of advanced technologies among sophisticated users—the essential ingredient for creating launch markets for innovative products and entrepreneurial firms to serve them.

Third, European policymakers sought to locate production of key technologies in Europe. One objective was to maintain employment and healthy trade balances. A second objective was to increase technology transfer by forcing foreign firms to locate production within Europe in order to gain market access. The French government and some in Brussels believed that the Japanese advantage would be blunted if they had to produce in Europe with European labor practices and wage and overhead costs. Or at least Europe would be in a position to channel some of the Japanese advantage into their own industry by forcing technology transfer. If the European governments were right and could buy time for adjustment, European-owned production could be sustained. If they were wrong, at least jobs would be retained and technology transferred; local suppliers would learn from working with Japanese firms; local research and development (R&D) would build up fonts of knowledge and technology. Europe therefore ended up with a policy that essentially traded imports for foreign direct investment (FDI); that is, Europe discouraged imports but tolerated and often directed FDI.[6] The policy worked on its own terms. By the end of the 1980s, motivated by fears of being locked out of Fortress Europe, both U.S. and Japanese electronics firms had made substantial direct investments to establish production, distribution, and even R&D in Europe.[7] It is too early to tell which, if any, of its various goals Europe's FDI strategy will achieve; but in the short term, the strategy only exacerbated both of the problems that the first two policy choices—pushing established producers into highly contested markets and ignoring users—had failed to solve. The increased presence of U.S. and Japanese producers created even more competition for European firms in established market segments.

5. Ibid.

6. See Tyson, *Who's Bashing Whom*, chap. 6. See also the excellent article by Robin Gaster that discusses European FDI policies, "Protectionism with Purpose: Guiding Foreign Investment," *Foreign Policy* (Fall 1992).

7. Yui Kimura, "Japanese FDI in the European Semiconductor Industry," in *Does Ownership Matter? Japanese Multinationals in Europe*, ed. Mark Mason and Dennis Encarnation (New York: Oxford University Press, 1993).

In short, things did not work out quite as the Commission and European governments planned. The lesson of the past decade is that neither policies of promotion—such as the high-definition television undertaking—nor policies of protection—which encouraged FDI—served to preserve the position of established European producers in their own markets, let alone improve their overall position in global markets.

European corporate leaders and policymakers now wonder whether they can succeed where they failed in the 1980s: that is, can they create a competitive electronics industry? In this article, we will consider the nature of the challenges now facing this sector and how European policy might address them. To understand these challenges we must first turn to the broad transformations occurring in the international economy.

REGIONAL POLITICS
IN A GLOBAL ECONOMY

Though the world may be globalizing, it still has a geography.[8] The economic world is slowly dividing into three powerful trading groups: Asia, North America, and Europe.[9] These three groups together constitute close to 70 percent of global gross domestic product (GDP), with the U.S. and European shares each at

about a quarter of global GDP, and Asia's share growing very rapidly.[10] Contrary to the common perception that trade is spread widely among the nations of these regions, a large part of trade takes place only within the regions. For example, interregional trade makes up only a small part of the GDP of the Asian and European regions. For America, foreign trade as a part of GDP has grown in the last quarter century, but Canada and Mexico still are its first- and third-largest trade partners, respectively. Alternatively, consider the pattern of trade growth. Trade within Europe has long been growing more rapidly than external trade; trade within Asia since the second half of the 1980s has likewise grown faster than trade with other regions.[11] In

8. Winifried Ruigrok and Rob van Tulder, "The Ideology of Interdependence" (Diss., University of Amsterdam, 1993).

9. This argument is widely disputed. For a view parallel to ours, see Lawrence B. Krause, "Trade Policy in the 1990s: Good-Bye Bipolarity, Hello Regions," *World Today*, 46(5) (May 1990). In our view, the difference is largely one of vocabulary.

10. In 1987, Japan alone accounted for 12.4 percent of global GDP, and Japan plus the East Asian newly industrializing countries accounted for 15.8 percent. These figures are based on data in Bureau d'Information et Prevision Economique, *Europe in 1992* (Paris: BIPE, 1987). Since these data were published, the Japanese share has risen.

11. Trade within the European Economic Community has grown faster than the trade between the European Community and the rest of the world since the establishment of the European Community in 1958. From 1967 to 1987, the ratio of intraregional trade to interregional trade rose from .79 to 1.15. Colette Herzog, "Les trois Europes," in *Europe: Economie prospective internationale*, La Documentation Française 43 (Paris: CEPII, 1989). Discounting intra-European trade, Europe's percentage of world exports and imports dropped drastically: exports from 44.6 to 13.8 percent and imports from 42.6 to 11 percent. Ibid. Trade within Asia has grown faster than trade between Asia and other regions since 1985. *The Rising Tide: Japan in Asia*, special supplement, *Japan Economic Journal*, p. 4 (1990). See also Takashi Inoguchi, "Shaping and Sharing Pacific Dynamism," *The Annals*

fact, as we look at these three regions, what is surprising is not the extent of trade connecting the regions but the persistence of regional autonomy despite it.

Trade relationships between the regions are very different. Overall, the trade relationship between the United States and Europe is remarkably balanced, despite the ever flaring trade wars over chicken or soy beans or the debates over aircraft subsidies and public procurement. A quick glance at the trade numbers suggests not only an enduring, healthy trade balance but that the trade flows have responded to exchange rate changes. As the United States turns inward to its own economic regeneration, and Europe to its political as well as economic reorganization, there is certainly a risk that the domestic preoccupations of each will give particular squabbles some general significance and undermine a fundamentally balanced relationship. But the balanced trade relationship between the United States and Europe is very different in character from the balance between Asia, on the one hand, and Europe or the United States, on the other. Both American and European trade with Asia is growing very rapidly. American trade with Asia is as great as

trade with Europe. But both Europe and the United States massively import from Asia while their export and investment positions in Asia are remarkably limited. Of course, all of Asia has a deficit with Japan, as Japanese components and subsystems are assembled throughout Asia into final product for export out of the region.[12] The entrenched export surpluses—those directly between Japan and Europe or America and those indirectly between them through other Asian exporters—generate a more fundamental structural problem that expresses itself as a series of bilateral quarrels and makes the international trading system unstable. In our view, the objectives of multilateralism are ultimately at risk.

Trade is certainly not the only activity that connects the regions. Consider the often talked-about multinational corporations and financial institutions. Though these firms roam the globe, each has a home—a country that necessarily shapes its character and both constrains and directs its choices.[13] Each home has a distinct industrial and technological base and a developed domestic regional market. Economic strategies and responses to new competition are generated within particular places, rather than by world corporations that stand outside a home base. Multinational corporations may someday

of the American Academy of Political and Social Science, 505:46-55 (Sept. 1989). By 1988, intra-Pacific Basin trade had risen to almost 66 percent of the region's total trade, from about 54 percent in 1980. See Lawrence B. Krause, "Pacific Economic Regionalism and the United States" (Paper prepared for the symposium "Impact of Recent Economic Developments on US-Korea Relations and the Pacific Basin," University of California at San Diego, 9-10 Nov. 1990).

12. Japan's trade with the rest of Asia in 1989 surpassed its trade with the United States, more than doubling since 1982 to over $126 billion. *The Rising Tide: Japan in Asia,* special supplement, *Japan Economic Journal,* p. 4 (1990).

13. See "Everybody's Favourite Monsters," a survey of multinational corporations, in *Economist,* 27 Mar. 1993.

be able to act without national constraint, but not yet. The present international economy may be more global, but that does not end the importance of place—community, district, nation, or region.

FDI also reveals patterns of regionalization in the world economy. FDI grew much faster than did world trade between 1983 and 1989, expanding at a rate of almost 30 percent, compared to under 10 percent for world exports.[14] Roughly 80 percent of the flows during this period took place between the advanced industrialized countries, suggesting simple integration. But if we look more closely, a regional pattern reemerges. As Sylvia Ostry notes,

A significant aspect of the 1980s FDI wave is what appears to be the emergence of regional strategies by the triad's [multinational corporations], leading to the likely formation of investment blocs and thereby also hastening intra-regional trade integration. The clustering pattern which is emerging among the countries shows each region dominated by investment from a single triad member: the Americas by the United States; Asia by Japan; and Eastern Europe as well as selected African countries by the [European Community]."[15]

That is, the transnational corporate investment flows are themselves shaping three global regions.

FDI influences much more than simple ownership or corporate position in several markets. FDI powerfully drives trade as well. FDI is not just a substitute for trade in which cars or videocassette recorders that were once produced in Japanese factories or American factories are now produced in European factories. Rather, FDI opens up a wedge that often expands trade as subsystems and production equipment are shipped from the home country of investing corporations to the host country where production subsequently takes place.[16] Majority-controlled FDI is an impetus to exports from the home country of the investor. Moreover, in some places like Japan, minority foreign investment stimulates exports from the host country as foreign firms buy into a source of product.[17] Consider, for example, Chrysler's original investment in Mitsubishi as a means of obtaining models to fill out its product range in the United States.

In sum, patterns of trade, finance, and FDI indicate that three regional groups are emerging. Whether or not the three economic groups come to constitute rival blocs will depend on politics within each group and the politics of their economic relations. But even if the regions do not evolve into regional blocs, the emerging economic geography will powerfully influence each region's strategies to maintain competitive industries and develop the technologies necessary to support their growth.

14. Sylvia Ostry, "Foreign Direct Investment in East Asia" (Paper, Center for International Studies, University of Toronto, and the Berkeley Roundtable on the International Economy, 1992).

15. Ibid., p. 14.

16. See Dennis Encarnation, *Rivals beyond Trade: America versus Japan in Industrial Policy, 1925-1975* (Tokyo: Charles E. Tuttle, 1982).

17. Ibid.

TECHNOLOGY VERSUS APPLICATIONS SKILLS: WHAT STRATEGY FOR EUROPEAN ELECTRONICS?

If the world economy conformed to the popular image of symmetrically interdependent globalization, there might be no need for detailed European electronics policies. In that world, technology would flow rapidly across national borders and regional boundaries. Europe's size and wealth would ensure that a significant proportion of advanced activities occurred there. But the reality of asymmetrical regionalization implies something entirely different. Technology will not necessarily flow smoothly between the regions or, in particular, from Asia to Europe. There is no guarantee that relevant technologies will be available in a timely fashion within Europe's borders. Local technological capabilities will need to be nurtured within Europe if only to ensure that European countries and companies can bargain on strong terms for access to markets, technologies, and investment opportunities in the other regions. Europe's size and wealth will continue to depend principally upon developments within Europe.

What, then, should Europe do in electronics? The answer turns on the role that technologies play in industrial competitiveness. There are two extreme views. Each leads to different policy choices. The first focuses on applications expertise, the second on development and production know-how.

Proponents of the first view argue that while production and employment in a growing sector are impor-tant, it is the capacity to apply the new technologies that is ultimately decisive in international competition. In their view, Europe must first and foremost be able to effectively absorb, diffuse, and apply these technologies. The kinds of capacities that enable an economy to absorb, diffuse, and apply technology are, if not broader and deeper than the capacities required to produce the technology, certainly more difficult to create and maintain.[18] But if we adopt this vantage, evaluating the precise technology position of a nation becomes very difficult. How can one measure, evaluate, and quantify the mechanisms that allow timely and efficient application of innovative technology, for example?

In this first view, a country—or a region—need not be a major producer of electronics or other advanced technologies in order to sustain a competitive position; new technologies will always be readily available in the market and can be bought, albeit at a somewhat higher price under some circumstances. To remain in a strong position, a country or a region must only be able to apply these technologies quickly and effectively. Thus producers of Danish hearing aids and Italian music boxes can compete effectively based on their sophisticated applications know-how if they are assured access to microelectronics technology.

The competing view, and really the dominant view in most European dis-

18. See Gerd Junne, "Competitiveness and the Impact of Change: Applications of High Technologies," in *Industry and Politics in West Germany*, ed. Peter J. Katzenstein (Ithaca, NY: Cornell University Press, 1989), p. 250.

cussions, is that only an intimate knowledge of the most advanced products permits a timely flow of technology and intermediate product into final product. In this case, the reality of a regionalizing world figures prominently. Intimate knowledge could only come from local production and local R&D, or it might even require local development, production, and ownership. For example, a strength in consumer electronics or computer-aided design (CAD) tools would require early command of advanced component technologies. In turn, advanced electronic products would increasingly turn on CAD tools and the components that go into consumer products. The French socialist notion of technological *filieres*, strands of technological development in which the different activities or steps in production are inextricably interconnected, represents the most extreme version of this concept. The extreme versions of the argument for domestically located intimate knowledge should not discredit the general observation that different production steps do depend on each other. Europe's dilemma is that American and Japanese firms, not indigenous European producers, are the primary source of advanced electronics technology. Broadly speaking, a firm's technology supply base constrains its strategy. Consequently, Europe's dependence on foreign suppliers raises concerns about both political autonomy and constraints on economic development.

European governments continually ask themselves how they should manage this dependence. Should Europe willingly accept imports to maintain lower prices, or should it restrain imports to encourage local producers—even if that involves penalties for the users who would employ the products? Or, instead, should foreign producers be encouraged to develop and make products in Europe to ensure closer links between foreign producers and European suppliers and to encourage technology transfer? If the foreign firm only wholesales commodity products or produces standard products largely from imported components in automated factories, then there will be limited technology transfer or learning within the home industry. The same would be true, of course, if a national firm merely assembled imported technological parts. Even if the foreign firms conduct local R&D, that may not be sufficient to ensure technology transfer. The projects undertaken may be so narrow and specific to particular products that the host country's broader technology competence is not nurtured.

Theoretical arguments alone cannot resolve this matter. In practice, the country's composition of electronics production, the types of final products, and firms' market strategies determine what access to emerging technology is required for them to be competitive. On balance, European governments have reluctantly and nervously accepted foreign substitutes for local production when there is no alternative, but they have paid very high prices to support the market entry or reentry of local producers.

The two vantage points that have been outlined are complements. The first emphasizes applications knowhow while downplaying concerns about foreign supplies of technology and focusing on users. The other emphasizes the need for intimate access to rapidly evolving cutting-edge technology and focuses on producers. It is vexing that, depending on the circumstances, the prescriptions of either view may be correct. Consequently, the appropriate policy balance—between emphasizing user application, diffusion, and the creation of sophisticated markets, on the one hand, and promoting directly the development of particular products, technologies, or supplier firms on the other—is very difficult to specify and will be even harder to implement.

Can we proceed further in answering when governments or companies that have become dependent on suppliers in another country, particularly another region, should be concerned? The critical issue becomes the terms on which technologies are available. The concepts of an industrial and technological supply base and the architecture of that supply base can help. Borrus defines the supply base as

the parts, components, subsystems, materials and equipment technologies available for new products and process development, as well as the structure of relations among the firms that supply and use these elements. The supply base shapes the possibilities confronting users by enabling or deterring access to appropriate technologies in a timely fashion at a reasonable price.[19]

Logically, supply bases act as a structural constraint on individual company choices. In this sense a supply base regulates firm choices in the same manner as the structure of an industry, as a set of constraints or opportunities. The supply base can be understood as an element of industrial structure or organization external to the firm that defines the choices of the firm.[20] The supply base describes the technologies—the parts, components, subsystems, materials, and equipment technologies —necessary for product development and production in a range of activities, and it describes their interconnections. A supply base consists of a set of interrelated activities; when they are tightly linked—that is, mutually dependent and reinforcing— they constitute a development bloc.[21]

The concept has intuitive appeal. It does not identify which of those elements or activities are critical to ensure production or to create competitive advantage and profit. It does not show us precisely where value is added and what positions are competitively defensible. That can only be determined by a separate, competitive analysis of an individual industry and of its firms' strategies, that is,

19. Michael Borrus, "Re-Organizing Asia: Japan's New Development Trajectory and the Regional Division of Labor" (BRIE Working Paper #53, Berkeley Roundtable on the International Economy, 1992).

20. Paolo Guerrieri, "Technology and International Trade Performance of the Most Advanced Countries" (BRIE Working Paper #49, Berkeley Roundtable on the International Economy, 1991). Seen from the viewpoint of a supply base that underpins final production, it is not surprising that Guerrieri finds that export competitiveness in production equipment is linked to the competitive position of firms in the final goods sector in which the equipment is used.

21. Erik Dahmen, "Development Blocks in Industrial Economics," *Scandinavian Economic History Review*, vol. 1 (1988).

by an analysis of the terms on which a given industry's firms compete and create advantage.

The strength of the supply base concept, however, is that it allows us to see how distinct sets of technologies develop in a region or a nation and how access to those technologies then becomes a pressing issue for firms and governments. For example, most of the hardware elements of the new electronics supply base are emerging in Asia, whichever measures and definitions we might use. We must ask, What access will American and European companies, firms with homes outside the region, have to these technologies? Variations in market and institutional arrangements permit us to make systematic distinctions in the accessibility of technology supply bases. A market consisting of many flexibly specialized small firms all in shifting horizontal relations, each supplying components and know-how to one another, has a very different architecture from a market in which concentrated suppliers compete with their customers; the latter describes the vertically arranged Japanese *keiretsu* in which component suppliers also produce the final product.

The architecture of supply is a tool for helping firms and governments judge when dependency is acceptable or dangerous and how to proceed in either case. Borrus argues that they must worry about their supply sources as follows:

When suppliers have the ability to exercise market power or to act in concert to control technology flows, or when markets and technologies are not accessible because of trade (and investment) protec-

tion, then the architecture of supply can significantly constrain competitive adjustment to the disadvantage of domestic industry. Such an architecture is emerging today. . . . A small number of foreign suppliers, principally Japanese, are more and more driving the development costs, quality, and manufacture of the technological inputs critical to all manufacturers.[22]

For Europe, the question thus becomes, How is access to the supply bases of high technology changing? Today, most of the electronics technologies crucial to Europe have their home base in the United States and Asia. Our American preoccupation with the Asian supply base must not obscure for us Europe's concern with its dependence on American suppliers of components and subsystems. IBM, after all, not long ago defined for the computer industry proprietary standards and, indeed, the very trajectory of its development. Not so long ago American companies firmly controlled the component segments of these industries. However, the rise of Japanese competitors to the top ranks of the industry, the expansion of the Asian supply base, and the changing character of the electronics industry changes Europe's problem. Now, one might argue, dependence on America can be offset by Asian sources. But American component suppliers were usually not in competition with their European customers, and product technology was relatively accessible. With an increasingly Asian—usually Japanese—supply base, suppliers do compete with their customers in a wide range of products.

22. Borrus, "Re-Organizing Asia," p. 26.

To better pose the European problem, let us return to the three distinct economic regions of Europe, North America, and a Japan-centered Asia.[23] Each has, in fact, its own regional supply base with different capacities and dependencies on other regions.

A critical issue for corporate strategy and government policy then becomes how these three supply bases are linked together, that is, how technology flows between the regions.[24] Technology flows can become strategic. We must, of course, distinguish between scientific knowledge, formal and more specifiable, and technological knowledge, more implicit and less easily specified, noting that flows of scientific knowledge are much more open and much more international. Let us specify four mechanisms of technology flow. First, industry technology flows through communities. Such technological communities are inherently more local and national than international. Second, technology can flow through markets. Computers, microprocessors, robots, and plastic materials all embody technology. Technological know-how is trans-

ferred with the sale of product or license. But national markets are often protected, and the flows of technology through products is distorted. Not all buyers have equal access; local buyers are likely to have some initial advantage. This is particularly important when production and design supply bases are in the same region as launch markets for innovative products, as is now the case in Asia for electronics. Launch markets are where innovative products are first sold. Not only is demand there the greatest; firms there usually find the technology required to design and make advanced products. Outsiders will have to develop new products with technologies sourced away from home and may even have to launch them in markets away from home.

The third mechanism of technology flow is the multinational corporation. These firms may act as bees sampling pollen in each of the three regions, but they are likely to make honey at home base, keeping the real expertise and markets in their domestic base. Many of the recent international technology deals and alliances between companies reflect different corporate capacities, capacities that differ because of their distinct home supply base.

The fourth mechanism of flow is corporate networks. Increasingly, companies are developing long-standing arrangements among themselves, a trend that may or may not offset the tendency toward giant corporations. These arrangements are seen as new kinds of networks, developed to respond to an era of rapid technological change, product development, and market evolution. They can take sev-

23. Michael Borrus and John Zysman, "Industrial Competitiveness and American National Security," in *The Highest Stakes: The Economic Foundations of the Next Security System*, by Wayne Sandholtz et al. (New York: Oxford University Press, 1992).

24. John Zysman, "Trade, Technology and National Competition," *International Journal of Technology Management*, 7(1-3):161-89 (July 1992); or see John Zysman with assistance from Laura Tyson, Giovanni Dosi, and Stephen Cohen, "Trade, Technology and National Competition," in *Technology and Investment*, ed. Eurico Deiaco, Erik Hornell, and Graham Vickery (Stockholm: Royal Swedish Academy of Engineering Sciences, 1990).

eral forms: supplier networks, which include subcontracting, original-equipment-manufacture or original-design-manufacturing arrangements, and procurement of intermediate inputs; production networks; customer networks; and technology networks.[25] Managing these networks can prove to be a strategic weapon by providing early access to, and influence of, key technologies.

If a firm does not have a technology, it can (1) develop technology in house (hierarchies); (2) buy on the open market (markets); and (3) team up with others (joint ventures and networks). The circumstances in which each has advantages have been widely discussed. In-house projects are needed for proprietary technologies critical to a particular company. But accumulating knowledge exclusively through internal investment is neither desirable, due to the inefficiencies of hierarchy, nor feasible, due to the limitation on resources. Markets are attractive means of assuring access to commodity products. Alliances may be attractive for projects that are too expensive or that require technologies not under a firm's control. When to adopt which tactics? A firm must assess its own technological capabilities, evaluate the capabilities and position of its competitors, and ask questions such as (1) could the firm become dependent on outside sources for critical technologies by alliances or procurement and thus unable to sustain product or production advan-

tage—that is, does it undermine its own critical capacities; (2) will the firm transfer technology to competitors by joint deals; (3) can the firm, by contrast, learn critical new technologies from a partner?[26]

Should regionalization of the global economy change a company's decision? Implicitly, one issue is whether the risks of cross-regional sourcing of components, subsystems, or production services in the form of contract manufacturing are greater than obtaining them within the region. Networks concentrated in a particular region may better serve firms that have that region as home base in the delicate problems of technology development, technology protection, and technology transfer. An outsider may be disadvantaged.

There are no general rules that can guide decisions for companies and government about when to buy or develop and on what terms. But the objectives of a national and corporate technology policy can be made clear. The objectives must at a minimum be access and access on a timely basis on terms at least equal to one's competitors.

With these concerns, let us return to the European electronics industry. For much of high-volume digital electronics as well as the mechatronics and mechanical components that support final product, the core supply base is in Asia and is dominated by Japanese firms. Companies in Europe and the United States often find that these networks in the supply

---

25. See the interesting paper by Dieter Ernst, "Networks, Market Structure and Technology Diffusion: A Conceptual Framework" (BRIE Working Paper, Berkeley Roundtable on the International Economy, in press).

26. Indeed, these networks may be permanent features that represent mechanisms to manage technological diversity in an era of rapid technological change.

base are closely linked to their competitors.

There are two significant implications for Europe from the discussion so far. First, the character and sophistication of the market for final products are critical. The market itself is an instrument of industrial policy, perhaps the most powerful one available to a government. A highly sophisticated market will induce producers to respond innovatively. An immature market is a handicap for local producers. So, ironically, protection for producers that serves to limit the development of the market may ultimately serve to undermine, not promote, the industry. The second implication for Europe is that the competitive position of national or regional producers of particular products may not be the central question. Crucial issues are the character of the regional supply base, the access to supply bases outside of Europe, and the ability to apply technology and combine components into systems whether those technologies are initially developed in Europe or not.

WEAKNESSES IN
EUROPEAN ELECTRONICS

Before considering how Europe might reformulate its policy, we must briefly overview the industry as a whole, not just a discussion of one or two sectors. In the presentation that follows, we move from areas of clear European weakness that have been the focus of policy debate to areas of potential strength that should be the basis of any rebuilding strategy. Several themes will emerge in the overview. One, common to all the sectors, with very few exceptions, is the vir-

tual absence of a European presence in the Japanese market. Another is Europe's tendency to eschew niche markets where competitive advantage might be created in favor of policies to promote producer positions in internationally significant segments. This tendency has prevented European firms from defining their own strengths.

Semiconductors

The semiconductor sector is the most evident area of European weakness. Europe represents only 20.0 percent of the world market for semiconductors, compared to 26.6 percent for the United States and 36.0 percent for Japan. In part, that difference in use of semiconductors reflects Japanese and American exports of equipment embedding components to Europe, but, more important, it reflects very low overall use of electronics by Europe. As a consequence, European producers in 1991 held only 10.0 percent of world semiconductor production, compared to 38.4 percent for the United States and 46.4 percent for Japan. The European producers hold less than 40 percent of their own market. More than 30 percent of European use is supplied by foreign companies manufacturing in Europe. The rest is provided by imports. The trade deficit in active components was $4.15 billion in 1990.

The European market weakness is even deeper than these aggregate figures suggest. There are no robust European producers, and Europe does not have an entrenched position in any segment of the sector. Consider commodity memories, which are standard and depend on production skill. In dynamic-random-access-memory products that drive the advancing edge of process technology, only Siemens remains in the game at all, and only courtesy of junior-partner alliances with Toshiba and IBM —alliances from which it shows no signs of ever graduating to full partnership. Moreover, the equipment that underlies production is dominated by Japan and the United States.[27] The positions shifted in favor of Japan in the 1980s and have shifted somewhat back toward the United States in the last several years.

In microprocessors, American producers dominate. The Europeans have no independent position either in traditional all-purpose processors or in the new reduced instruction set computing.

One area of European semiconductor strength is in application-specific and customized chips that are adapted to particular market needs and usually made with processes that are not state of the art. But Americans, and now the Japanese, have established extensive and substantial production facilities in Europe. Both have expanded their operations in anticipation of political restrictions that would close the market to them.[28]

European policy has sought to remedy the situation, but, if any-

thing, it has made it much worse. Support has gone to those activities that encourage European firms to compete directly with American and Japanese firms in the main industry segment, but not to those that would underwrite and develop European market strengths.

Consumer electronics to high-volume high technology

The next area of weakness is consumer electronics. The Japanese control more than half of the world market in consumer electronics. But Europe still holds a competitive position, especially within its own market. Though the two leading companies are Japanese, Philips and Thomson are in the third and fourth positions, and Nokia, Grundig, and Bosch have strong positions in Europe.[29] European-owned producers control 34 percent of the European market—significantly more than American-owned producers' control of the U.S. market.[30] Moreover, European firms can be innovative. Philips has introduced significant new products to the market from the videocassette recorder through digital tape in 1992.

European industry has seemingly withstood the Japanese challenge in consumer electronics better than the American industry. The question is whether the European position is, in fact, defensible. Vulnerabilities persist. The enormous losses posted by

27. Jay Stowsky, "From Spin-Off to Spin-On: Redefining the Military's Role in Technology Development" (BRIE Working Paper #50, Berkeley Roundtable on the International Economy, May 1991).

28. Didier Huck, "Composants electronique" (Paper prepared for the seminar "Les Nouvelles Armes du Defi Industriel," Paris, 7-9 Sept. 1992), pp. 5-6.

29. Thierry Triomphe, "Electronique grand public" (Paper prepared for the seminar "Les Nouvelles Armes du Defi Industriel," Paris, 7-9 Sept. 1992).

30. *Panorama of the EC Industry* (Lanham, MD: UNIPUB, 1990), sec. 10-17ff.

Philips in recent years certainly evidence the need to reformulate basic corporate strategy. The European market for consumer electronics is $28.4 billion, but European producers provide only $15.8 billion—a trade deficit of $12.6 billion. In other words, Europe is a huge importer but exports almost nothing to the rest of the world. The deficit is, in fact, growing at least as fast as the market itself.[31] Moreover, Japanese factories in Europe provide 28 percent of European production.[32] Of course, the Japanese market has been effectively closed, first by policy and then by a mix of business practice and distribution arrangements. In addition, the Japanese have often employed determined low-cost pricing strategies that sometimes drift into dumping. But the Japanese product strengths and production advantages are real. It is our judgment that, without protection, Asian producers would capture a much higher share of the European market. Overall, the European producers do not appear cost-competitive, are generally slower and less effective at establishing new product niches, and spend less on R&D than do their Japanese competitors. In any case, evidence shows that the Japanese firms are more profitable.[33]

The impending round of competition in consumer electronics will be of huge significance for the European electronics industry in general. Very simply, many of the components and subsystems that are the core of the new consumer electronics are cut-ting-edge products that define the new category of high-volume advanced digital technology.[34] "The development and application of a broad range of subsystem, component and machinery and materials technologies are increasingly being driven by high-volume electronics that boast leading edge sophistication and extremely high quality at remarkably low costs."[35] The product set that uses these products include lap-top, note-book, and hand-held computers, optical disk mass storage systems, smart-cards, portable faxes, copiers, printers, electronic datebooks, portable and cellular telephones and pagers, camcorders, electronic still cameras, compact disc players, hand-held televisions, controllers for machine tools, robots and other industrial machinery, and embedded automotive systems like those for antiskid braking, engine, transmission and suspension control, and navigation.

As high-volume electronics production begins to use the sophisticated technological inputs that industrial systems share, it begins to drive common technological development. By spreading the huge development costs across many more sales, high-volume markets can support the development of advanced technologies previously initiated only by public spending. Consumer markets demand much lower costs, costs that are achieved through rapid attainment of economies of scale, learning, and the other attributes of the new

31. Triomphe, "Electronique grand public."
32. Ibid. Indeed, 32 percent is by Asia as a whole.
33. Ibid.
34. Michael Borrus and Jeffrey Hart, "Display's the Thing: The Real Stakes in the Conflict over High-Resolution Display" (BRIE Working Paper #52, Berkeley Roundtable on the International Economy, 1992).
35. Ibid.

manufacturing. The associated product development and process skills permit the technology to be cycled much more rapidly. Cost savings and rapid cycle times permit expanded R&D, broader experimentation, and the capturing of new opportunities for additional technological learning. The final result is a new technological development trajectory—new generations of cheaper but sophisticated technologies emerging from high-volume consumer applications but applicable across the board in professional and military product and therefore essential to the success of all other industries that produce or use electronics.

To create a defensible market advantage in consumer electronics, Europe must recognize that, at the moment, the points of leverage and advantage in new product lines are dominated by the Americans and Japanese. First, the Japanese control components and subsystems that allow them to differentiate their products and production systems that not only create cost advantage but also allow flexible quick-response approaches to marketing. Their strong position rests on intense technology development and on the control of the flow of technology to suppliers and potential competitors, that is, the control of the supply base. The Asian region's production network appears to be a hierarchy dominated by Japan. Advanced products and most of the underlying technologies are controlled by Japanese companies, with labor-intensive and standard technology production in the periphery of the region and often under the control of Japanese industry.

Next, consider America's competitive advantage. American companies have used skills in product definition, design, and marketing to maintain market position. Amazingly, after having ceded the television and related product markets to Japanese and some European companies, new American firms are beginning to redefine the character of consumer electronics. The American position rests on the ability to define dramatically new products that become new industries, such as the Apple II a few years ago or the Apple Newton today. Control of product design, definition, and marketing has often allowed American firms to force component and subsystem technology, no matter how sophisticated, to be sold as commodity products. Similarly, other American firms have created proprietary standards in a supposedly open-system world that have allowed them to capture monopoly or semi-monopoly profits. Arguably, European firms such as Philips have innovated in the definition of new products, but they have fallen short in solving the design, manufacturing, and standards problem. Europe must determine why this is the case. Part of the cause certainly lies within the companies, that is, in their limited ability to bring new product to market. But part of the problem also lies in the character of the primary market, the European market, that the companies are addressing.

These relative strengths—components and product definition—suggest the pattern of deals between Japanese and American firms. The Americans create distinct product definitions, which are often produced for them by the Japanese. The Japanese often then produce next-generation design improvements, which the Americans often then distribute under their own labels. There is seemingly little room for European companies unless they are able to find new and innovative product strategies.

It will be very difficult for European firms to build positions of long-term advantage in consumer electronics. Equally important, it will be hard for them to use this sector as a foundation on which to build broader competitive advantage. The supply base problem, described earlier, will not be resolved by wishing the re-creation of the entire electronics *filière* in Europe. Europe must secure access to the Asian supply base and work with American producers to maintain an open international supply base for producers from all regions. But securing access to other regional bases will mean little if the Europeans do not work to capture the product definition, design, and marketing game. Developing Europe into a cutting-edge market to promote the launch of sophisticated new products requires policies of diffusion, not just producer support.

The computer industry

The weakness of the European computer industry is legendary; the measures of its weakness are extensive.[36] Europe imports roughly one-third of its computer and information technology needs.[37] European firms control only 34 percent of their market; the rest—whether by import or local production—is controlled by foreign firms. By contrast, American firms control 92 percent of the American market, while Japanese firms control 84 percent of the Japanese market.[38]

But the weakness is even deeper when we look beyond these general figures. The microcomputer segment of the industry is controlled by American firms, with the largest European being Olivetti, with 5.5 percent of the market in 1991.[39] Bull has become a player by buying Zenith, but Zenith hardly gives it a powerful position in the market. The minicomputer segment is dominated by IBM and DEC, while Bull and Siemens hold only 10 percent each of the market. In mainframe systems, the European position is a bit stronger, but each of the main European companies is substantially dependent on Japanese or American suppliers for major parts of their product line. Fujitsu now owns ICL, which has 7 percent of the European market. Bull depends on NEC and IBM; Hitachi supplies Olivetti; Fujitsu provides for Siemens.[40]

If anything, the European position has deteriorated over the past ten years. The Japanese have come to challenge the Americans, increasing their share of the world market in the

36. The European computer market is much smaller than the American market; computers are simply not as widely used. The per capita figures for the installed base of personal computers illustrate this fact: in Europe there is one personal computer for every ten people;

in the United States, there is one personal computer for every four. Dataquest, Inc., "PC Europe" (Data report, Dataquest, 1992).

37. Catinat, "L'informatique et les automatismes," p. 11.

38. Ibid.

39. Dataquest, Inc., "PC Europe."

40. Ibid.

period from 1984 to 1990 from 6.5 percent to 18.0 percent as the American share descended from 62.7 to 47.4 percent.[41] The Europeans might comfort themselves with explanations that American success rested on military spending—except that this was only the case in the very early years —and that Japanese successes rested on a large, coherent, and highly protected domestic market. The fact is, however, that the Europeans largely missed the commercially based workstation and microcomputing revolutions that are transforming the very character of the computer industry. European firms, often badly organized and insensitive to market requirements, did very poorly with a difficult situation.

Government policy did not help. If anything, it made matters worse, as Zysman has argued for many years.[42] As many observe, national policies created a fragmented European market that was slow to adopt new technologies. More important, policymakers sought to imitate the product mix and industrial structure that they saw in the United States. They reasoned from the structures they wanted to the strategies they wanted the firms to adopt. The policies then pushed European firms directly into market segments dominated by the American giants. Bureaucrats could only, by the nature of the situation,

play catch-up; they could not play the entrepreneurial role of imagining and inventing new industrial futures. And the catch-up game was difficult in the fragmented European market. Firms were discouraged from finding their own distinctive technological avenues and, consequently, the possibility of innovative breakthroughs that could permit European firms to become leaders. These views are beginning to find expression in Europe.[43] In sum, the result has been a deep and enduring technological dependence in virtually all segments of the industry.

Europe made its first mistake by never even debating the notion that a sophisticated market could be the best possible assistance to computer producers. Policies for the diffusion and use of advanced technology never received the same attention and weight as did producer-oriented support.[44] The symbolic consequence of producing particular products, not the broad economic gain from widespread adoption of new technologies, was the emphasis of policy debates. This is particularly significant now because the European position in systems integration—the development of large-scale networks of computers to apply to specific problems— is much stronger than in the hardware included in the systems.[45] European companies have a strong position in their own market. Equally important, the customized and skill-intensive nature of systems integra-

41. Ibid., pp. 7-8.

42. John Zysman, *Political Strategies for Industrial Order: State, Market and Industry in France* (Berkeley: University of California Press, 1977); idem, *Reviews of Innovation Policies France (Note by the Secretariat)* (Paris: Organization for Economic Cooperation and Development, 1986).

43. Catinat, "L'informatique et les automatismes," p. 8.

44. Ibid.

45. Ibid.

tion means that the fundamental technological know-how can grow up in Europe even if the company selling the service is American. Systems integration can create the sophisticated market. But there is, in any case, no vision in the policy community about how a solid position in systems integration can be used to rebuild a base in computer hardware. More generally, European firms have not been able to define strategies by which they would be able to capture distinct proprietary positions that would generate monopoly-like profits or at least would insulate themselves from a pure cost-based and production-centered strategy. Doing so will almost certainly come from an exploration of the competitive interplay between software and hardware, but for now Europeans have not found distinctive solutions that will allow them to capture powerful competitive positions that can be translated into standards and proprietary technologies, or found standards and proprietary technology that can be the base of competitive advantage.

Why defense electronics cannot defend the European position in commercial markets

Defense electronics cannot defend the broader European position in electronics. As in the United States, the emerging high-volume digital technology industry described previously is likely to make the military electronics industry ever more dependent on advances in the commercial industry. At the Berkeley Roundtable on the International Economy, we have explored this issue in both the American and Japanese economies.[46] We have argued that

a completely alternative military technology development trajectory is emerging from the innovations in production and consequent reshuffling of markets. . . . This alternative drives technological advance from commercial rather than military applications. Technology diffuses from civilian to defense use rather than vice versa, a trajectory characterized as "spin-on" in contrast to its predecessor. The new alternative is prospering most fully in Japan, where an increasing range of commercially developed technologies are directly, or with minor modification, finding their way into advanced military systems. In particular, militarily relevant sub-system, component, machinery, and materials technologies are increasingly driven by high-volume commercial applications that produce leading-edge sophistication, with extremely high reliability but remarkably low costs.[47]

As argued previously, the high-volume electronics industry is beginning to drive the development, costs, quality, and manufacture of technological inputs critical to computing, communications, the military, and industrial electronics. The basic technological requirements of new consumer products now approach, equal, or at times surpass those needed for sophisticated military applications. They have also begun to share a common underlying base of components, machinery, and materials technolo-

46. See Steve Vogel, "The Power behind Spin-Ons," in *Highest Stakes*, by Sandholtz et al.; Jay Stowsky, "From Spin-Off to Spin-On: Redefining the Military's Role in American Technology Development," in ibid.
47. See Borrus and Zysman, "Industrial Competitiveness," p. 31.

gies. There are several significant implications. First, by spreading the huge development costs across many more units, high-volume markets can support the development of advanced technologies previously initiated only by military spending. Second, price-sensitive consumer applications demand that the unit cost of the underlying technology components be very low.[48] The necessary low costs can be achieved only by the scale, scope, and learning economies of revolutionary production approaches. The end result is that new, militarily relevant generations of cheaper but sophisticated and reliable technologies emerge from high-volume commercial markets.

POTENTIAL STRENGTHS
IN EUROPEAN ELECTRONICS

The weaknesses are abundant, but there are some clear strengths. They are reviewed in turn.

Telecommunications

Telecommunications is the most evident European electronics strength, and the major firms have been very successful. At least until the late 1980s, the European equipment makers held onto the bulk of the European telecommunications market. The share of European telecommunications equipment provided by European suppliers has likewise remained high. Of course, national ministries or their agents served as monopoly buyers, a situation not different from the recognized monopoly of AT&T, but many of the European firms have es-

48. Ibid.

tablished themselves as major global competitors with substantial strengths. Some of the companies have been important innovators and have become leading-edge final producers creating sophisticated home markets. Alcatel led the way to digital switching in France, which was the first country to take this significant step. Ericsson helped the rapid diffusion of cellular telephony in Sweden; indeed, Ericsson has been remarkably successful in international markets by carefully identifying market possibilities, understanding the needs of potential customers, and pursuing them carefully for years. Siemens, a $7.3 billion company, remains entrenched in the German market while already establishing a real presence in the United States. Given this strength in the telecommunications sector, there are two major issues. First, can the Europeans maintain their position of strength in Europe and extend that into world markets? Second, can telecommunications be the foundation from which to rebuild the rest of the European electronics sector?

Foreign firms are not poised to capture a major piece of the telecommunications equipment markets in Europe. The Japanese firms are not distinctively strong in this sector and are unlikely to represent a powerful challenge in the next few years. Similarly, American equipment firms are not likely to displace their European rivals in the near future. The Europeans not only are quite competitive but also benefit from intimate relationships with their users. Client markets, particularly the switching market, depend on the firms' close and careful interaction with the buyer because the systems are inherently customized. The sales and the work require a sophisticated and permanent commitment to the customer. The American firms are only now beginning to establish those liaisons.

Nonetheless, as the telecommunications service markets are deregulated and at least some competition in services is introduced, the European equipment companies and network providers must confront two problems to hold position. First, there has been a burst of new peripheral equipment such as cellular telephones and palm computers, many with communications capacity. The new consumer electronics, high-volume high-technology digital equipment, is invading telecommunications. That, of course, opens up the market to firms other than established telecommunications companies, to consumer firms with whom the Europeans have had trouble competing.

Second, and more important, telecommunications policy in the European Community has reached the end of a phase, as Peter Cowhey and John Zysman have argued.[49] This now completed phase involved changes that separated regulation from operation, a round of marginal liberalization that did not alter the dominant position of the telecom operators, and efforts, mostly timid, at European harmonization. That period of re-regulation overlaps the move toward

a single market. Together, the result was a dissolution of purely national supplier cartels linked to national public service providers. Those national cartels have not been replaced by an open and competitive European market. Rather, a European-wide oligopoly of equipment suppliers, albeit with room left for some American companies, has been established. The continued privileges of the now privatized and semi-autonomous telephone companies is essential to that oligopoly. The European experience is not unique. One might note that the breakup of the Bell system in the United States has not eliminated the purchasing biases in favor of American companies, though those biases have eroded.

The Commission of the European Community now finds itself in a stalemate. The Commission initiated the policy with support from large users and built a complex support base from the national governments. That support base, however, has not been strong enough to push forward to a next round of policy. Those in the Commission who created the first round would clearly like a second and more ambitious phase. That next round of policy would involve some European-level regulation, efforts at liberalization that cut into the basic monopoly rate base, and the implementation of innovative services. If those regulatory changes come, they will involve not only a shift of position between European producers but also entry for American and Japanese firms. For now, the debate appears as a struggle with established producers and network suppliers on one side and telecom users concerned

49. Peter Cowhey and John Zysman, "European Telecommunications at the Crossroads" (Paper, Berkeley Roundtable on the International Economy, 2 Apr. 1992).

with capturing the competitive advantages that early implementation of new network-based strategies can provide, on the other. There is a distinct possibility, however, that the debate will become more urgent.

Revolutionary changes in telecommunications network use are taking a new form to which European users, equipment suppliers, and network providers will be compelled to adapt. The early signs are clear; the implications, dramatic.[50] A broadband network future is arriving much faster than anticipated. The new broadband networks open dramatic service possibilities that are enormously attractive, and, indeed, in the few settings where the new networks are being fully implemented without serious constraint, the network traffic is expanding as rapidly as 20 percent a month, and the rate of increase is accelerating.[51] In just a decade, the telecommunications system of suppliers and providers could look very different from the way it does today. The notion of ISDN (integrated system digital network) with a single integrated digital network may give way to a system with multiple networks linked together—not just because competition creates fragmentation (as some fear), but because each of the networks will have quite distinct characteristics. Each network may be optimized for particular use. Flexible networks may be adapted not just to shifting needs, but readapted continually as firms learn

from using them and producers get feedback.[52] The established telecommunications operators may have trouble adapting without substantial pressure and real regulatory change. Set aside the importance of the networks to the economy. For the equipment makers, those new networks are essential; they represent the innovative market of tomorrow. In sum, the Europeans have a strong foundation in telecommunications, but their position in the next generation of competition will rely on well-formulated and forward-thinking network policy and firm strategy.

The European telecommunications system from equipment suppliers to network providers—present and potential—seems well positioned to maintain control of European markets. But can success in telecommunications be the foundation from which to rebuild the rest of the European electronics sector? Here we have our doubts. The hope is that telecommunications companies can create demand for European suppliers of components and subsystems. This will not be automatic by any means. Consider the components sector. Telecom equipment suppliers in Europe generate a huge demand for semiconductors. That demand is still largely filled by foreign-owned companies, whether they produce in Europe or not.[53] Similarly, there is a hope that, as computing and telecommunica-

50. François Bar and Michael Borrus, "The Future of Networking in the U.S." (BRIE Research Paper #4, Berkeley Roundtable on the International Economy, Sept. 1992).

51. Ibid.

52. François Bar and Michael Borrus, *Information Networks and Competitive Advantage*, OECD-BRIE Telecom Project, Vol. 1 (Paris: Organization for Economic Cooperation and Development, 1989).

53. Jean Philippe Dauvin et al., "Le future de l'industrie europeene des semiconductors" (Paper, Thomson Groupe, May 1991).

tions converge toward distributed computing, telecommunications networking skills and experience with digital switches would provide an opportunity for Europeans to establish a competitive position in computers. However, neither AT&T nor Siemens has managed to switch over from a telecom base to a major computer position. Nor has IBM been able to move from its dominant position in computers to a strong position in telecom. The reason seems to be that the business problems and user requirements are distinct in each sector so that business organizations and technologies generated in one segment cannot be directly applied to another. Telecommunications may continue to be a bastion of European electronics strength, but it is not evident that it can nurture a rebirth of the industry as a whole.

Professional and industrial electronics

Industrial and professional electronics is a second area of real European strength. In this sector, the applications know-how rooted in the fundamental and deep scientific, technological, and industrial traditions of Europe matter the most. In a range of areas—from machine tools to hearing aids and automobile electronics—European producers are in fact quite strong. Consider automobiles, for example. The largest automobile electronics firm in the world is Bosch; 3 of the leading 5 companies are European and so are 4 of the leading 10. Or consider machine tools, which is an industry made up of a myriad of smaller producers.

Here Italy and Germany rank among the world's largest exporting nations. Indeed, when we look at production equipment in general, we find that the European position in global markets is very strong. These are all sectors in which the creative application of electronics has been and will increasingly be critical. They are sectors that depend on access to advanced electronics but that also represent a market for innovative producers.[54]

The same two questions that we posed in the telecommunications section confront us once again. First, can the Europeans maintain their market position? There are a number of competitive risks. The most serious is that the bulk of this sector—automobile electronics and production equipment such as machine tools—depends on demand from the rest of the industrial economy. If imports of autos displaced European production, there would be a problem for equipment producers as well. Imports, by definition, dampen the domestic demand for equipment from European-owned producers. Substituting imports with FDI may preserve European final-assembly producers, but this substitution could still cut demand for production equipment. If foreign-owned producers import production equipment or bring their suppliers of equipment or components with them, then demand for European producers is dampened in the same way. As evidenced in the American case, Japanese companies —the principal new investors—do have a propensity to create an enclave economy inside the host country.

54. Ibid.

Second, will European firms be able to weather Japanese production innovations that have proven critical in a range of consumer durable sectors? The American machine tool and robotics companies specializing in standard equipment were unable to respond to the more specialized and differently conceived Japanese products, for example. In that case, the Europeans defended their positions more effectively. They held market niches based on more specialized equipment in the first place. But now a new challenge looms. The Japanese are attempting to implement functions in electronics that the Germans implement mechanically. If there is long-term inherent advantage in electronic approaches, the Japanese will be well positioned. But it is not even that microelectronics underpins Japanese automation equipment. Rather, there is a different approach to the production line and the place of tools in the line. The difference, in our view, is driven by the primary final goods in the two countries: volume consumer durables in Japan and capital equipment in Germany. The result is that the functions and design of tools are different. There is likely to be a serious challenge.

Assume that the European producers do retain their competitive edge in production equipment and professional electronics. Can this be a foundation from which to rebuild the rest of the sector? Automobile electronics will be an increasing portion of the electronics market as the use of electronically controlled active chassis, engine operations, safety systems, and entertainment and comfort systems expands and grows

in value. Factory automation will become increasingly rooted in electronics. The demand for electronic components will thus expand, creating new opportunities. The question is whether the European companies can seize them. The risk and concern must be that the weakness in the broader electronics sectors will endanger the European competitive position in these segments where European companies hold defensible positions. Recall that in automobile electronics, the European semiconductor industry provides only about a quarter of the European demand.[55] However, the one real strength of the European semiconductor industry is, as we noted, application-specific or custom circuits. These are the types of circuits critical to differentiating industrial products. Consequently, Europeans here can easily import commodity memory and even standard microprocessors if they can differentiate their electronic functions. The question of whether strength will underpin weakness or weakness will drown strength remains open.

LESSONS OF THE EUROPEAN ELECTRONICS CASE: FORMULATING POLICY IN A REGIONAL WORLD

The surge in Japanese FDI, huge subsidies demanded by many European producers, the outright takeover of major European companies by American and Japanese competitors, and the failure of other companies have all contributed to a reformulation of European policy. Past policy of support for weak producers has failed to regenerate industrial posi-

55. Ibid.

tion in those sectors defined as critical. Past preoccupation with American dominance seems dated given the rise of Japanese electronics companies and increased Japanese investment in Europe. What are Europe's policy choices today? And how are these choices shaped by the regionalizing global economy?

The emergence of three competitive regions has changed many of the issues facing European industry. For years, the Europeans worried about American domination of the computer industry, and in particular about IBM's domination of mainframe markets. American firms will certainly continue to define or powerfully influence the definition of core products in the computer and the consumer electronics industry, but today Europe must also reckon with Japan (and Asia more generally), now a dominant force in the component and volume electronics markets. One might say that Europe has fallen into third place in the global electronics competition, suffering dependency on not just one but two competitive regions. On the bright side, however, Europe may now be able to exploit a regional rivalry—led by the regions' central powers, Japan and the United States—and, using some of its existing strengths, it may now be able to heal the weaknesses of its producers. In formulating policy for electronics, two questions confront the Europeans and, with a complex web of industrial alliances linking the several regions and thus creating multiple dependencies, the Americans and Japanese as well. First, can policy help assure a strong supply base for sustained develop-

ment? Second, should European policy try to bolster Europe's position in weak sectors thought to be critical or try to build from strength in those areas with a defensible position?

In considering the first question, we must recognize that in the short term—if at all—Europe cannot hope to re-create under European control the various elements of a sophisticated electronics supply base. Indeed, no single region can construct an entirely independent supply base. Consequently, assuring leading-edge technology becomes a matter of securing access to other regions' supply bases. European policy must make certain that critical products and components are available in open, competitive markets, that is, it must ensure that European producers have market access to all supply bases of components, subsystems, production equipment, and skills.[56] Since many of those elements are available in the electronics industry only in the United States or Japan, it is essential that Europe maintain access to both supply bases. Diversity of supply is essential to guard against exploitative dependency; several suppliers in at least two economic regions ought to be a policy goal.

Ideally, of course, it would be best to have evolving technology close to home to profit from any spillovers. But for the moment, this is not a realistic scenario for many segments of the European electronics industry. For now, Europe must settle for

56. See Borrus, "Re-Organizing Asia"; Kenneth Flamm, "Semiconductors," in *Europe 1992: An American Perspective*, ed. Gary Clyde Hufbauer (Washington, DC: Brookings Institution, 1990).

maintaining alternative regional sources; that is, it must maintain a healthy U.S.-Japanese competition by playing suppliers in the different regions off one another. Europe could, however, establish itself as a critical test ground if it manages to transfer much of the technology early.

Henceforth, Europe must be concerned with how supply bases are linked and how technology flows from one to another. Regionally structured supply bases change the problem of technology management for both governments and corporations, not only in Europe but all over the industrialized world.[57] They force firms and governments to be concerned with the architecture of supply in the home regions of their rivals. At issue is no longer just access to export markets in general but access to technology and to markets that may be critical to the launch of new product.

The second question—whether European policy should try to bolster Europe's position in weak sectors thought to be critical or try to build from strength in those areas with a defensible position—can also be posed in the following way: should policy support weak producers in their efforts to entrench their market position or try to foster the diffusion and spread of advanced electronic applications? It would be congenial to argue that government policy should do both. This seems to make market sense: help buyers to expand the market and producers to supply it. However, the policies conflict when support for producers results in higher prices or reduced supply for clients, the final producers, as is the case with the semiconductor tariff. It is important to remember that Japanese policy protected final producers but generally allowed imports of intermediate goods required for production. (Of course, FDI by importers who might establish a strong market position in Japan with local production was blocked so local Japanese producers could later attempt entry into these sectors.)[58]

Policies to support the diffusion of advanced technology are important to support general economic development, to speed application of technology, and to maintain the competitive position of final producers (users). A deep, diverse, and sophisticated user base is a means to induce supply from local sources, a means to create competitive producers, a mechanism to incite innovation. Powerful general-purpose suppliers of chips or computers might be attractive symbols, but they are not likely to be built simply by European policy. A network of sophisticated suppliers to users is needed to create the foundation of skills and equipment from which breakthrough innovations might emerge. A web of advanced users would mean that there was pressure on suppliers to generate sophisticated responses. As important, a sufficient European demand would

57. John Zysman, "Regional Blocs, Corporate Strategies, and the End of Free Trade," in *The Impact of Globalisation on Europe's Firms and Industries*, ed. Marc Humbert (London: Pinter, 1993).

58. Pierre Buigues and Alexis Jacquemin, "Foreign Direct Investments and Exports in the Common Market: Theoretical, Empirical, and Policy Issues," in *Does Ownership Matter?* ed. Mason and Encarnation.

allow innovative products to establish a sufficient home base that they might set a global standard.

Computers and semiconductors were often thought to be the core technologies of the information era. Without them, it was argued, position in all other electronics sectors would be blocked. This takes us back to the dilemma posed at the beginning of this article: for effective application of technology, will arms-length market access of advanced technology suffice, or is intimate involvement with the producers required? The dilemma is false; there must be a balance. A strong application position can create a foundation for strength in the production of underlying components. Worldwide, this trend is evident; strength in semiconductors—and in other component technologies—often reflects the final products and market position of the customers, whether the customers are internal or external to the firm. While the situation is obviously reciprocal and some draw the conclusion that semiconductor technology permits final product strength, we would argue that final market position in fact begets semiconductor strength. Final market strengths should therefore be the basis for formulating a strategy to induce innovation in supplier or intermediate industries.

ANNALS, *AAPSS*, **531**, January 1994

An Assessment of the EC Future

By MARTIN J. HILLENBRAND

ABSTRACT: The European Community is presently experiencing a period of relative gloom due partly to the current economic stagnation in Europe but also to doubts about the Maastricht Treaty and the inability of the Community to do anything effective with respect to the war in the former Yugoslavia. There are, however, longer-term indications of a more robust Community, particularly as the dynamic impulses generated by the unified market implementing the Single European Act begin to work through European economies. Dramatic changes in Eastern Europe and the former Soviet Union have presented new problems reflected, for example, in the dilemma of deepening or widening the Community. The near collapse of the Exchange Rate Mechanism in July-August 1993 and continuing speculation on the monetary exchanges may actually provide a further argument for monetary union. Community relations with the United States have remained ambiguous, with continued American support for European integration in the abstract clashing with specific trade disputes.

A former professional diplomat, Martin J. Hillenbrand has served as U.S. Ambassador to Hungary (1967-69), Assistant Secretary of State for European Affairs (1969-72), and Ambassador to the Federal Republic of Germany (1972-76). He is currently Dean Rusk Professor of International Relations at the University of Georgia and codirector of the Center for East-West Trade Policy. He has written, edited, and coedited several books and contributed to numerous others, most recently Europe and the Superpowers *(1991) and* Export Controls in Transition: Perspectives, Problems and Prospects *(1992).*

SPECULATION about the present state and the future prospects of the European Community provides a never ending subject for politicians, pundits, professors, and just plain journalists. This reflects recognition that the organization to a considerable extent will determine the future of Western Europe and perhaps at least a part of Eastern Europe. But it also reflects a tendency today to emphasize the negative, the many difficulties that inevitably make human efforts fall short of the plans and projects that we elaborate.

One thing that has become apparent in the past 15 years is that the mood within the Community, whether optimistic or pessimistic, is closely related to the business cycle in Western Europe.[1] This is not strange, for economic slowdown inevitably breeds talk of "Europa sclerosis," the threatened breakdown of the Exchange Rate Mechanism (ERM), and the impossibility of ever achieving the goals of the Maastricht Treaty (also known as the Treaty on European Union). The Community has been passing through such a period of gloom and negativism as the economies of its member countries have stagnated. With the advent of economic upturn, we may confidently expect a more optimistic mood. Meanwhile, of course, the implementation of the

Single European Act of 1986, which took place at the beginning of 1993, will have been injecting dynamic new impulses into intra-Community trade and eventual economic growth.

This is the wisdom of experience. Changing moods linked to the state of the European economy do not mean, however, that the Community has not faced and sometimes mastered real problems in the past or that it still does not have a long way to go to achieve the aspirations of those who see it as the sole hope for the effective organization of Europe to meet the undoubted economic and political challenges of the future. Supporters of European unity have from the outset brought to the task a peculiar mixture of idealism and economic hardheadedness. The founding fathers—Jean Monnet, Konrad Adenauer, Robert Schuman, Alcide de Gasperi, and others—did not have their heads collectively in the clouds, but they did share a common dedication to the cause of unification as well as a realistic adaptability in the face of reverses. The bitter disappointment involved in the collapse of the European Defense Community and European Political Community treaties in 1953-54 turned them, after a few years of adjustment, to the idea of a European Economic Community embodied in the Treaty of Rome of 1957.

1. Ever since my assignment in 1952 to the Bruce Mission in Paris, a primary function of which was to persuade the French to ratify the Treaty Establishing a European Defense Community, I have followed closely, both as an official and as a scholar, the process of European integration. Unless otherwise indicated, this article is based largely on my own recollections, impressions, and continuing personal contacts.

INSTITUTIONAL ADJUSTMENTS

During the past 15 years, the institutions of the Community (now called simply the European Community), most notably the European Commission, have admittedly developed a certain brittleness. The Commission, ensconced in its Brussels headquarters, has become the focal point of criticism for alleged inflexibility, insensitivity, and, worst of all, a lust for power. Yet it was thought from the outset of the Community that, to the degree it developed supranational powers, they would be vested in the Commission as the executive branch of the organization. Even a reluctant French government during the period of the de Gaulle presidency conceded that as far as the Common Agricultural Policy was concerned, the Commission should essentially exercise the powers in the area handed over by national governments. The Common Agricultural Policy was, of course, much desired as a source of protection for French agriculture.

It was perhaps inevitable that the Council of Ministers—and, of course, the European Council—should emerge as the definitive repository of executive and legislative authority in the Community, the latter necessitated by the unwillingness of member countries to grant any substantial powers to the Community Parliament. The Maastricht Treaty itself did not contemplate, even at the end stage of its implementation, the kind of supranational political organization envisaged in the abortive 1953 Draft Treaty to Create a European Political Community.

THE FUTURE OF MAASTRICHT

During the two years following its adoption, the Maastricht Treaty suffered from the coincidence of bad times, abnormally high Bundesbank

interest rates, the consequent near collapse of the ERM, the inordinate profits made by speculators free to operate on the currency exchanges, and the general demoralization caused by the inability of Europe to do anything effective to stop the slaughter in the former Yugoslavia. It was not a propitious time for a bold new stroke in the direction of economic unity.

The debate over whether the broadening or the deepening of the Community should receive priority has worked its way out to the pragmatic conclusion that, in a measure, it can both enlarge and move toward greater unity at the same time. The magic formula, agreed at the Edinburgh summit of December 1992, was that new members must accept the Maastricht approach.[2] This amounted to an implicit acceptance of a two-tier community or, to use a different metaphor, of an inner core of countries prepared to move faster toward greater unity than other member countries. The Maastricht Treaty made the same assumption in that only those countries that meet the stipulated "convergence criteria" will be able to advance toward full monetary union. This whole subject had been one of intense discussion and scornful rejection within the Community since Willy Brandt first suggested it as a likelihood some twenty years ago.[3]

2. See "Cheery Faces," *Economist*, 19 Dec. 1992, p. 48. For a description of the Maastricht Treaty, see Martin J. Hillenbrand, "European Community: Prospects and Problems," *Global Review*, 1(1):8-9 (Spring 1992).

3. He was Chancellor at the time, and I was the U.S. Ambassador in Bonn. Having incited a negative reaction, he did not press the point.

The question of what is to become of the Maastricht Treaty remains, of course, fundamental to the future of the Community. Will those member countries that meet the "convergence criteria" be prepared to move ahead, when the time comes, toward full implementation? Much will, obviously, depend on the mood of peoples and their leaders during the years ahead, and that will, obviously, be largely influenced by the state of European economies in the latter part of the decade and, to an extent, by what has happened in the meantime in Eastern Europe and the former Soviet Union. Chaos there reflecting the continued inability of the West to bring about peace and assist in at least some progress toward economic reform may well revive the present negativism. After all, apart from its economic provisions, Maastricht was also supposed to bring about greater political and military cooperation within the Community—areas with respect to which the situation in the former Yugoslavia and elsewhere have only demonstrated the present impotence of Western Europe.

CRITICISMS OF MAASTRICHT

There are, I believe, some reasonable grounds for longer-term optimism, but it may be useful to note arguments made by opponents of Maastricht that go beyond the mood of the moment. The question raised by Wynne Godley and others is whether economic union with a single currency managed by a Community central bank can really function in the absence of any central political management or commensurate political institutions—in other words, a federal European government.[4] There is obviously some point to this question. Its logic was precisely that of Foreign Minister Paul Henri Spaak and Heinrich von Brentano in their advocacy of a European Political Union in 1953. The counterargument, of course, is that economic union of the kind contemplated will inevitably lead to a greater measure of political union as the logical connection between economics and politics asserts itself. This was clearly the hope of Jean Monnet in his advocacy of the European Economic Community in 1957.

A significant negative factor for the future of Maastricht is that neither Chancellor Kohl nor President Mitterrand is likely to still be active politically as the climactic years for the implementation of the treaty roll around. No one conversant with the primary causal factors operating in the Community during recent years could deny that, without the combined effort of these two leaders, Maastricht, the Edinburgh summit, and the required steady pressure over a period of years within the Community could not have been achieved. Despite the criticism of Commission President Jacques Delors for his *dirigiste* tendencies, his leadership was also an essential ingredient in the movement toward unity. He, too, will in all probability have gone on to other things by the late 1990s. Mitterrand's and Delors's

4. See Wynne Godley, "Maastricht and All That," *London Review of Books*, 9 Oct. 1992, p. 3.

French Socialist Party suffered heavy reverses in the parliamentary elections of late March 1993, and no one in France believes the former will run again for the presidency in 1995.[5]

The degree of commitment to European integration that their successors will have obviously remains an open question. There is no a priori reason, however, why it should be insufficient to provide continuing leadership toward implementation of the treaty, particularly if circumstances are more propitious than at present.

There has been a good deal of talk during the past decade about the need to democratize the Community. In practice, this meant increasing the powers of the European Parliament. The Maastricht Treaty provided some additional functions for that body, but these fell considerably short of what proponents had hoped. The record of the Assembly created by the Treaty of Rome has been largely a source of frustration at the unwillingness of member governments to grant it significant legislative authority. The institution of direct elections in 1979—rather than selection by appointment—raised, at least for a time, the quality of representation but did not allay the basic frustration of those members who wanted to see the Assembly acquire a truly legislative role. Here, too, it would seem, an effective parliament is likely to develop only as part of a real move toward a supranational political community.

THE SINGLE EUROPEAN ACT

With all the hubbub over Maastricht, implementation of the Single European Act at the end of 1992 attracted relatively little attention. Many skeptics had predicted that governments would never accept and ratify the some 280 directives proposed by the Commission as necessary to achieve the purpose of the act, which itself had come at a time—1986—when "Europa sclerosis" and "Europa pessimism" were all the talk. In reality, nearly 95 percent of the directives had been approved as 1993 approached.[6] There are, of course, some problems and unanticipated difficulties. For example, the elimination of all border controls within the Community would make it possible for terrorists and other criminals to circulate freely without fear of detection. Moreover, contraband goods barred from export to certain rogue countries, and even to Eastern Europe under existing restrictions of the Coordinating Committee for Multilateral Export Controls, could exit the Community via the member country with the least effective export control system. Given these possibilities, it seems inevitable that some sort of continuing surveillance system will survive at border crossings even if formal passport and cargo controls have disappeared.

Unless, however, all conventional theory about trade and its relationship to economic growth is egregiously wrong, the new impulses that the unified market will inject into the Community should help to mitigate

---

5. See *Le Monde*, 29 Mar. 1993.

6. Axel Krause, "The Single Market Takes Off," *Europe*, p. 19 (Feb. 1993).

the current economic stagnation and drive the economies of member countries into a new cycle of economic expansion.

EUROPEAN POLITICAL COOPERATION

As former German Foreign Minister Genscher described it, European Political Cooperation (EPC) between the 12 member states of the Community has become "a central instrument of the pursuit of national interests and European integration."[7] A series of Foreign Ministers' and summit conferences during the 1970s established the operating framework for such cooperation—to the considerable chagrin of Secretary of State Henry Kissinger, who wanted an American *droit de regard*—and the 1980s were filled with further confirming intra-Community agreements. The Single European Act provided an international treaty basis for EPC, and the process of coordinating foreign policy within the Community has involved numerous meetings of various levels of officialdom on a regularly scheduled basis. Apart from other occasions when they regularly come together as the Council of Ministers, Foreign Ministers meet at least six times a year within the EPC framework.

Cynics have questioned whether all this activity actually adds up to very much, and there is a feeling among more balanced observers that meaningful political cooperation requires something more than what

has been achieved so far. As one wag put it, however, if it has accomplished little else, all this traveling around to respective capitals by ministers, state secretaries, and numerous other officials has at least contributed to lowering the normal operating deficits of European airlines and rail systems. From my own observation, I would add that there is inherent merit in a consultative process that brings together officials on a regular basis; it creates both better understanding of national positions and a network of personal relationships that makes problem solving at least somewhat easier.

ADJUSTING TO CHANGE IN THE EAST

Among the problems with which Kohl, Mitterrand, and other European leaders have had to contend has been the need to adjust to the dramatic post-1989 changes in Eastern Europe and the former Soviet Union.[8] These removed almost overnight the propulsions of the Cold War that had undoubtedly provided an additional motive for the unification of Western Europe, but they also added an enormous array of new problems and uncertainties for the West.

The immediate post-1989 reaction in the Community, as elsewhere, was one of euphoria. It was also a time of relative economic growth. No one had any real idea of how difficult the transition to market-oriented economies would be and how severely the fledg-

7. *European Political Cooperation (EPC)*, 5th ed. (Bonn: Press and Information Office of the Federal Government, 1988), p. 14.

8. Pierre-Henri Laurent, "Western European Integration and the End of the Cold War," in *The End of the Cold War*, ed. David Armstrong and Erik Goldstein (London: F. Cass, 1991), pp. 147-64.

ling new democracies in Eastern Europe would be tested. The assimilation of the former German Democratic Republic into the economy of the Federal Republic of Germany, which to the government in Bonn first appeared deceptively easy, became an enormous drain on West German resources—resources a part of which, it was hoped, would be available to help the former Soviet Union and Eastern Europe. An observer of the German government today could legitimately conclude that it is suffering from systemic overload. Some would say the same applies to the institutions of the Community.

Although the Community was prepared to consider enlargement of its membership after implementation of its 1992 program, it was thinking essentially of those countries of the European Free Trade Association (EFTA), such as Sweden, Austria, and perhaps Norway, that were relatively advanced economically and already enjoyed through EFTA a special trading arrangement with the Community. The troublesome application for membership of Turkey was on hold. Now other countries to the east, especially Poland, Hungary, and Czechoslovakia (split in two at the beginning of 1993) also wanted to join. The feeling in Brussels was that their economies were still too fragile and noncompetitive internationally to make full membership practical, but that some sort of special association arrangement could be made to assist the entry of their products into the Community market.[9]

What, of course, Western European countries have come only slowly to appreciate is that the collapse of the centrally planned and dysfunctional economies to the east did not automatically bring an improvement in the condition of populations with a low standard of living and with access to only shoddy goods and inferior foodstuffs. They did not sufficiently anticipate that the transition to market-oriented economies would be difficult and might actually for a time lead to a period of acute hardship and systemic breakdown. The end result of this process might be a return to a more authoritarian type of regime that promises restoration of the "relative stabilities" of the old order. For what it is worth, a Gallup survey of 18 countries commissioned by the Community confirmed that most East Europeans are "deeply disillusioned with democracy and half believed they were better off under communism." Of the Russians, who were generally the most pessimistic, one-third expected their country to return to a dictatorship.[10]

The Community's inability to make any effective contribution to the bloody mess in the former Yugoslavia has dramatically underlined the political helplessness of the Community. Its attempt to mediate through Lord Carrington failed, and as an organization it stood by passively while efforts at mediation under U.N. auspices took over. It could be argued that one should not criticize the Community for failing to achieve something that it was not created to do, and that Franco-Ger-

9. For a somewhat different point of view, see "Europe's Hard Core," *Economist*, 21 Nov. 1992, p. 72.

10. *Atlanta Journal and Constitution*, 25 Feb. 1993.

man efforts to establish a European military capability—opposed by the United States—were still too primitive to be relevant. But the feeling of incapacity, whatever the excuses, could not help but depress morale within the Community.

THE NEAR COLLAPSE
OF THE ERM AND
THE EUROPEAN
MONETARY SYSTEM

During the 1980s, the ERM, the principal component of the European Monetary System, experienced some rocky moments but generally provided an oasis of exchange rate stability in the worldwide regime of floating exchange rates. In September of 1992, however, the ERM reached a point of crisis as the high domestic interest rates maintained by the German central bank provided a field day for speculators betting that the Bundesbank would attempt to support weakening currencies like the Italian lira and the British pound on the international exchanges, thus driving them up temporarily against the deutsche mark. When the inevitable crash came as central bank intervention dried up, profit taking on a massive scale would begin. Never mind that both the Italians and the British had to withdraw from the ERM and let their currencies float downward despite the domestic political fallout. Only massive intervention by the Bundesbank and Banque de France prevented similar unbearable downward pressures from developing on the franc.[11]

The traumatic change—some would say "collapse"—of the ERM on 1 August 1993 necessitated by speculative pressures against the French franc will at the very least further delay implementation of the Maastricht Treaty. Some would argue that the member states of the Community have demonstrated that they are simply not ready for the concerted actions required to move toward the Maastricht goals.

One argument nevertheless likely to become more and more compelling is that monetary union will bring to an end the speculation with regard to member-country currencies that sends the equivalent of hundreds of billions of dollars worth of what used to be called hot money sloshing around between the world's currency exchanges—a process that makes speculators immediately rich and central bankers crazy. The combination of the communications revolution and enormous international liquidity has made such a partial system as the ERM almost unmanageable during periods of stress. Since no one is advocating a return to strict national exchange controls, only a single currency for those members of the Community that eventually meet the "convergence criteria" can bring order for them out of the present chaos on the exchanges.

---

11. By chance, I happened to be in Paris, Frankfurt, and London during the fateful week beginning 13 September 1992, when all this came to a head. The group of American institutional investors I was accompanying met with central bank officials in both Paris and Frankfurt and in London with the Minister of State of the British Treasury.

U.S. RELATIONS
WITH THE COMMUNITY

The same ambiguities that characterized earlier U.S. relations with the Community have continued through the 1980s and up to the present. They may well survive this century. There has seldom been any doubt about the verbal commitment of the United States to greater European integration. Successive administrations have reaffirmed U.S. support for such integration. The standard formula used to be that the United States was prepared to accept the economic disadvantages that European political integration might involve because of the greater political advantages of such unity. The first report of the Nixon administration to the Congress, dated 18 February 1970, deleted this formula and replaced it with some vaguer language about partnership.

Despite such verbal refinements, U.S. policy has, during the more recent past, continued to endorse the idea of European unity while sometimes balking at its specific manifestations and while reserving the right, when our ox is gored economically, to protest vigorously and to defend our interests by all available means. American protests over Community "misbehavior" have been most consistently directed at various aspects of the Common Agricultural Policy but have also included steel and, most recently, European subsidization of the Airbus, which is now competing in world markets with the products of Boeing and McDonnell Douglas.

From the 1950s on, American officials have, paradoxically enough, tended to think of the Community, when it branches out of the purely economic area, as a possible threat to the cohesion of the Atlantic Alliance. This feeling of uneasiness has seldom been a major problem in the concrete except in the Kissinger period and, much more recently, in the steady American opposition to the incipient Franco-German attempts to begin the process of implementing the military aspects of the Maastricht Treaty by forming a joint military force of admittedly modest dimensions. Protagonists of the North Atlantic Treaty Organization (NATO) attacked the very idea as subversive of the Western Alliance, but the French and Germans nevertheless persisted. Their joint force, however, is essentially still embryonic since the German part thereof cannot yet be used except within the strictly defined limits of the NATO treaty.

At a perhaps more abstract level, it is fair to say that the United States had never been able to work out a consistent theory of its relationship to the European Community that went beyond such metaphorical expressions as dumbbell or two pillars. President Kennedy tried, but he quickly exhausted the ingenuity of his speech writers. I would suggest, however, that short of America's joining the Community—a most unlikely development—there are some intermediate relationships worthy of exploration.

A fundamental statistical reality, despite all the emphasis these days on the priority status of the East Asian market, is that, under normal circumstances, the United States should run a favorable balance on both trade and current account with the European Community. When we do not, it is primarily a function of an overvalued dollar, as during the Reagan administration, or an asymmetrical relationship of the business cycles of the United States and Europe. Our foreign imbalances are not due to any closure of the European market but to seemingly irremediable deficits with Japan, China, and the Four Tigers.

A FINAL THOUGHT

The past decade and a half have been a period of great progress for the European Community interlarded with much doubt and pessimism along the way. The years 1992-93, for the various reasons already discussed, have seen more emphasis on the negative rather than the positive. Nothing is assured in the unpredictable years ahead, but it does not require unrealistic optimism to envisage the development of an ever stronger and more integrated Community, though one certainly doomed, in this less than perfect world, to fall short of its most comprehensive goals. An American policy that assumes failure of the Community, or allows disputes over individual problems to tarnish our entire relationship, not only will run counter to the underlying thrust of policy during the postwar era but will, in my view, be contrary to our national interest.

Book Department

INTERNATIONAL RELATIONS AND POLITICS

BELLAMY, RICHARD. *Liberalism and Modern Society*. Pp. x, 310. University Park: Pennsylvania State University Press, 1992. $40.00. Paperbound, $16.95.

ACKERMAN, BRUCE. *The Future of Liberal Revolution*. Pp. viii, 152. New Haven, CT: Yale University Press, 1992. $18.50.

Liberalism, in Richard Bellamy's account, has shown since John Stuart Mill an ineluctable tension between its ethical foundation and the socioeconomic institutions of modernity. Liberal theorists avoided this tension only by idealizing market relations and assuming that individual life plans would naturally harmonize. When such relations and harmony failed to materialize, liberalism began to unravel.

Bellamy traces this unraveling through nineteenth- and early-twentieth-century European liberal theorists and does so nationally to show the historical and particularistic nature of liberalism. Specifically, he examines J. S. Mill and T. H. Green, Emile Durkheim, Vilfredo Pareto and Benedetto Croce, and Max Weber, who showed how liberalism crumbled under the weight of bureaucracy: the evolution of capitalism resulted in a diminution of individual freedom through the need for increased bureaucratic management and a concomitant regimentation of everyday life. Necessary bureaucratic hierarchies deprived most people of self-directed action. Weber thought that the liberal characteristic of autonomy could be attained therefore only by a select few. For the masses, a Schumpeterian democracy—obviously, not Weber's phrase—was all that remained.

Bureaucracies necessitated action in accordance with formal procedures and rules. According to Bellamy, Weber "reconceived liberalism in realist terms as a set of procedures and institutions" and not as a set of rights or as principles of justice. Bellamy sees in this reconceptualization an opening for generating "democratic liberalism," as opposed to liberal democracy.

Bellamy's democratic form of liberalism is neither neutralist nor communitarian, faults he finds in contemporary liberal theories. Additionally, unlike contemporary liberalism, which Bellamy claims relies, or has relied, on social homogeneity to regulate public interactions, democratic liberalism recognizes and accepts pluralism: the pursuit not only of different and divergent goods but also of contrasting and "contradictory kinds of reasoning."

But Bellamy's democratic liberal alternative is underdeveloped at best and, at worst, rests on questionable assertions about the nature of modern societies; the impact of technologies and innovations and of functional differentiation and specialization; the decline of autonomy and the rise of complexity and expertise; and the impossibility of "a revived liberal moral community." While liberal democracy requires moral consensus, democratic liberalism "gives central place to fair procedures that favor the expression and temporary conciliation of a plurality of ideals." How this is to be accomplished without falling into the problems of liberal democracy Bellamy does not say.

Nor does he argue in detail, after superb critiques of various liberal theorists, just how democratic liberalism differs from liberal democracy. While he does not mention him by name, Bellamy would surely include Bruce Ackerman among liberal democratic theorists. Yet in *The Future of Liberal Revolution*, Ackerman speaks directly to Bellamy's concerns. Bellamy thinks that liberalism has been unable to address modern social pluralism. Ackerman, confronting exactly this pluralism, seeks to build in the United States, in Europe, and throughout the globe liberal states "dedicated to our equal right to be different . . . we may become something more than strangers but less than friends. We may become

liberal citizens." The purpose of liberal principles and constitutions is to provide political institutions and safeguards that will both protect our rights—including the right to be different—and provide the democratic procedures for expressing our differences.

Contra Bellamy and following from Ackerman's reading, liberalism is not "a doctrine which is neutral between different conceptions of the good" (Bellamy, p. 218). Rather, liberalism wants the state, as Ackerman points out, to strive to achieve structural conditions that can guarantee "undominated equality," to use Ackerman's term. To do so requires, both here and abroad, liberal revolution, that is, "the democratic adoption of considered constitutions . . . [that] define affirmatively the principles that will mark off the 'new era' from the 'old regime.' " Thus the terms "revolution" and "constitution" describe what Ackerman calls the two faces of liberal political transformation.

Like Bellamy, Ackerman needs to say more about democratic procedures, especially those envisioned during and after a liberal revolution. He also needs to say more about the "self-conscious and deliberate majority" whose support is crucial before a revolutionary change in the constitution. But he argues strenuously and concretely that the use of liberal revolution in the current political predicaments of Eastern Europe is essential if those burgeoning democracies are to survive the rampages of nationalism and avoid a loathsome retreat into authoritarianism.

JACK CRITTENDEN

Arizona State University
Tempe

JOWITT, KEN. *New World Disorder: The Leninist Extinction*. Pp. ix, 342. Berkeley: University of California Press, 1992. $30.00.

Few reprint collections should be published as books. This one by Ken Jowitt, cumulative and consequential, is an obvious exception. Though his somewhat poetic use of terms presents a few initial obstacles to clarity, even to comprehension—"world liberal capitalist democracy" having in common with "Holy Roman Empire" the contradiction implicit in every word, and the "Leninist extinction" having little to do with V. I.—the persistent reader will be rewarded with a genuinely comparative, original, and intellectually captivating analysis of the political plate tectonics of the late twentieth century. *New World Disorder*, foreseeing various conflicts, is lively, lucid, diverse, and broadly informed. This book definitely reads at least 8 on the Richter scale. Even though he has committed some social science here, auguring, I fear, far too well, if one cannot study with Ken Jowitt, one should at least beg, borrow, buy, or purloin this book.

T. C. SMITH

Mankato State University
Minnesota

MacNEILL, JIM, PETER WINSEMIUS, and TAIZO YAKUSHIJI. *Beyond Interdependence: The Meshing of the World's Economy and the Earth's Ecology*. Pp. xx, 159. New York: Oxford University Press, 1991. $24.95.

PORTER, GARETH and JANET WELSH BROWN. *Global Environmental Politics: Dilemmas in World Politics*. Pp. xv, 208. Boulder, CO: Westview Press, 1991. $43.50. Paperbound, $10.95.

Environmental issues are very much on the agenda of international politics despite the present disinclinations of some prominent international leaders. The two books reviewed here convey the broad range of those issues and discuss the numerous international institutions and agreements that have been established to deal with them. Both books provide an extended list of acronyms for these institutions and agreements, Porter and Brown's list running to three pages. It would seem that almost no major international organization has avoided a significant involvement in environmental matters. More than that, a whole array of organizations has been created to address what finally now commands some of the attention it deserves.

The authors of these two books are in general agreement on the main themes. The planet as a whole now faces a wide variety of problems that can be effectively resolved only if addressed internationally and collectively. These issues include global warming, depletion of the ozone layer, the destruction of tropical forests and the variety of human threats to biodiversity, acid precipitation, desertification, and human overpopulation. *Beyond Interdependence* is, essentially, a well-argued update of *Our Common Future*, the report of the Brundtland Commission, and *Global Environmental Politics* is a well-written introductory textbook on the conduct of environmental politics in the international arena.

MacNeill, Winsemius, and Yakushiji's central theme is captured in their title. The world, they argue, is no longer merely economically interdependent. We are also ecologically interdependent, and the global economy and ecology are inextricably linked as well. The desperate economic situation of the poorer nations currently leaves them little choice but to put biodiversity at risk. But economic growth in its traditional forms and patterns is not a solution. As the authors put it,

Since 1900, the world's population has multiplied more than three times. Its economy has grown twentyfold. The consumption of fossil fuels has grown by a factor of 30, and industrial production by a factor of 50. Most of that growth, about four-fifths of it, [has] occurred since 1950. Much of it is unsustainable (p. 3).

Beyond Interdependence convincingly makes the case that the interdependence of the world's economy and Earth's ecology will alter both our patterns of governance and the underlying logic of economic decision making. Indeed, we must fundamentally change economic incentive patterns such that all nations cease the overexploitation of resource stocks (soils, forests, fisheries, species, and waters) and global life support systems (especially the atmosphere and climate). Here the book is at its best. It demonstrates how some nations contribute to ecological decline out of poverty, others out of wealth. It also outlines one of the root causes of these problems: misdirected governmental subsidies that accelerate the overexploitation of forests, waters, and energy. The case made for change regarding these and other destructive policies is beautifully articulated. A less explicit and detailed case for curbing human population growth is also clearly stated, to the authors' credit.

Global Environmental Politics is much more a guide to international environmental organizations and what they have done in recent years. It also carefully examines a wide variety of international environmental issues from the unsuccessful attempt to ban whaling to the 1991 gulf war. The latter is considered in relation to a rethinking of many national security issues as environmental security issues. The range of particular issues covered is most impressive and includes conservation issues such as the ivory trade, resource issues such as tropical timber, and health issues such as the international trade in toxic wastes. Contemporary international relations undergraduates can get a very up-to-date look at the new environmental dimension of modern diplomacy. As Porter and Brown note, environmental issues are no longer regarded as "low politics—a set of minor issues to be relegated to technical experts."

Both of these books are surprisingly and admirably tough-minded. All of the authors are experienced hands in international and governmental circles. Both books accept that profound economic and political changes are implicit in the many environmental problems we now must confront collectively on a global scale. Neither steers away from addressing controversial questions with perhaps one exception. Neither book is quite prepared to argue that we in the industrialized nations must be prepared to do with less, be it less than we have now or merely less than we might otherwise have. Is it not possible that the long-term global future now requires such a perspective?

ROBERT PAEHLKE

Trent University
Peterborough
Ontario
Canada

AFRICA, ASIA, AND LATIN AMERICA

AMOS, DEBORAH. *Lines in the Sand: Desert Storm and the Remaking of the Arab World.* Pp. 223. New York: Simon & Schuster, 1992. $21.00.

This first book by Deborah Amos arouses hopes that it is the first of many. There are numerous memoirs of Desert Storm and the Gulf crisis of 1990-91 and she can bring no really startling insights to the topic, but she does contribute a great facility with language and a cheerful magpie's aptitude for collecting anecdotes. The book is thoroughly enjoyable and immensely readable.

This is not without perils. Investigative journalists with her prose ability are beguiling, and the danger is that we will accept a great deal of plausible opinion as fact. At the time of the freeing of Kuwait, did the royal family really prevent its own army from having modern weapons because of a fear that they would be used against the dynasty? Did the spicy conversations reported take place in exactly the way that Amos describes? The total absence of footnotes, the reliance on the remarks of taxi drivers and waiters, and the seamless mixing of incident with innuendo mean that *Lines in the Sand* will not be a hollowed source book for scholars.

However, while intoxicated just a bit by language, she has succeeded in capturing the theater of the absurd that is the modern Middle East. An American jeep goes by festooned with a pair of purple panties. Saddam keeps his dead troops in deep freezers so the daily number of fatalities can be spread out. Iraqi Foreign Minister Tariq Aziz smilingly tells Kuwaiti Prime Minister Sheikh Saaed al Sabah that he has obtained the dirty movies kept in al Sabah's office. The Americans argue with Muslim holy men about the propriety of Saudi soldiers' cutting their beards so they can wear gas masks. The inhabitants of small towns on the war front guzzle Diet Pepsi and consume great quantities of Pringles potato chips and Twinkies.

There are occasional errors of fact; surely, the Gulf states donated more than $2 million a year to the Palestine Liberation Organization. And not everyone will appreciate such a breezy approach to history. The Syrians, for example, are described as having "the smell of past combat," and we are assured that "it was an odor that tickles the olfactories of the American military." The dour Saudis who "paw through the mail" of the American soldiers miss the blowup sex dolls, and there are chuckles over consuming pork sausage so close to holy Mecca. There is enough irony for more than one sitting: after liberation the Sri Lankan women who are so shamelessly exploited as nan-

nies and maids are airlifted back to clean up, dressed in smocks that announce, "Building a New Kuwait," while Kuwaiti youths sport T-shirts with "Holy War" and "Holy Shit" logos.

Deborah Amos remarks, "As far as I could tell, the only direct benefit of the Iraqi occupation in the so-called nineteenth province was to drive down the price of whiskey in Kuwait City." Permeating the book is a note of despair that is justified. "We've all wasted our lives," asserts one Palestinian. "We are all shaped by misery." The Kuwaiti playwright Abdul Aziz al Musalem stages "Desert Storm" a year after the return. "The theme," writes Amos, "was this: No matter what government rules in Iraq, the Iraqis would be back." Indeed, they may return, and if they do who will protect the Gulf sheikhdoms?

PAUL RICH

Stanford University
California

BONNER, ARTHUR. *Averting the Apocalypse: Social Movements in India Today.* Pp. vi, 467. Durham, NC: Duke University Press, 1990. $52.50. Paperbound, $17.95.

EMBREE, AINSLEE T. *Utopias in Conflict: Religion and Nationalism in Modern India.* Pp. xii, 144. Berkeley: University of California Press, 1990. $17.95.

If ever a book was prophetic, Ainslee Embree's *Utopias in Conflict* is, even though it consists of essays from earlier periods, from 1968 to 1987. I write as the Ayodhya conflict presents India with a crisis: will the "alternative utopia," in Embree's terms, of the radical right Hindutva forces win over the secular state of India's constitution? What will be the effect of the most serious Hindu-

Muslim riots since partition? Does Embree's analysis of the conflict offer understanding or hope? Certainly, his observations that "the truly astonishing factor in Indian civilization is the endurance and persistence of its style and patterns" and that Hinduism's "encapsulation" of other religions is neither "toleration, absorption, nor synthesis" help us analyze the current Hindu-Muslim conflict.

For some of Embree's other observations—such as the erosion of traditional values, a 1968 opinion—we will have to wait even longer, as we will have to for a clearer idea of what actually is immutable tradition—certainly, such traditions as music, dance, and regional language creativity are by no means eroded but are even stronger. Moreover, while the European comparison is useful, the triumph of nationalism there is belied by current events; at least for some parts of Europe and the rest of the world, ethnicity triumphs over nationalism.

In some ways, this collection of essays is a summation of Embree's study, comparable to W. Norman Brown's *Man in the Universe*. Embree is more pessimistic, but his graceful, easy prose is considered and provocative in many areas. But most important, if violence in India is not "senseless and random" but "a way of changing things," then we have cause for both hope and fear. The presentation of Muslim and Sikh demands as well as the current Ayodhya crisis as a conflict of utopian ideas is based on Embree's long and careful study of Indian history and, in my opinion, must be considered by those analyzing the current situation and predicting India's future.

Arthur Bonner's *Averting the Apocalypse* is an important book, one that should be consulted by those interested in grassroots movements in India and in the future of India. Bonner has given us a work with two strong points: (1) stories of an unusual assortment of activists

working locally in Bombay, Gujarat, Bihar, Andhra, and Tamil Nadu, whom Bonner allows to speak for themselves; and (2) a series of premises for "averting the apocalypse" that many predict for India.

As a journalist, Bonner interviewed and looked closely at the work of a number of activists whose movements have gone pretty much unnoticed. I list here some of the areas covered because they offer teachers and those interested in development information not available elsewhere. In Bombay, there were the Society for Promotion of Area Resource Centers (SPARC) in the slums, work with prostitutes, and Annapurna (meals for workers prepared by slum women). Bonner found work with tribals in Thane; trees for the Western Ghats; biogas toilets in a Christian Dalit community in Gujarat; the Narmada project; the Self-Employed Women's Association (SEWA) in Ahmadabad (the only well-known grassroots women's project) and several other Ahmadabad projects, including efforts to confront police rape; a Ganges fishermen's movement; a grassroots literacy program in Andhra and various imaginative village development programs in that state; efforts to help the so-called little slaves of the Mirzapur carpet factories and the child match workers in Madras; and a swami working against suttee and other violent traditions.

Bonner's premises should be considered as both guideposts and warnings; I find them thoughtful and provocative. They are as follows:

1. India's social movements are concerned entirely with the poor, and the percentage of women leaders is high.

2. Political theories based on charismatic leaders and institutionalized parties no longer have meaning.

3. Even though it was through the instrumentality of Gandhi that power

was transferred from the British to the elite and although Gandhian centers are "museums of memorabilia," many grass-roots leaders are based in the Gandhian tradition.

4. The welfare approach has been abandoned in favor of empowerment by those who are actually helpful.

5. Fifteen percent of India is Brahmanic, an amalgam of caste, class, and consumerism; 85 percent is poor and depressed.

6. Gramschi is the theorist who best explains the Indian condition.

7. The question is not whether India will continue to exist or not—there are too many institutions in place for India to disappear—but rather what kind of India will survive into the twenty-first century.

8. "Sacrifice is the hallmark of Indian culture," as an activist in Andhra tells Bonner, and one has only to give volunteers "a social cause and a direction."

I think the reason a work of this quality, concern, and imagination has not been given the consideration of Naipaul's million mutinies is that it just tries to do too much. Each interesting interview with an activist is preceded by general history and myriad statistics and news notes. Overall statistics on Bombay do not do much but create horror, with nothing of the vitality revealed in, say, Mira Nair's *Salam Bombay*. Other segments read like modern-day Katherine Mayo. Bonner has in general done his homework, unlike that other pessimist-optimist, Naipaul, but chapters such as that on the origin of the tribals are superficial. I know what he is trying to do, and I admire his intent to set up an overview of the problems each activist deals with, but he would have been better advised to stick to his journalistic expertise and not attempt to cover all of India's ills historically and sociologically in one book. Nevertheless, the book should be in college libraries and used as one consults an encyclopedia.

ELEANOR ZELLIOT

Carleton College
Northfield
Minnesota

BUDDE, MICHAEL L. *The Two Churches: Catholicism and Capitalism in the World System*. Pp. 172. Durham, NC: Duke University Press, 1992. $29.95.

KIRK, JOHN M. *Politics and the Catholic Church in Nicaragua*. Pp. xiii, 246. Gainesville: University of Florida Press, 1992. $34.95.

The two works reviewed here have as their focus the relationship between Roman Catholicism—defined at the levels of the hierarchy and the parish—and politics, with primary attention devoted to religion and politics in Latin America. The volumes are cast at markedly different levels of analysis: Budde's *Two Churches* is geared to the level of world systems theory, which resembles, at least superficially, Alasdair McIntyre's general theory of holes; the Kirk volume is a detailed historical case study of church-state relations in one country.

Budde's system-level analysis is organized around the prediction that, over time, the Roman Catholic Church will become an anticapitalist force in world politics. Budde's principal basis for this prediction is demographic: Church membership in Latin America is growing much more rapidly than in other regions of the world, and the Latin American Church is a source of political and economic radicalism. As the response of the Church hierarchy comes to reflect these emphases, the Vatican will have a much more Latin—and therefore, socialist—set of priorities than has traditionally been the case. Budde argues that, although considerations exist that operate in the opposite direction, the forces favoring the dominance of a Latin American "anticapitalist direction" are "more fundamental, [and] more deeply rooted, than those undermining it." Forces undermining the ascendancy of the "preferential option for the poor" enunciated at Medellin and Puebla—such as the ambivalence of John Paul II toward liberation theology—are dismissed as "merely contingent," and not structural in nature.

I found Budde's case rather unpersuasive. Even assuming the correctness of his demographic data, which I do not question, Budde's prediction is based on a questionable assumption and ignores the varied experiences of the Church in Latin America. The implicit assumption, which I find unwarranted, is that the policies of the Catholic hierarchy will necessarily shift as the result of changing membership patterns among the laity. The notion that the Catholic hierarchy is a representative institution, responsive to the desires of the laity, is one that, to say the least, requires careful scrutiny. Even if the worldwide membership of the Catholic Church increasingly over-represents Latin America, it does not follow that Vatican policies or priorities will change as a result.

Second, the equation of Latin American Catholicism with anticapitalism ignores the historical experiences of a number of countries. While Budde's account of the "People's Church" fits admirably in nations such as Brazil and Chile, the notion that the Church is a source of radicalism at the parish level does not apply well to other Latin nations. Indeed, in countries such as Mexico and Venezuela, church-state relations resemble a form of quasi establishment, with relatively few overt conflicts between clergy and government. This is not to say that there may not exist anticapitalist forces at the parish level in such nations; how-

ever, it does suggest that the connection between economic radicalism and Roman Catholicism in Latin America is more complicated than Budde's broad-brush treatment would indicate.

John Kirk's useful volume on church-state relations in Nicaragua is, by contrast, much more narrowly focused and much more detailed. Kirk shows that the Church was always a player in Nicaraguan politics but that the Church's role has changed over time. For most of Nicaragua's history, the Church was a source of accommodation and compliance with the state—an opiate, in Marxist terms. However, the Nicaraguan Church was frequently—at the pastoral level—or occasionally—at the episcopal level—a source of opposition to the Somosa and Sandinista regimes.

Kirk's account of Catholicism's dynamic political role in Nicaragua is a particular historical narrative and simply relates a chronology of events. Kirk does not settle on a general analytical framework but emphasizes actors and events unique to Nicaraguan history, such as the appointment of Miguel Obando y Bravo as archbishop in 1970 or the election of Ronald Reagan as President of the United States in 1980. In so doing, he demonstrates the efficacy of particular—perhaps even accidental—contingencies dismissed as epiphenomenal in Budde's more ambitious account. While it might be possible to relate the actions of particular actors to more systemic considerations, Kirk's account strongly suggests that unintended side effects of particular decisions shape the changing face of the relationship between Caesar and Christ.

Taken together, these two related volumes illustrate the problems in doing social science at different levels of analysis. Budde's general description of Catholic politics in Latin America does not correspond to Kirk's more detailed history of one Latin American country. While there is a place in the social sciences for both broad-gauged general theory and smaller-scale case studies, it is of some importance that the more abstract analyses be firmly grounded in the particulars of history. Budde's systemic account would have benefited enormously from more attention to analyses such as those offered by Kirk.

TED G. JELEN

Illinois Benedictine College
Lisle

FRANKO-JONES, PATRICE. *The Brazilian Defense Industry*. Pp. xiii, 262. Boulder, CO: Westview Press, 1992. Paperbound, $32.50.

This book is the latest offspring of a series of studies that started in the 1970s and looked closely at the Brazilian state as agent of industrial development. Highly nationalistic, the military regime that ran the country from 1964 until 1985 pursued the import-substitution policies adopted by civilian governments since 1945. Large public investment, made possible through heavy foreign borrowing, favored local producers protected by prohibitive tariffs. Foreign participation was called in when technology transfers were required. This recipe was successfully applied, as eloquently demonstrated by the work of Patrice Franko-Jones, in the defense industry.

This case is remarkable, not only because Brazil has managed to produce sophisticated weapons but mostly because it has suddenly emerged as an exporter of armaments. Franko-Jones's study provides a detailed account of the structure of the industry and of its major achievements. The description is certainly the strength of the book, but the work is so meticulous that the reader soon becomes exhausted by the accumulation and repetition of details, while the theoretical contribution remains limited. The de-

fense industry does not reveal much to someone who is acquainted with recent works on the Brazilian economy. Franko-Jones should have used this particular case study either to discuss in depth the Brazilian model of industrial development or to present a systematic comparison with defense industries in other underdeveloped nations.

The most original part of the study, chapter 6, shows how the state has contributed to the development of an indigenous technological capacity. Unfortunately again, the Sabato Triangle, presented to explain the relationship between the research and development center, the producer, and the final user, is dated. This could have been a golden opportunity to test Soete's hypothesis on technological leapfrogging or Freeman's national systems of innovation. A comparison between the Air Force Research Center (CTA) and CEPEL (Electricity Research Center) would have contributed to show the distinctive pattern of the Brazilian quest for technological autonomy. Also the technological justification of the infant industry argument could have been considered.

More disturbing is the fact that the early, and short-lived, success of the defense industry stopped suddenly in the late 1980s, and the firms involved soon dived into financial quagmire. In 1991, Embraer, the firm producing planes for both civilian and military uses, had an estimated debt of US$680 million, and 4000 workers were laid off between 1989 and 1991. Engesa, the tank producer, owes US$450 million and had to be saved from failure by Imbel, a state enterprise controlled by the armed forces (*Veja*, 8 April 1992). Brazil has been losing customers on foreign markets while local demand has collapsed due to a catastrophic economic situation. This reality projects a shadow of skepticism on the whole process of the protective nurturing of a defense sector; this skepticism is not dissipated by the last chapter, which tries to make sense of the crisis.

This book shows that, through the strategy of forced growth imposed by the Brazilian state, some real breakthroughs in advanced industrial production have been achieved at a considerable cost to society. The volume thereby unwillingly confirms that the creation of a defense industry may not be an adequate development strategy.

PHILIPPE FAUCHER

University of Brasilia
Brazil

Université de Montréal
Quebec
Canada

KEDOURIE, ELIE. *Politics in the Middle East.* Pp. 366. New York: Oxford University Press, 1992. $56.00.

This detailed study by the late, much published professor of politics emeritus of London has been a dozen years in the making according to an early note in this book. One can see why, for it contains a careful digest of political events from about 1800 onward in most of the modern nation-states, except Israel, that were once the Ottoman Empire. Arabic, Persian, and Turkish sources were consulted painstakingly to cross-reference the largely English books and journals of the end notes and suggested readings. Elie Kedourie produced for a readership of politicians, diplomats, and people of commerce a summary of the swirling currents of Middle Eastern politics and religion that helps to explain contemporary configurations of power in those lands. He did this not only with dispassion and clarity but in a distinguished English style.

To say Middle Eastern has been, by and large, to say Islamic ever since the Prophet's death in 632. An early chapter, "The Legacy," spells out the total coincidence of religious faith and political organization in an *umma*, or a people that was ethnically tribal, as were most of those it conquered. The Christians, Jews, and other religionists within this orbit formed no part of this people, each being a *milla*, or community of inferior status but protected and given a degree of autonomy by the *umma*. A paradox of the yielding of the *millet* system to nineteenth-century constitutional guarantees of equality was that the protected religious communities found themselves in a worse condition, since Muslims have no conception of faiths on a par with Islam politically or otherwise.

The oriental despotism that had preceded the spread of Islam shortly overtook it, making the caliphate, or succession to the Prophet by one in his place, a legatee of the system. Medieval jurists like Ghazzali confirmed the de facto state of affairs by describing the tyranny of a sultan or the interpretation of the *shari'a* by an unjust *imam* as the lesser of two evils. Order at least was assured, a better condition than anarchy. Two isolated verses in the Quran (III.159; LXV.6) would be cited seven and eight centuries later in support of consultation by a ruler as an authentic Muslim tradition, but the idea had little support in the sources or in practice.

The central chapters of the book trace the step-by-step efforts by reformers in what have come to be Egypt, Syria-Palestine, Turkey, Iraq, and Iran to impose European political settlements on people who continued to think in Quranic terms. The reforms were not only inspired from outside the culture—namely, from Europe—but were calculated to shore up the power of autocrats by a show of attention to the popular will. What came of them was chiefly a tangle of bureaucracy that outran anything known in Great Britain,

France, or Italy, where most of the "democratic" schemes originated. The failed attempts at constitutionalism under, first, the Young Ottomans (from 1867) and then the Young Turks (from 1897) are given a complete airing. So are the secularization of Turkey under Mustafa Kemal (Atatürk) and the subsequent reaction in modern Turkish politics. Egypt, Iraq, Syria (with Lebanon and Jordan), and Iran under the Pahlavis and Khomeini come in for their share of chronicle and analysis. The intervention of England and Russia is never absent from these accounts. Only Libya and the countries west of it are not examined and brought up to date in these pages.

Kedourie concluded his narrative "of one hundred and fifty years of tormented endeavor to discard the old ways" which had ceased to satisfy, leading only to the mixed fortunes of various constitutional and military governments, with the laconic comment, "The torment does not seem likely to end soon."

GERARD S. SLOYAN

Temple University
Philadelphia
Pennsylvania

KIM, BYOUNG-LO PHILO. *Two Koreas in Development: A Comparative Study of Principles and Strategies of Capitalist and Communist Third World Development.* Pp. x, 138. New Brunswick, NJ: Transaction, 1992. $32.95.

VOGEL, EZRA F. *The Four Little Dragons: The Spread of Industrialization in East Asia.* Pp. x, 138. Cambridge, MA: Harvard University Press, 1991. $16.95.

Byoung-Lo Philo Kim begins *Two Koreas in Development* ambitiously by arguing that a social scientific study of the two Koreas, one Communist (the North)

and one capitalist (the South), can illuminate the differences in these two developmental models. That is, because both Koreas share the same background, they make a perfect social scientific laboratory, since extraneous factors can be eliminated. Not surprisingly, dependent development in the capitalist south is shown to be preferable to autarchic development in the north, allowing Kim to conclude that, contrary to a great deal of academic writing, dependency need not be so bad after all. Kim then proceeds to compare the two Koreas along social, economic, political, and military lines.

This study originated as a doctoral dissertation at Rutgers University, and many of the features of a dissertation are retained. In fact, too many features are retained. For example, an extended treatment of other divided nations and various theories of development, certainly appropriate for a dissertation, are here but have little relation to the main body of the work. It also seems that there was little in the way of revision, for on p. 66 the term "this dissertation" appears. Moreover, there is an inordinate amount of time spent arguing over the reliability of different statistical measures, there is inconsistent romanization of Korean words, there is a great deal of repetition, and there is a need for a native speaker of English to proofread the manuscript. Much of the blame here must be shared by the publisher.

In short, while this book does highlight the differences between North and South Korea, it does not offer much that would not already be known by the reader who is familiar with Korea. Furthermore, questions that would intrigue a Korea specialist, such as how to explain the prevalence of military rule in the south versus civilian rule in the north, remain unanswered even though the author's approach implicitly promises answers to them.

Ezra Vogel's small book on the four little dragons—South Korea, Taiwan, Hong Kong, and Singapore—appears to derive from a series of lectures, for this is not an in-depth examination of the topic, nor is it an extensively researched work —the notes appear to be an afterthought. As a result, the introduction and the conclusion, which provide an overview, hold more interest than do the three short individual chapters that deal with these four units (Hong Kong and Singapore are treated together in a single chapter). Readers seeking a thorough treatment of the individual national experiences should look elsewhere.

That being said, Vogel, who has looked at this problem for a number of years, concludes that there is no single theory or factor that can explain the rapid rise of these economies, a refreshing view to a historian who appreciates multicausal explanations. Some of the factors he cites include a free and expanding trade system; abundant and cheap labor supplied by refugees, immigrants, and rural-to-urban migrants; labor-intensive export manufacturing; a strong state; U.S. aid; a sense of urgency; the availability of the Japanese model; a consumer desire for textiles and later electronics; the information revolution and technology sharing; and multinational corporations. He also tackles the problem of Confucianism head on, arguing that these states have jettisoned those aspects of Confucianism that hindered industrialization, such as an anticommercial bias, but have made use of those aspects that promoted industrialization, such as a meritocratic elite and the importance of the group. Some recent trends he notes that augur the end of this era include an end to cheap labor; protectionism; a divergence between national goals and industry goals; more vocal labor unions; and democratic development.

In sum, while this volume barely qualifies as a book in the usual sense, it does illustrate and isolate many of the relevant factors common to the industrial growth of these four economies.

WAYNE PATTERSON

St. Norbert College
DePere
Wisconsin

LARDY, NICHOLAS A. *Foreign Trade and Economic Reform in China, 1978-1990.* Pp. x, 197. New York: Cambridge University Press, 1992. No price.

In the 1980s, the Chinese economy was transformed from a closed and decrepit entity, a shadow of its grand socialist promise barely able to feed itself, into one of the world's fastest-growing and most dynamic trade powers. Nicholas Lardy explicates one aspect of this remarkable story, China's foreign trade policy and its relationship to domestic economic reform. He defines his study rather narrowly, eschewing not only political questions but also foreign investment issues. The limited scope is compensated, however, by the rich detail and subtle analysis of contemporary Chinese trade reform, making this one of the best available economic treatments of the topic.

In the opening chapter, Lardy sets the analytic stage with a concise outline of alternative trade regimes as understood by development economists and a brief description of China's rise as a trading state. From the economic literature, he draws the argument that export promotion is generally a better means of fostering economic growth than import substitution, a point that appears to be borne out in the coincidence of China's gradual trade liberalization and its rapid economic expansion in the 1980s. Lardy does not take this relationship as given, however; he makes it his research question: "To what extent has China's shift toward a more open trade policy contributed to the growth acceleration observed in the first decade of reform?"

The second chapter examines China's prereform trade policies. Here Lardy begins to explore foreign trade prices and foreign exchange policies, his main concerns. The closed trade regime of state socialism created a befuddling pricing problem: "When domestic prices diverge from international prices it is possible that a country whose international trade is in balance (i.e., the value of exports equals the value of imports, both measured at international prices) could experience either a surplus or a deficit measured in terms of domestic currency." This is the heart of the matter for Lardy. Throughout the book he demonstrates how financial losses or gains from trade arising from the disjunction of domestic and international prices are a driving force in Chinese policy debates, producing economic inefficiencies and bureaucratic politics. Foreign exchange problems are related to pricing practices in that, under state socialist import substitution, foreign exchange was strictly controlled in order to insulate domestic prices from international influences and the exchange rate was systematically overvalued to reduce the price of desired imports. Such were the difficulties Chinese leaders faced in 1978 as they set out to open China to the world economy.

China's efforts to reform the inefficiencies of state socialist trade policy are the focus of chapter 3, the longest section of the book. Lardy makes a number of ironic points, to the effect that liberalization initially brought increased use of trade licensing and tariffs, policies usually associated with protection. But the central themes are foreign exchange policies and trade prices. He does an excellent job detailing the stopgap efforts to decentralize the use of foreign exchange and to devalue the exchange rate, including one of the best accounts of the economics of foreign exchange swap centers that I have seen (pp. 57-66). He also identifies changes in pricing policy that mark a significant turning point in trade reform.

In chapter 4, Lardy assesses the efficiency of China's trade reforms. He is careful, arguing that not all the necessary data are available for a definite conclusion, but he points out that financial problems in the early 1980s suggest that more extensive domestic price deregulation was needed to maximize gains from trade. He picks up on this theme in the fifth, and final, chapter, holding that further improvements in the efficiency of foreign trade rely upon domestic economic liberalization. More than price reform is needed, in his view; labor and capital markets must be developed, and macroeconomic forces better managed. His illustration of these points in a comparison of Shanghai and Guangzhou provides telling insights into a keen economic rivalry.

By way of conclusion, Lardy returns to his initial question and answers in the affirmative: China's opening to the world economy has contributed significantly to domestic economic growth. While reiterating the further efficiencies that could be attained, he asserts that China's approach to economic reform has been more successful than that of the Soviet Union and Eastern Europe. China's "gradual but sustained development of markets" has produced superior economic results compared with the "big bang" of rapid adjustment attempted by other reforming socialist states. He may be right. But before China is made a model for others to emulate, the political costs, not a part of Lardy's masterful economic study, must be weighed.

GEORGE T. CRANE

Williams College
Williamstown
Massachusetts

SCHWARTZ, STUART B. *Slaves, Peasants, and Rebels: Reconsidering Brazilian Slavery*. Pp. xiv, 174. Champaign: University of Illinois Press, 1992. $34.95.

Stuart Schwartz, professor of history at the University of Minnesota, is author of the major work *Sugar Plantations in the Formation of Brazilian Society, Bahia, 1550-1835* (New York: Cambridge University Press, 1986) and one of the leading scholars of Latin American and Brazilian history. In *Slaves, Peasants, and Rebels*, he presents five essays reconsidering aspects of slavery and the slave society in Brazil. Based upon extensive primary research, as well as deep knowledge of the secondary literature in Brazil as well as on slavery in the United States, these essays were written primarily within the past several years, with occasional revisions and enlarging based upon more recent materials. As are all recent scholars of slavery everywhere, Schwartz is sensitive to "the role of slaves in shaping their own lives and in the construction and operation of the Brazilian slave system," while aware of "the pervasive and pernicious nature of slavery as a social and economic system." This meant that while "slaves were independent historical actors able to mold their own destiny at will, masters too were limited, sometimes, by the actions and attitudes of slaves."

Schwartz's essays are able to balance these concerns with masters and slaves in an excellent manner, demonstrating the complexities of the ongoing slave systems as well as their variations over time and space. After an introductory essay reviewing the major recent writings on slavery in Brazil, the next four essays deal with specific subjects, including the nature of slave labor, emphasizing the adaptive capabilities of the slave economy and the interaction of slaves and masters in setting work routines; the nature of slave resistance, presenting interesting information on Palmares and other of the large *quilombos* (fugitive communities); and godparentage patterns among slaves, using baptism records as a guide to understanding the slave communities. There is also a key essay relating the plantation system to foodstuff production by small, peasant producers, which provides useful material for describing Brazilian social and political history, as well as directing attention to a similar set of connections in other slave and free-labor economies that have recently been underplayed.

While the essays deal exclusively with Brazilian topics, a strength is that Schwartz is also able to draw upon the questions and analysis of recent research on slavery in the United States, thus providing for very useful comparisons and contrasts that will make this book important to a wider audience. This volume will also be of interest to all concerned with the human interactions under nonfree—as well as free—labor systems and those involved with the historical study of slavery and slave societies.

STANLEY L. ENGERMAN

University of Rochester
New York

TERRILL, ROSS. *China in Our Time: The Epic Saga of the People's Republic, from the Communist Victory to Tiananmen Square and Beyond*. Pp. 366. New York: Simon & Schuster, 1992. $25.00.

In this book, interesting vignettes outnumber well-argued interpretations of major events, making the volume a good read for generalists eager to taste life in the People's Republic and for specialists ever alert for colorful and entertaining stories.

Author of five earlier well-received books on China, Ross Terrill first visited there in 1964, two years ahead of the Cultural Revolution, and as an Australian citizen eight years before Nixon's visit opened the door for Americans. He returned almost two dozen times, once while Henry Kissinger stole into China in 1971 to negotiate the Nixon breakthrough and again in 1989, arriving on the very eve of the Tiananmen massacre.

Not only because Terrill enjoyed go-between status in Chinese eyes and thus peripherally participated in key events himself but also because he made it a regular practice to interview other participants, his accounts are more personal than most. For example, he recalls an evening at the cinema in 1973, viewing a documentary: "Deng [Xiaoping] appeared clumping toward the camera, and the packed cinema erupted in 'oohs' and 'ahs.' . . . They did not cheer him—the habit of six years was not cast aside in one moment—but the excitement at his return was palpable." That is a priceless eyewitness account that speaks volumes.

Terrill's portrait of the status of the foreign guest trying to probe China is among the best in the literature. "The term 'friend' was used as a suction pump designed to draw off from the visitor all juices of objectivity." Overhosting, vagueness, allegory, and even ideology, more than silence or outright falsehood, were the familiar retreats of hosts not wishing to pursue a subject candidly. "The word 'revisionism' was the linguistic whore of Communist history; it meant everything and it meant nothing."

In many passages, new color is added to the well-known. Kissinger, presented, unsurprisingly, as more of a realist than a man overwrought by moral postures, would ask Terrill, "What should we talk to the Chinese about?" instead of the more usual question presented, "When

are the Chinese going to become worthy of our recognizing them?"

Foreign Ministry mandarin Zhou Nan, in Terrill's account, took China's profound naïveté about American politics at the time of the Nixon breakthrough to a new level. Expressing disbelief that Daniel Ellsberg had acted alone in releasing the Pentagon Papers, he asked, "Is it the Morgans who are behind him? Or the Rockefellers?"

On the true toll of official violence in June 1989, Terrill writes of a teacher who could not recover the body of his son, shot near Tiananmen Square on 4 June, until he certified in writing that the death was due to natural causes; of Friendship Hospital's destruction of many records of its treatment of the wounded to impede later police investigation of democracy-movement participants; and of a student treated by the Red Cross that day for a bullet wound to the stomach whose medical record makes no mention of a bullet wound. Official accounts of the Tiananmen incident may accurately reflect the records, but the records hardly mirror events.

GORDON BENNETT

University of Texas
Austin

EUROPE

GABRIEL, RICHARD A. and KAREN S. METZ. *From Sumer to Rome: The Military Capabilities of Ancient Armies.* Pp. xxi, 182. Westport, CT: Greenwood Press, 1991. $45.00.

BAUMGARTNER, FREDERIC J. *From Spear to Flintlock: A History of War in Europe and the Middle East to the French Revolution.* Pp. xii, 355. New York: Praeger, 1991. $45.00.

Set side by side, these two books would offer any scholar concerned with the historical evolution of war and politics a great deal of information and a number of theoretical suggestions.

Of the two books, *From Sumer to Rome* is the more based on original sources, blending insights from anthropology and written history, delving into issues of technology, strategy, medicine, and even psychiatry. Perhaps this is because there were fewer existing works attempting to sort out myth from reality on the warfare of the Egyptians, Persians, and Greeks. While the product is a shorter book, it still comes across as the more ambitious academic undertaking. The study delves at times into the macroscopic overall relevance of military developments, but it includes much more information—often in quite surprising detail for the early period it covers—than can be tied to any general theory. The book is a little less chronological than it might be, if the reader is to sort out trends and deterministic patterns, and after the first two chapters, it is broken into functional chapters on weapons, death and wounds, and medical care.

While the first study ends with the quite remarkable development of discipline achieved in the Roman Legion, *From Spear to Flintlock* offers a synthesis, in effect, of a great many of the works that have been written on all of Western warfare up to the French Revolution. Included in more detail here are capsule descriptions of major wars and military campaigns, and of many of the major battles, interspersed with a host of references to changes in the technology and the tactics.

Neither of these books can be accused of reducing or oversimplifying all of the military trends surveyed into some single theme or single variable. This makes the books more inclusive as sources and stimuli for any other scholars—the bibliographies in each of the books would themselves be of the greatest value—but comes at the price of leaving dangling many of the threads of possible causal connection between war and politics.

A political scientist reading either of these volumes may thus come away a trifle disappointed that no grander theory of state building or international regime development is brought to the surface in these surveys. Yet the political, economic, and social trends are definitely outlined in both of these works, side by side with the trends in military practice.

GEORGE H. QUESTER

University of Maryland
College Park

TILLY, LOUISE A. *Politics and Class in Milan, 1881-1901*. Pp. xii, 355. New York: Oxford University Press, 1992. $49.95.

Louise Tilly rightly observes that Karl Marx's views on working-class formation long dominated studies of the Italian workers' movement. A logical progression from industrialization and proletarianization to class consciousness and the political organization of Italian proletarians has thus been the theoretical mainspring of such scholarship. The studies of more intellectually supple scholars after 1945, however, undermined the Marxist assumption that the industrial transformation of Italy preceded the founding of the Socialist Party. Immiserization and the capitalist-induced disintegration of the peasantry more powerfully shaped the formation of the Italian working class than did structural changes in the economy.

Tilly argues, however, that both Marxist and non-Marxist studies of the Italian working-class movement are similarly flawed. Though conceptualized at the national level, they are too heavily dependent on unsystematic data from one place or industry to make a case for the entire country. They also feature narrowly linear and mechanistic explanations of the process of working-class formation. She therefore offers her study of workers' experience in Milan during the two decades before 1900 as a corrective. She also wants to make the important points that the process of industrialization is inherently regional in nature and that working-class formation in pre-1900 Italy was a contingent and ongoing political process in which the actions of strategically placed individuals and groups served as "the engine of change, not the unfolding of a logic inherent in economic change."

Tilly's monograph is an important contribution to Italian labor history. Its chapters on capital and labor movements in Lombardy, conditions of life and work, and Milanese workers' institutions and collective action constitute the most coherent and fully developed picture of working-class experience that we have for any Italian region. Yet it has the same shortcomings that its author attributes to earlier studies of the Italian working-class movement. Focused on Milan—the most important city in the early process of Italian industrialization—its conceptual point of view is inevitably national. Its explanatory perspective, moreover, is linear since it tells the story of Milanese working-class formation as a progression from mutual aid societies, resistance leagues, and chambers of labor to the successive creation and history of the Italian Workers' and Socialist parties after 1875. Finally, Tilly has rigidly organized her analysis according to Ira Katznelson's well-known notion of a fourfold layering of class formation. The result is a book no less "mechanistic" than earlier Marxist-oriented studies that Tilly reproaches for being uncritically dependent on the abstract theories of the man from Trier.

JACK E. REECE

University of Pennsylvania
Philadelphia

VAN OUDENAREN, JOHN. *Détente in Europe: The Soviet Union and the West since 1953.* Pp. xi, 490. Durham, NC: Duke University Press, 1991. $60.00. Paperbound, $29.95.

Researched with the support of the Kennan Institute for Advanced Russian Studies and the RAND Corporation, John Van Oudenaren's *Détente in Europe* is a detailed study of the process of détente between the Soviet Union and the West, which he believes started not in 1949, as Marshall Shulman has contended, but in 1953. Concluding in 1990 with the reunification of Germany, it comprises a discussion of Soviet political leaders from Stalin to Gorbachev; European, Soviet, and international institutions; Soviet attitudes toward the European Economic Community; the art and politics of diplomacy; the practice of summitry; procedural disputes; the role of parliaments, trade unions, peace movements, religious organizations (Protestant, Catholic, and Orthodox), and Soviet-European and Soviet-American cultural contacts in furthering the process; human rights issues; arms control negotiations and agreements and disagreements; the relationship between the Soviet and the world capitalist economies; and Gorbachev's desire to go "beyond détente" as an incentive to "new thinking" and the idea of a "common European home."

Van Oudenaren does attempt to explain how domestic affairs reflect upon and are reflected in international relations. Curiously, however, he neglects the role of American, Soviet, French, and other Jews in both retarding and promoting détente. On the other hand, the book is excellent on the details of détente. That also may be its chief defect. Striving for balance and objectivity, Van Oudenaren explains actions and events in terms of immediate circumstances and consequences. As a result, the reader may be unable to ascertain which causes were more important in the ultimate undoing of the Soviet Union.

The answer to that question may lie hidden in the chapter on economics. It appears to me that the Soviet Union could not create an open and civil society—a free flow of goods and information within the Soviet Union—without a free flow of goods and information from the world economy to the Soviet Union. Such a flow did not and could not exist because of the Cold War and because the world market economy was in fact a capitalist political economy. Unable to obtain access to much technological and scientific information, deprived of most-favored-nation treatment in its trade with the United States, frustrated in its efforts to establish a high-capacity petroleum pipeline by Japanese, U.S., and North Atlantic Treaty Organization embargoes on the sale of large-diameter pipe, discriminated against by the European Economic Community and the European Free Trade Association, the Soviet Union was unable to profit from membership in the world economy without first undoing the structures that it had put in place in order to function as a closed economy.

TRAIAN STOIANOVICH

Rutgers University
New Brunswick
New Jersey

UNITED STATES

BAHRE, CONRAD J. *A Legacy of Change: Historic Human Impact on* *Vegetation of the Arizona Borderlands.* Pp. xviii, 231. Tucson: University of Arizona Press, 1991. $29.95.

In our attempts to understand global environmental change, natural scientists often underestimate the potential role of human impacts. In a challenge to conventional climatic explanations, geographer Conrad Bahre argues that historical vegetation change in the American West resulted primarily from human exploitation. Bahre's plea is well-taken. While Western scientists may be comfortable ascribing widespread vegetation alterations in other parts of the world—desertification in the African Sahel and the Middle East—to human land use, we rarely apply these same explanations to changes in our own backyard.

Dramatic changes in the vegetation of southeastern Arizona over the last 120 years include destruction of riparian habitats, decreased grass cover, and expansion of woody shrubs into rangelands. Following the subjugation of the Apache, mineral discoveries, and the completion of the Southern Pacific Railroad came a vast influx of Anglo-American settlers in the 1870s and 1880s. Rangelands were overgrazed, fires were suppressed, and massive amounts of wood were cut for fuel and construction. By the early 1900s, much of the land near these settlements had been ruined.

Much of our knowledge of historical vegetation comes from photographs taken around the turn of the century. Bahre uses repeat photographs, as well as early travelers' accounts and surveyors' notes, to document vegetation change. He argues convincingly that much of Arizona's "pristine" vegetation already had been impacted heavily prior to the initial photographs.

A period of extreme drought in the early 1890s—in which 50-70 percent of southern Arizona's livestock died—has led researchers to suggest that climate, or climatic change combined with overgrazing and fire suppression, created an environment that favored increases in woody plants and lowered the water table to initiate stream incision and degradation of riparian vegetation.

Much of Bahre's study is a reinterpretation of the now-classic study of vegetation dynamics by J. R. Hastings and R. M. Turner, *The Changing Mile* (Tucson: University of Arizona Press, 1965). Hastings and Turner argue that not only are xerophytic shrubs invading grasslands, but oak woodlands also have retreated upslope. Both of these shifts are explained best by an increasingly arid climate. Bahre suggests that anthropogenic causes explain the invasion of woody scrub best, and he argues that there is no evidence for a directional shift of oak woodlands. I urge readers to return to the original photographs in Hastings and Turner's book and decide for themselves. Bahre's book will not put the debate to rest, but it will force students of historic vegetation change to reassess the significance of human intervention.

PATRICIA FALL

Arizona State University
Tempe

FJELLMAN, STEPHEN M. *Vinyl Leaves: Walt Disney World and America.* Pp. xvii, 492. Boulder, CO: Westview Press, 1992. $45.00. Paperbound, $18.95.

To some degree it inverts the normal positioning of cart and horse for academic reviews to begin with personal comments. But Fjellman's discussion of the Disney simulacrum of America is so self-consciously idiomatic, so replete with borrowings from a multitude of others, and so cynically fascinated—admiring while condescending—with the Disney concept that I necessarily remark the point.

Fjellman examines Walt Disney World (which he calls "WDW"—he is fond of acronyms) of Orlando, Florida, and the "commodified" late-twentieth-century United States that gives WDW a singular and representational authentication. His America is "postmodern" and is the end product of consumer-goods-oriented mass production, aided by scientifically designed advertising and distorted history—or, as he often calls it, "Distory," the Disney version of history. The vinyl leaves realistically adorn an artificial tree in WDW, but they are an obvious paradigm. He is fond of jargon, infrequently defined and occasionally impenetrably dense except to inducted specialists or devotees. For Fjellman, "Disney's task . . . is deeply metaphysical: it is to capture time and thus annihilate it, by seducing its audience into willing complicity with corporate authority and control. Let Exxon and AT&T do it, and all will be well." Pseudo education and quasi fiction, disguised as entertainment, are placed at the service of ideology, express or implied.

The author spends many chapters guiding the reader through an extraordinarily detailed excursion of WDW. He admits to being captivated by the technical, philosophical, and artistic skills that have produced this recreational park of many thousand acres. For me, the absence of any maps or other visual material is an obvious weakness; wordy descriptions, using a limited and somewhat trite vocabulary, become redundant. Fjellman occasionally assumes others' familiarity with his own experiential or emotional stereotypes, to the extent that the reader gets the impression he is being nudged in the ribs over a not clearly defined joke. There are too many flatly ex cathedra judgments without evident data referents. Similarly, there is a surprising absence of referents about the size of spaces or costs of services, surprising since the writer is impressed by numbers. The physical extent of WDW, described late in the book, comes late for the reader who has not experienced the place.

At the same time, making intensive and extended use of the work of other writers—there are scores of seemingly pointless page citations—Fjellman challenges ethically and morally the underlying commercial and mercenary conception of the park. This mixture of ideas and sources is so generously and amorphously spread throughout the book that I repeatedly wondered where the author's own intellectual boundaries fell.

Walt Disney and all his works take a real beating in this volume. Fjellman has given readers an intensively mined bibliography of much of a large literature of this genre. Disney's success at placing enormous sums and much high technology at the service of intensely ideological capitalism and nationalism is recorded redundantly. If this be the point of the book, the book is a success. Fjellman's intent appears to have been to depict America as the self-imposing world model of glitz; will this be reinforced by the Disneylands in Japan and France?

PHILIP B. TAYLOR, JR.

University of Houston
Texas

GIBSON, MARTHA LIEBLER. *Weapons of Influence: The Legislative Veto, American Foreign Policy, and the Irony of Reform*. Pp. xi, 188. Boulder, CO: Westview Press, 1992. $38.50.

For fifty years, the legislative veto helped to moderate the inevitable conflict between the executive and legislative branches of the American government. It enabled the Congress to exercise a higher degree of control over executive actions, while giving the President more latitude in the execution of policy. In 1983, however, in the case of *Immigration and Naturalization Service v. Chadha*, the Supreme Court ruled that the legislative veto was unconstitutional.

In one of the best studies of the consequences of this decision, especially in foreign policymaking, Martha Liebler Gibson examines the pros and cons of the decision, within the broader context of executive-legislative relations, and concludes that on the whole it has contributed to the exacerbation of conflictual relations. In the *Chadha* case, she argues, "the Court effectively used *legal* means to nullify one of the most important *political* accommodations between Congress and the executive in the twentieth century." "The ruling . . . changed the structural context of congressional-executive interaction, transforming it from one of grudging yet effective cooperation into one marked by increasingly rigid and inflexible conflict." But she also demonstrates, through a series of four case studies, that the impact of the *Chadha* decision varied greatly in different issue areas.

The case studies, constituting more than half of the book, deal with major aspects of U.S. foreign policy in which the conflict between the President and the Congress was particularly obvious. The issues are (1) U.S. arms sales to the Middle East, (2) most-favored-nation trade status, (3) nuclear nonproliferation policy, and (4) the War Powers Resolution of 1973. In the first case—a "strategic-salient issue"—the *Chadha* decision, in Gibson's judgment, "seriously undermined the basis for cooperation between the president and Congress over arms sales to the Middle East," whereas in the case of the War Powers Resolution, "the loss of the legislative veto has had no practical impact on congressional-executive relations in foreign policy making." Incidentally, the four case studies may be recommended to anyone who is interested in concise and well-crafted analyses of four major issues in post-World War II American foreign policy.

Unfortunately, the focus on the impact of the *Chadha* decision on foreign policy, and the volume's high price, will greatly limit the distribution of this volume. It deserves a wider readership than it will probably receive.

NORMAN D. PALMER

University of Pennsylvania
Philadelphia

JENSEN, JOAN M. *Army Surveillance in America, 1775-1980*. Pp. ix, 325. New Haven, CT: Yale University Press, 1991. $29.95.

During the 1960s, many antiwar activists suspected—or hoped—that the Army was spying on them. Joan Jensen traces the growing role of the Army in internal security from the Revolution to 1980. Most of her book is devoted to the period of growing acceptance of Army surveillance—the last decade of the nineteenth century and the first two decades of the twentieth century. In her account, Jensen, a professor of history at New Mexico State University, displays a solid grasp of the various manuscript collections as well as the relevant secondary literature.

Throughout the nineteenth century, civilian and military authorities displayed an ambivalent, even hostile, attitude toward military surveillance of the civilian population. Labor unrest in the latter part of the century began to give ammunition to those who wished to use the military to spy on Americans. It was, however, the Cuban insurrection and the American reaction to it that led to an expansion of the Army's role in rooting out spies, or alleged spies. Jensen uses the career of Andrew Rowan as a case study to illustrate changing attitudes at the turn of the century and immediately beyond. Although Rowan celebrated his own exploits as a spy extraordinaire, the government and the American people were initially less certain of the validity of his exploits. But in 1922 Rowan received the Distinguished Service Cross for his efforts in Cuba, symbolic of an official change in attitude toward spying.

It was Ralph Van Deman who achieved the first effective internal security machinery for the Army. Spurred on by the Philippine insurrection, trouble on the Mexican border, fear of organized labor at home, and the pressures emanating from the war in Europe, the War Department gave in to those who thought it necessary to examine the conduct of their fellow citizens. The perceived need to safeguard industrial production during World War I led to a scheme of volunteers recruited to spy on their fellow workers. Many of the recruits were detectives on furlough from firms that provided antilabor detectives to industrial concerns. The attitudes they brought with them influenced the military, and gradually the Army, swayed by fears of wartime disloyalty, came to suspect the motives of most civilians. Van Deman played a crucial role in organizing the various surveillance programs. During World War I and the 1920s, the Army began to wholeheartedly accept a more antagonistic role toward the civilian population. From the 1920s through the 1970s, the Army continued and expanded its surveillance of suspected Americans. During World War II, and especially during the Cold War, both the Army and many civilians came to accept the necessity of continued surveillance of American citizens.

Dating from the founding, Congress had accepted a need for military surveillance of the civilian population grudgingly. In 1878, for example, Congress passed the Posse Comitatus Act, which was designed to limit military involvement in labor disputes. Other legislation followed, but, dating from the early twentieth century, Congress was unable for many years to curtail the growing military role in domestic affairs.

Jensen's account of the growth of the Army's program of domestic spying is a complete one. The reader is left with a gnawing feeling that there is more to the story, however. What of the civilian response? Was it inevitable that the Army would increase its surveillance efforts as she seems to imply? Answering such questions might be the subject of a different book, but they are an important part of the relationship of the military to American society. They are also an important part of explaining how far government should go in delving into the conduct and views of American citizens.

JOHN M. THEILMANN

Converse College
Spartanburg
South Carolina

LICHT, WALTER. *Getting Work: Philadelphia, 1840-1950*. Pp. xiii, 317. Cambridge, MA: Harvard University Press, 1992. $39.95.

This study of job-seeking and hiring practices in Philadelphia is a comprehensive account based on fresh research that makes a major contribution to American urban and labor history. Walter Licht, professor of history at the University of Pennsylvania, has provided a labor study of remarkable scope and depth.

As demonstrated here, the process of getting a job in industrial Philadelphia has been anything but simple. Labor supply and demand, available jobs, personal initiative, questions of skill and training, unions, schools, agencies, and government regulation have influenced hiring opportunities. At the end of his study, Licht concludes that one remedy for present-day employment problems is that of "reviving the institution of apprentice-

ship on a massive scale." But scarcely any assertion here escapes qualification. Citing the importance of "context, time, and place," Licht writes that in the employment experience, "the structural weighs more heavily than the personal and institutional."

In almost every phase of this study, Licht separates out the particular experiences of African American and German American workers in Philadelphia. African Americans faced the greatest obstacles in getting work. Racism, he argues, "made the black experience in Philadelphia extraordinary," and the state had a special impact on employment in efforts to end discrimination. German Americans demonstrated a greater personal agency in securing employment. They engaged in apprenticeship, and their older members became a dominant part of the skilled trades. Discussion of these groups is illustrative of Licht's ethnic and cultural approach.

The chapter on initial employment, "Entering the World of Work," is especially engaging. Here we find that "the socioeconomic standing of the family" proved to be the greatest determinant of a young person's success as a worker or student. Licht makes particular use of the studies of Philadelphia workers by Gladys Palmer, including her 1936 Works Progress Administration survey, held in the Urban Archives at Temple University. The separate chapters on schools, agencies, firms, the state, and losing work include analyses that rest on a strong statistical base.

Greater attention is given to twentieth-century labor trends than to those of the nineteenth century, but Licht's study is so broad that it offers insights into many varied elements of Philadelphia's business and industrial development. Whether Philadelphia's labor history may be more unusual, or more typical of a national pattern, this book should prove an invaluable resource for the history of getting work in an American industrial city.

RONALD E. SHAW

Miami University
Oxford
Ohio

LINK, ARTHUR S. et al., eds. *The Papers of Woodrow Wilson*. Vol. 66. Pp. xxiv, 576. Princeton, NJ: Princeton University Press, 1992. $57.50.

LINK, ARTHUR S. et al., eds. *The Papers of Woodrow Wilson*. Vol. 67. Pp. xxvi, 650. Princeton, NJ: Princeton University Press, 1992. $57.50.

As this series moves toward a close, it continues faithful to its mission of presenting Wilson whole. Volume 66 cov the year 1920 from August to Deceml 23; the next volume picks up the Dece ber tale and continues to 7 April 1922. This is less slow and deliberate than before but still substantial in its own right. It is relevant to recall how firmly the editors have held to their standards of clarity and form. Individuals are identified almost beyond need. Middle names and dates of birth and death, when available, are set down for the use of future scholars working on the Wilson presidency and life.

The highlight of the present volumes is the evidence of Wilson's full return to mental stability. As debilitating as was his loss of physical strength and energy, following his physical and partly mental collapse due to speech making across the country in behalf of his League of Nations panacea for war, for a while scholars as well as contemporaries had to notice some confusion in his thinking and memory. This shocked some of his visitors, such as Ray Stannard Baker and his physician, Dr. Grayson. They were forced to main-

tain Wilson's fantasy of running for a third term in 1920, despite the argument that serving would hasten his death.

Wilson not only reorganized his aides —Cabinet members, wife, secretary, and others—into a smooth-running assembly but, incredibly, contemplated running for the presidency in 1924.

Mrs. Wilson emerged not as a *grise éminente* to a dependent Wilson. She was a loving spouse intent on serving her husband's wants. Joseph Tumulty, ever faithful, and, John Randolph Bolling, Wilson's brother-in-law, turned significant matters requiring answers over to such worthies as Newton D. Baker, Bainbridge Colby, Louis D. Brandeis, and George Creel, the latter handling details involving publishers of Wilson's own writings.

With his old skill, Wilson coped not only with momentous matters involving sible war with Mexico and explosive tters in the Balkans and the Soviet ion. He also gave personal attention to tne details of the house he had planned to have built for his and his wife's retirement. He even recalled "several years back" paying a particular craftsman for furniture made "in the mission style." The furniture maker had himself forgotten all about it.

Wilson was liable to impatience. He tried to find a law that would keep motorists from passing him, the President, on the road in Washington during his precious auto rides. He called Colonel Harvey, who had begun Wilson's rise to the presidency but was now a Republican, a "skunk," and Herbert Hoover "no friend." Department of Justice head A. M. Palmer had been long thought responsible for Eugene V. Debs's lengthy incarceration for treason during wartime. But there is here evidence that, the war being over, Palmer recommended release of Debs.

Wilson's deep commitment to the League of Nations divided all the outside world into those following Wilson and those opposed. Henry Cabot Lodge, leading the opposition and following tradition, joined those in Congress waiting on the President at the opening of Congress. Wilson, who found Lodge's presence an "affront," elaborately explained to his visitors that he could not, because of illness, shake their hands as in the past—all to avoid shaking Lodge's.

During these years, Colonel House could not have an audience with Wilson, not because he was debarred from the White House by Wilson's wife but because Wilson now saw House as having taken too much upon himself during the Peace Conference, but then without reproof by Wilson. Also during this time, Wilson actually acquired admission to the District of Columbia bar. He and Colby opened law offices in Washington and New York as Wilson & Colby. As reported in the press, the two saw several potential clients. Wilson considered delivering his State of the Union Address in person but accepted Dr. Grayson's negative judgment.

Meanwhile, Wilson had moved into his soon famous S Street home, before which congregated an enormous crowd, whom he offered gestures of appreciation. He attended Cabinet meetings, which discussed such large topics as Poland's future. He also attended programs at a local theater and was cordially noticed by the public as he entered with a cane but without other support.

His presidency ended, Wilson had a sense of being isolated. He had R. S. Baker in his house researching what would be Baker's documented account of the Peace Conference. Wilson was well aware that the major nations in the League of Nations were pursuing national goals rather than those that placed world peace at the forefront. But though he was continuously hailed as a savior and martyr by his followers, one has to go beyond these distinguished volumes to remember that the era was the 1920s and the Harding Administration.

LOUIS FILLER

The Belfry
Ovid
Michigan

SORAUF, FRANK J. *Inside Campaign Finance: Myths and Realities.* Pp. x, 274. New Haven, CT: Yale University Press, 1992. $27.50.

This self-consciously revisionist study of the way election campaigns are funded in the United States refutes most conventional wisdom on the subject. Contrary to the assertions of most high-minded people, journalists, and many members of Congress, Frank J. Sorauf concludes, after careful study of the records of the Federal Election Commission, that there is little if any relationship between private giving to candidates for office and the public activities of elected officials. He dismisses such slogans as "the best Congress money can buy" as only the most recent, failed, effort by descendants of the Progressive tradition to take the politicking out of government. His exhaustive research also reveals the surprising conclusion that little relationship exists between the frantic efforts of candidates and officeholders to raise money and the propensity of donors to give. Setting campaign finance in a historical perspective, Sorauf notes that Americans like to give money to political candidates —it offers them a vicarious, and sometimes real, sense of participation in the affairs of the state. He argues that substituting public finance for private funding might have the unintended consequence of further alienating some people —those who like to donate to candidates —from a political system that many believe is already badly out of touch with popular desires.

So far so good. As a study of the ways donations have, or have not, affected elections, legislation, or executive behavior, *Inside Campaign Finance* provides a bracing breeze of realism to an overheated debate. The discussion of campaign finance, however, needs to go further. The current unhappiness with the supposedly baleful role of money in American politics is a symptom of much larger dissatisfaction with the apparent breakdown of legitimate government. A longer book with a broader perspective might have looked at three other questions. First, some of the loudest complaints about campaign finance have come from elected officials themselves. Many claim to find it a degrading and time-consuming experience constantly to shake the tree for money. While fundraising may not affect lawmakers' votes, it does seem to alter the way they spend their time. Does that matter? Next, Sorauf has performed a good service exploding what he characterizes as myths about the harmful effects of the present system. It would have been useful to read his explanation of why this conventional wisdom became so widespread. Finally, Sorauf's informed speculation about why the issue of campaign finance came to be seen as a metaphor for what is wrong with American government would have improved an already good book.

ROBERT D. SCHULZINGER

University of Colorado
Boulder

STEIN, STEPHEN J. *The Shaker Experience in America: A History of the United Society of Believers.* Pp. xvii, 554. New Haven, CT: Yale University Press, 1992. $40.00.

Stephen J. Stein's critical history of the United Society of Believers—the Shakers—offers a model denominational history that is usable and enlightening for all students of American culture. Stein traces the Shakers from their first ill-recorded appearance in the British North American colonies on the eve of revolution to their equally intriguing position in contemporary America, poised between extinction and new directions. Stein's treatment has several outstanding strengths: his prodigious research, his analysis of major phases of Shaker history in relation to a broader U.S. history, and his insistent distinction between myths about Shakerism and Shaker realities.

In this last aspect particularly, Stein makes a distinguished contribution. While picking up the theme of insider-outsider relations that is threaded through the book, part 5—on the "rebirth" of Shakerism, 1948 to the present—might stand alone as a fascinating, and, in places, astringent, analysis of the cultural strains that have contributed to an often profit-generating fascination with a selective vision, or set of visions, of the Shakers. Prosperous Americans have opened their checkbooks ever wider for authentic Shaker furniture—Oprah Winfrey paid a record-breaking $220,000 for one piece. Householders of more modest means have bought or assembled reproductions. Stein offers shaded portraits of several of the middlemen who have profited handsomely from their focused appreciation of Shakerism. From beginning to end, Stein explodes simplifying images and ideas of Shakerism, narrating, for example, some of the Shakers' extensive engagements with the speculative economy of the Gilded Age. Just a little less satisfying is Stein's account of the evolution of the Shakers' complex theology; to be fair, the reader may finally feel somewhat at a loss as to what the Shakers stand for religiously and ideologically because the Shaker faith is and has been fluid and nonmonolithic.

To what extent has the handful of remaining Shakers become what other Americans would have them be? Stein leaves us finally aware of our own nostalgia for a fixed Shakerism that never was; in so doing, he helps us to understand that despite the mortality of the last covenanted members of the society, there are a number of futures possible for Shakerism—its adherents and institutions, its ideologies, and its myths.

MINA CARSON

Oregon State University
Corvallis

SOCIOLOGY

LÓPEZ, GERALD P. *Rebellious Lawyering: One Chicano's Vision of Progressive Law Practice.* Pp. ix, 433. Boulder, CO: Westview Press, 1992. $48.50. Paperbound, $16.95.

In *Rebellious Lawyering*, Gerald P. López presents his vision of how public interest law should be practiced. He believes that "lawyering itself [has] to be remade as part of any effort to transform the world."

López contends that most public interest lawyers unintentionally perpetuate the system that they fight against because of the way they practice law. Legal training encourages a regnant view of lawyering that permeates our culture. Lawyers control all efforts to solve the legal problems presented to them and depend primarily on litigation and other traditional legal actions as ways to solve these problems. They are viewed as the critical actors in any legal problem, who deserve deference because of their special knowledge.

As an alternative, López offers his idea of "rebellious lawyering," a practice that challenges the regnant view by working with—as opposed to for—the people in the community, collaborating with other organizations active in social struggle, educating clients to help themselves in problem solving, and allowing oneself to be educated by those within the community. This view of lawyering "demands that lawyers (and those with whom they work) nurture sensibilities and skills compatible with a collective fight for social change."

Most of this book explains how the idea of rebellious lawyering would work in practice. López offers fictional accounts of the operation of a nonprofit community law office, a small for-profit office, and of persons involved in lay lawyering and community organizing. Through the construction of imaginary office memos, journal entries, and a position paper on community organizing, he explores the ways in which lawyers and others interested in social change can practice rebellious lawyering. These stories give life to the theory that begins the book.

This book will be found wanting by those who assign legitimacy to a work according to the extent to which it relies on citation of scholarly sources. Missing is the extensive citation found in most legal writing. While there is an impressive bibliography on progressive lawyering, the text itself is written in an informal, narrative style. This format supports López's goals of challenging orthodox thinking and reaching an audience of community activists as well as lawyers.

Rebellious Lawyering is a provocative book that challenges public interest lawyers to alter the way they think about themselves and their work. It should be of interest to all who are interested in the law and social change.

KATY J. HARRIGER

Wake Forest University
Winston-Salem
North Carolina

MARCUS, GEORGE with PETER HALL. *Lives in Trust: The Fortunes of Dynastic Families in Late Twentieth-Century America.* Pp. ix, 380. Boulder, CO: Westview Press, 1992. $45.95. Paperbound, $16.95.

Have inherited wealth and the creation of descendant upper-class families given rise to an economic elite that shapes social and economic policy in twentieth-century America? Social scientists have debated whether America is a class society, whether power derives from wealth or organization, and whether the source of power is primarily economic or political. The divisions over these issues underpin the pluralist and elitist interpretations of American politics and economy. Adopting a cultural and familial approach, George Marcus and Peter Hall propose a different model of dynastic families. According to their theory, external factors—the role of trustees in addressing inheritance and tax laws and the public interest in information about prominent wealthy families—have shaped descendant generations' attitudes toward their family. The creation of dynastic families, Marcus and Hall posit, is essentially a cultural development and not principally economic or based on class values. Not their wealth alone but a shared family experience deriving from their prominence as descendants of wealthy families led to the phenomenon of dynastic families. While the Marcus-Hall model does not significantly revise the conflict between pluralists and elitists over the relationship between wealth and power in twentieth-century America, it proposes to move the debate away from the focus on economic class and institutions that has heretofore defined the interpretive debate.

The authors, however, do not successfully document their theory of dynastic families. *Lives in Trust*, in fact, is not a jointly authored monograph by a cultural anthropologist (Marcus) and researcher of philanthropy (Hall). Marcus is the principal author, as Hall's contribution is confined to a jointly authored summary epilogue and a detailed chapter on the Rockefeller family. Hall's Rockefeller chapter, because it is thoroughly grounded in primary sources and carefully analyzed, is the most solid essay in an otherwise episodically organized, often disjointed, and highly speculative book. Marcus's attempt to employ the skills of a cultural anthropologist to explicate how descendant generations develop shared cultural traits fails, primarily because his speculative observations are rarely documented or tightly reasoned. Basing his model of the dynastic family on personal observations about two Galveston families—Kempner and Moody—and speculative reactions to newspaper articles and books about other wealthy families—Hunt, Bingham, and Getty—Marcus invariably offers sweeping, unsupported speculation about how descendants came to share common values. Furthermore, he fails to establish the representative character of the disparate families—notably, the Hunts, Binghams, Gettys, Moodys, and Kempners—who are the subject of his commentary while his narrative about these families is episodic. Because of these research deficiencies, his chapters, which constitute the bulk of the book, do not substantiate Hall's more narrowly focused study of the Rockefeller family. The resultant impressionistic ethnographic analysis adds little to the debate on whether wealth has given rise to a class system that shapes the politics and economy of twentieth-century America.

ATHAN THEOHARIS

Marquette University
Milwaukee
Wisconsin

SKOLNICK, ARLENE. *Embattled Paradise: The American Family in an Age of Uncertainty*. Pp. 284. New York: Basic Books, 1991. $23.00.

Embattled Paradise is an interesting book, but it could be more aptly described as an overview of popular culture since World War II than as an investigation of American family trends. The inclusion or exclusion of topics in the book is highly idiosyncratic. For example, Skolnick states at the outset that she intends to focus on middle-class families in order to examine the changes affecting most Americans. In practice, this means, unfortunately, that she almost completely ignores the familial experiences of blacks, the group that has undergone the most drastic alterations in family structure (as well as Hispanics). Puzzlingly, Skolnick devotes more attention to the New Left, communes, and open marriages, which affected no more than a minute fraction of the middle class.

Even when Skolnick addresses family issues, the focus is all too often on the depiction of family life through movies and television, or else on what various writers have said about the family. This sort of material has its place, but it should take a place at the end of the line behind the rich evidence available on the actual behavior of family members and polling data concerning their opinions on various family-related issues. Similarly, Skolnick devotes too much attention to media fads while neglecting important issues that garner few stories. For instance, *Embattled Paradise* scrutinizes the controversies surrounding *The Greening of America* and *The Culture of Narcissism*, books of dubious historical importance and even less relevance to the family. However, the growing importance of grandparents—who often supply financial and other support to their divorced children and who must be cared for when infirm by children struggling to raise families themselves—is ignored.

Skolnick's assessments of the causes and implications of various family trends are generally sound, and she persuasively debunks the myths of the "good old days." One of the book's theses is that changes in family behavior are primarily a positive adaptation to altered economic and social conditions in the last half century. Although this is often true, Skolnick understates the personal tragedies associated with out-of-wedlock births, which now account for more than one of every four births. The hard truth is that most of these families suffer serious and lengthy impoverishment. There is nothing positive about the rapid escalation of out-of-wedlock births, which shows no signs of slowing. Rather, it is one of the most deleterious social challenges facing the United States today.

FRANK GALLO

George Washington University
Washington, D.C.

ECONOMICS

ANDERSON, JEFFREY J. *The Territorial Imperative: Pluralism, Corporatism, and Economic Crisis*. Pp. xiv, 252. New York: Cambridge University Press, 1992. No price.

YARBROUGH, BETH V. and ROBERT M. YARBROUGH. *Cooperation and Governance in International Trade: The Strategic Organization Approach*. Pp. xi, 182. Princeton, NJ: Princeton University Press, 1992. $35.00.

Institutions are the vehicles through which economic policies are carried out. Generally, they are taken as exogenously given; analysts tend not to focus on the effects of institutional arrangements on economic events or the factors that generate the institutional arrangements themselves. The authors of these two volumes cast light on these subjects. Jeffrey J. Anderson examines the effects of differing political institutions on the design and implementation of regional economic policies, and Beth V. and Robert M. Yarbrough discuss the factors that determine the nature of the institutions that govern international trade.

Anderson begins his volume by noting,

We know little of the potential for the expression and pursuit of *territorial* economic interests in advanced democracies or of the specific circumstances under which sub-national actors—chronically underresourced in comparison to national actors—engage in politics about territory across territory. We are unaware of the consequences, if any, of the apparent lack of fit between interests based on territory and a political process tuned overwhelmingly to national policies. We possess little information on the distributive and redistributive conflicts that arise when market and territory collide, and the way in which such conflicts spill over into the political arena.

He sets out to examine "the patterns and the content of relationships among actors, both public and private, within and between the national and subnational levels" as exemplified by the making and carrying-out of regional economic policies—principally revitalization policies—in the Northeast and West Midlands of the United Kingdom and the Saar and North Rhine-Westphalia in Germany. He chooses these areas because of similarities between the economic situations of the nations and the regions. Both the United Kingdom and Germany are industrial countries. The Saar and the Northeast economies have been dominated by monostructural heavy industries, which have been in decline for some time; the West Midlands and North Rhine-Westphalian economies, on the other hand, are more broadly based and began their decline much more recently. Notwithstanding these broad similarities between the economies of the

nations and regions, however, Anderson notes a major difference in the political institutions of the two countries: in the United Kingdom, there is no strong regional governmental unit; in Germany, on the other hand, regional governments are, in some respects, more powerful than the central government in Bonn.

After carefully tracing and analyzing the histories of regional economic policies in the United Kingdom and the Federal Republic—including, importantly, regional efforts in the United Kingdom that failed because of the lack of a regional political structure—Anderson concludes, "Succinctly stated, constitutions matter. In the politics of regional crisis, the constitutional ordering of territorial political power distributes interests, resources, and capabilities across space."

The Yarbroughs note that people usually study the degree and nature of trade liberalization but not the institutional form of that liberalization. They ask the question "What can explain the historically observed institutional variety in efforts to liberalize or open the world trading system?" According to the authors, the key factor determining the nature of the institutional framework within which trade liberalization has occurred is the feasibility of engaging in opportunistic protection—the extent to which one party to an agreement can benefit by cheating on its commitment to liberalize trade.

They contrast the mid-nineteenth-century British policy of unilaterally opening the U.K. market to foreign goods with the reciprocal global liberal multilateralism of the General Agreement on Tariffs and Trade (GATT) adopted after World War II, the small-group liberalization characteristic of many free-trade areas and customs unions, and the small-group economic integration characterized by EC92.

In the mid-nineteenth century, the United Kingdom was the world's sole source of manufactures. The markets for these exports were assured, and an illiberal trade policy could only raise prices paid by the nation's producers and consumers. Hence self-help motivated British adherence to a liberal trade policy.

After World War II, the United States was the international hegemon. In contrast to the U.K. situation of a century earlier, however, the United States was not the only source of the goods it exported; it was not prepared to liberalize unilaterally. Since some nations might think they could benefit by violating the provisions of the GATT while others observed their obligations, the agreement incorporates both rules for liberalization and supranational enforcement mechanisms, neither of which was needed by the nineteenth-century United Kingdom.

Small-group liberalization, embodied in such structures as regional free trade areas and customs unions, is usually enforced primarily through the self-help motive. Investment in facilities designed to produce exports to other member states or other economic factors that are hostage to the continued observance of the agreement typically effect adherence to the pact. Usually, decisions to make changes in the regulations governing free trade areas or customs unions must be approved by a very large majority, if not all, of the member states. When members of customs unions or free trade areas desire closer economic policy coordination and integration than can be obtained in such a regime, they may establish a supranational body to enforce rules adopted less than unanimously. Such has been the history of the European Community since the mid-1980s. The Yarbroughs term this sort of arrangement "minilateralism."

Anderson and the Yarbroughs provide valuable insights into the relationship between institutions and the making of economic policy and the factors that determine the institutional structure through which economic policy is implemented. The authors' arguments are clearly and persuasively stated.

MICHAEL ULAN

Department of State
Washington, D.C.

FLEISHER, ARTHUR A., III, BRIAN L. GOFF, and ROBERT D. TOLLISON. *The National Collegiate Athletic Association: A Study in Cartel Behavior.* Pp. xi, 190. Chicago: University of Chicago Press, 1992. $24.95.

This book provides a detailed economic study of the National Collegiate Athletic Association (NCAA) in its dual role as a coordinating mechanism for intercollegiate athletic events and a regulator of academic standards for the student athletes participating in these events. It concludes that the NCAA acts as a cartel, exerting monopsony power over the labor input of student athletes while, at the same time, exerting monopoly power over the supply of college sports to the benefit mainly of an elite subset of academic institutions.

The primary value of the book is its considerable information concerning the NCAA, but its main theme that the NCAA is a monopolist-monopsonist is unconvincing. Although the authors disclaim the pursuit of normative objectives, the book nonetheless implies that college sports should be deregulated on both the product and factor sides of the market. Yet this analysis fails to recognize the joint-product nature of the NCAA's output. One of the products, the supply of intercollegiate athletic events, is indeed a for-profit output, but the other product, the preservation of academic standards for student athletes, is of a not-for-profit nature that does not fit well into cartel theory. All one needs to do to bring this point home is to compare the NCAA to professional, for-profit sports such as supplied by Major League Baseball, the National Football League, the National Basketball Association, and the National Hockey League. These professional sports organizations, unlike the NCAA, do not have the obligation of maintaining academic integrity at the nation's colleges and universities. Their markets are single-product markets. Imagine what would happen to academic standards if colleges and universities competed in an unregulated fashion with only the profit goal in mind?

Moreover, the book's primary contention that the NCAA exerts monopsony control over the labor input of student athletes is tenuous. Consider the case of a graduating high school senior who possesses considerable baseball-playing skills. What options does this young man have in the face of the NCAA, which the authors suggest is something akin to Darth Vader? The young athlete might sell his skills directly to Major League Baseball for an immediate monetary return. Alternatively, he might choose to showcase his talents at a member institution of the NCAA and, perhaps, gain greater financial remuneration at a later date while being given the opportunity for a college education as well. Where is the monopsony? The young athlete has attractive choices that are inconsistent with monopsony behavior.

A direct solution to the joint-product dilemma would be to divorce the dual functions, for-profit and not-for-profit, of the NCAA and return the colleges and universities to the exclusive supply of education. Probably not a bad idea! There would be no intercollegiate sports except at the not-for-profit, club level. Sports would be a professional domain in its entirety and universities could pursue the primary goal of education. Since this optimal solution is unlikely to occur, however, it may be advisable to stick with the NCAA in its present, joint-product role as the lesser of two evils.

BERNARD P. HERBER

University of Arizona
Tucson

KORNAI, JÁNOS. *The Socialist System: The Political Economy of Communism*. Pp. xxviii, 644. Princeton, NJ: Princeton University Press, 1992. $49.50. Paperbound, $14.95.

János Kornai has undergone a remarkable intellectual odyssey from the technocratic socialist planner of the 1960s to the (nearly) unequivocal advocate of laissez-faire capitalism of the 1990s. In his earliest major work published in the West, *Mathematical Planning of Structural Decisions* (1967), Kornai, then affiliated with the Computing Centre of the Hungarian Academy of Sciences, set forth techniques for applying mathematical programming methods to intersectoral investment decisions made by a central planning agency. As in the case of Russia, efforts made in Hungary—and other Eastern European nations—by mathematically sophisticated analysts to apply advanced mathematical methods to planning issues met with limited success. These methods remained generally incomprehensible to the real-world planners handling the day-to-day problems of the planning effort.

But the relative unimportance of mathematical programming in actual central planning may not have been a serious constraint on the performance of the planning system. Presumably, Kornai would now regard any serious effort to apply mathematical programming to planning decisions as probably worse than useless—not so much because of the conceptual weaknesses of the methods themselves but, rather, owing to the poor quality of the data that would necessarily be utilized in their implementation. The perception that underlies Kornai's new book, *The Socialist System*, is simply that any effort to achieve bureaucratic control over a national economy so badly distorts economic decision making and phenomena that the price and other data that are generated are useless for any sort of rational decision making, whether by individuals or by planning agencies.

The Socialist System is a magisterial description and evaluation of the Communist system of centrally planned socialism that prevailed in the USSR and Eastern Europe throughout the post-Stalin era. This economic system never worked as well as the Communist Party authorities wanted it to—they wanted their people to enjoy living standards higher than those in the advanced capitalist nations of Western Europe and the United States—and their perennial dissatisfaction was manifested by constant tinkerings with reforms, most of them aimed at reducing the constraints imposed on individual initiative and enterprise flexibility by the central planning system. The traditional Stalinist central planning system, however, proved remarkably resistant to fundamental change. To the amazement of the world, the overall Communist social system has recently been radically disrupted through a chain of events initiated by a crisis of confidence among the high-level leadership. What will eventually emerge in its place is still uncertain, with respect both to the economy and to the larger social system.

Insofar as socialism is concerned—that is, public ownership of capital and other nonhuman factors of production—the critical question is whether any type of market socialist system might exist that would be substantially superior to communistic centrally planned socialism as practiced in the USSR and Eastern Europe. The Austrian school of econom-

ics, represented by its major twentieth-century luminaries Ludwig von Mises and Friedrich von Hayek, has consistently maintained that true markets are impossible in the absence of private ownership of capital, making "market socialism" an oxymoronic term. Kornai endorses the Austrian viewpoint on the matter. In commenting on the 1930s debate between Oskar Lange, the founding father of the market socialist concept in Western economic thought, and Friedrich von Hayek, Kornai states, "Looking back after fifty years one can conclude that Hayek was right on every point."

This strong statement, coming from a scholar of impeccable academic credentials—now affiliated with Harvard University's Department of Economics as well as the Hungarian Academy of Sciences—and a veteran of decades of participatory experience with the Communist economic system, will be welcomed by all those who regard the socialist idea—at least in the public-ownership sense—as having been nothing more than a troublesome aberration in human history, an aberration that is now, thankfully, coming to an end. The basic message conveyed by the *The Socialist System* is that the inherent attributes of socialism will inevitably produce inefficiency, so that fundamental progress can be achieved only through wholesale privatization within the ex-Communist nations. Such wholesale privatization, which would effectively close the book on the real-world experiment with socialism initiated by the Bolshevik Revolution of 1917, is now anxiously awaited by the large majority of people in the West.

There is still a small minority of others in the West—such as this reviewer—who continue to believe that democratic market socialist social systems are feasible that would probably, if not certainly, be superior both to the oligarchic planned socialist social system of the USSR and Eastern Europe and to the democratic market capitalist social system of the United States and Western Europe. To these individuals, Kornai's endorsement of the Austrian dismissal of the market socialist possibility is regarded as premature, a consequence of being too close to the problem, of failing to consider possibilities with which the author is not personally familiar. Be that as it may, even the most die-hard proponents of socialism will have to concede that János Kornai's *Socialist System* is a compelling indictment of the only form of socialism with which humanity has had any significant real-world experience.

JAMES A. YUNKER

Western Illinois University
Macomb

LANE, ROBERT E. *The Market Experience.* Pp. viii, 630. New York: Cambridge University Press, 1991. $65.00. Paperbound, $24.95.

Shortly after election day in 1992, the President-elect announced nominations for a series of high-level economic posts; he also conducted an unprecedented economic town meeting to help lay plans for the new administration. Two important facts emerged. The economics profession now enjoys as much legitimacy and influence as the science community once possessed—perhaps more. Equally important, what economists profess is an almost theological faith in the market as guarantor of both equity and universal well-being.

Robert Lane, professor emeritus of political science at Yale, has an extensive list of contributions on the social and psychological motivations of voting behavior. In *The Market Experience*, he painstakingly examines the motivations of individuals who enter the labor force. What are the perceived benefits and costs? What value does the individual attach to economic equity among workers as a group or to the environmental consequences of the work that is done?

The Market Experience is an elaborate essay on the psychology of behavior, drawing upon a formidable social science literature. That literature describes behavior as the result of a very mixed recipe —perception, memory, cognition, motivation, attitude and value formation, social reference, social norms, ambivalence, and effective response.

Economics simplistically presumes, without proof, that behavior is governed only by greed and rationality. Further, economics assumes that success is additive, that more is better. The reality is that experience in the marketplace is emotionally complex and nonlinear. Market economics, then, cannot be the formula for attaining overall well-being.

Economics does not care whether you enjoy your work or hate it. Economics assumes you are indifferent about how your work—the things you make—affects others. A careless reader might imagine that welfare economics meets all these issues, but that branch of the dismal science is also founded on grossly unsophisticated behavior assumptions.

Lane dissects the individual's market experience with a very fine knife; then he surveys many generations of social science literature on each component. Always the message is that human beings are vastly more complex than economic models perforce assume. The market is irrelevant to most of those matters that human beings actually seem to care about.

Lane wants the reader to avoid jumping to the conclusion that the book is a humanist critique of market economics, that is, that a person should not be reduced to a commodity. Nor does he hold for the socialist critique, which blames the market for creating economic inequality. Since market economists would generally have us believe that private property and unregulated markets guarantee democracy, Lane archly observes that "equality is undemocratic . . . almost no one wants it." That should give the President's Council of Economic Advisers something to think about!

Though it is a lengthy treatise by today's standards, *The Market Experience* limits itself to individual or microeconomic behavior. At the end there is a hint that national or global matters—macroeconomics—will be taken up subsequently. Looking back in the history of economic thought, we find, however, that the larger picture came first. Adam Smith's purpose in writing his famous book was to explain not how people behave but what determines "the wealth of nations."

Smith argued that unfettered, selfish individual behavior tends to make a nation wealthy. Today's market economists have gone back to this prescription after two centuries of wandering in a wilderness of moralizing and statistics.

But just as economics lacks credible theory on individual behavior, Adam Smith's happy notion of a beneficent "invisible hand" is also no more than an incoherent article of faith. A market economy ignores the values of individuals and the objectives of society.

Lane provides a relevant observation attributed to Ruth Benedict. There are as many social values as there are roots of personal behavior, and they can be incompatible. A society can elect to pursue one value or at best a limited set. The rest are scuttled. "A society that chooses piety will likely forgo wealth; one that chooses honor in war will suffer the losses in war."

Turning people loose to make money, or to try to make money, is an idea that today has been vastly oversold. Such is the mundane summation of this thoughtful work. The book has flaws, mainly of style, and leaves important matters for another day, yet it has fundamental validity. Market economics is an intellectual quagmire.

WALLACE F. SMITH

University of California
Berkeley

LIBBY, RONALD T. *Protecting Markets: U.S. Policy and the World Grain Trade.* Pp. xvii, 152. Ithaca, NY: Cornell University Press, 1992. $26.50.

Given the current condition of the world trading system and negotiations about its future, it would be difficult to come upon a more timely book than Ronald T. Libby's *Protecting Markets*. Problems with agricultural trade in general and trade between the United States and the European Community (EC) in particular, are, in 1993, the major obstacles blocking a new General Agreement on Tariffs and Trade settlement. No one reading Libby's book can fail to understand why transatlantic agricultural trade is problematic. Nor will anyone come away expecting ready solutions, because Libby describes the political gridlock with great accuracy. Libby's is one of the best explanations of the recent politics of EC agriculture in print today.

Protecting Markets is mainly focused on the U.S. government's Export Enhancement Program (EEP), passed into law as part of the Food Security Act of 1985. Though complicated in its execution, the EEP is in essence an export subsidy mechanism designed to enhance the price competitiveness of U.S. commodities on foreign markets. It is targeted at the external markets of the EC. Libby not only approves of the EEP, but he also goes to some length to endorse the mercantilistic principles that lie behind it. Part of his approval is pragmatic, inasmuch as the documentation that he provides rather persuasively shows that the EEP had intended effects upon EC politics, policies, and trading behavior despite the fact that European officials deny this. Ideologically, Libby's position is highly controversial; it contradicts prevailing free-trade liberalism and is therefore destined to upset the orthodox community. Still, his position is also provocatively argued and has to be taken seriously.

Libby can be criticized for failing to conceptually elaborate the theory of modern mercantilism more than he does. This renders the book less of a social scientific contribution than it might have been. Then again, and surely unintendedly, the Libby study dramatizes in bold strokes the political-economic surrealism of the world today. At monumental cost to taxpayers, and to the dismay of consumers in Europe and the United States, our respective governments pay farmers to produce too much. They buy this surplus from the farmers, and this keeps food prices high at home. Then our governments pay trading companies to sell food overseas and they pay foreigners to buy it. Libby explains why our governments do this, but knowing is not very comforting.

DONALD J. PUCHALA

University of South Carolina
Columbia

OYE, KENNETH A. *Economic Discrimination and Political Exchange: World Political Economy in the 1930's and 1980's*. Pp. ixx, 235. Princeton, NJ: Princeton University Press, 1992. $35.00.

If there is one icon in the international political economy at present, it is the belief that an interdependent world requires open markets. Yet, at the same time, competitive pressures mount from various sorely beset local manufacturing and agricultural interests to raise import barriers, regionalize and cartelize production, or place all trade relationships on a case-by-case, quid pro quo basis. In response to this trend, advocates of further liberalization point to the disaster of the 1930s, when, as Kenneth Oye puts it, "discrimination was pervasive" and "commercial, financial, and monetary relations were organized along bilateral, regional, and imperial lines." Was the pattern of growing international trade discrimination, imposition of import quotas, and bilateral or regional preferences evident during the 1980s a harbinger of a new collapse in the global economy, a collapse likely to be worse than that of the thirties because of the growth in number and in vulnerability of new national economies since the Great Depression?

The answer is no, says Oye, associate professor of political science at the Massachusetts Institute of Technology and coeditor of the recent seminal volume on post-Cold War American political and economic policy needs, *Eagle in a New World*. After introductory sections on the philosophical and economic-theoretical bases of the principle of "unrestricted bargaining"—that is, open markets and trade—Oye's new book offers a concise analysis of the structure of international commercial relations, including its financial and macroeconomic underpinnings, in the 1930s and 1980s. The conclusion warns against the "perils" of drawing an "imprecise analogy" between the world economies of the two periods and notes that the world economy of the 1930s was aggravated by various "inappropriate *domestic* policies" that in turn adversely affected national and international recovery. An example of this wrong domestic policy in the 1930s, Oye notes in Keynesian fashion, was the lack of initiating expansive monetary and fiscal policies in the United States. Moreover, the weakness of the international monetary system in the 1930s had the effect of rapidly worsening the impact of various domestic crises around the globe.

Today, neither fiscal and monetary policies, either in the United States or among the other major world powers, nor the international currency control and rescue system that now prevails replicates the national centricities and operational ineffectiveness of the 1930s.

Still, Oye notes that there is a useful lesson to be learned all the same from the current fashion of invoking the imagery of an analogy between the 1930s and the 1980s, false though the analogy may be. That lesson is that the general fear of an international economic collapse created by "the mindless and shortsighted pursuit of narrow national interests" in turn gives potent impetus to the need for close international cooperation. In today's world, such cooperation, as Oye indicates, has a diplomatic and strategic dimension ("political exchange"). Protectionist and countervailing measures may well eventually contribute to a wider, multinational "openness."

This is a book primarily for the advanced student of international trade and monetary policies. Its jargon and assumptions likely would deter the general reader, though the thorough annotation and comprehensive bibliography also would give a beginning student a good place to start. It is to be hoped that Oye will cast the themes of this volume into a general article and so give his provocative insights greater currency.

JUSTUS M. VAN DER KROEF

University of Bridgeport
Connecticut

PISANI, DONALD J. *To Reclaim a Divided West: Water, Law, and Public*

Policy, 1848-1902. Pp. xx, 487. Albuquerque: University of New Mexico Press, 1992. $40.00. Paperbound, $19.95.

FELDMAN, DAVID LEWIS. *Water Resources Management: In Search of an Environmental Ethic.* Pp. xi, 247. Baltimore, MD: Johns Hopkins University Press, 1991. $38.50.

These two volumes are critical appraisals of U.S. water law and policy. Donald Pisani's book provides an important historical synthesis of the development of water law and public policy in the West between the discovery of gold in California in 1848 and the enactment of the Reclamation Act of 1902. It is part of the distinguished series Histories of the American Frontier. David Feldman's book is an essay on proposed reforms of water policy in the United States.

Donald Pisani details a rich variety of institutional experiments regarding water allocation that were tried in the arid western states in the nineteenth century. In particular, he outlines the gradual displacement of riparian water rights by the doctrine of prior appropriation that allocated water to first claimants and allowed them to transfer it to remote locations. The driving forces were the mining industry, which required water for placer and hydraulic mining, and irrigation projects, which transferred water to potential farm sites on arid land. Pisani also describes the adoption of various private, state, and federal programs for irrigation and reclamation. At the federal level, these projects involved enormous sums of money, and the political competition between private interests, state governments, and federal agencies for favorable legislation was intense.

David Feldman also discusses such programs, with brief references to the Garrison Diversion Project on the Missouri River in North Dakota and the attempted Blue Ridge Pump Storage Project on the New River in North Carolina. Both authors assert that a broader and more cohesive approach ought to be taken regarding water policy to make it more efficient and better directed to collective national interests, rather than to narrow special interests. For Pisani, a more unified, coherent approach to water could have resulted had the federal government played a greater leadership role, instead of allowing water policy to emerge in a haphazard way through competition between governmental jurisdictions. The laws and programs that resulted were often inconsistent and wasteful. Indeed, Pisani argues that the observed nature of water law was indicative of a broader failure of government to provide a framework for the long-term, sustainable development of the arid West.

Since water was the most valuable commodity in the region, it seems doubtful that any public policy could have escaped the demands of competing interest groups for its allocation and use. In fact, the real culprit was the failure to allow water to be transferred at low cost from one use to another. This smooth transition likely would have done more to promote efficient water use and sustained economic development than any of the programs Pisani seems to have in mind.

For David Feldman, the prescription for pork-barrel and environmentally unsound water projects is the adoption of a new ethic in the allocation and use of water. This ethic would promote fairness, broader community interests, and the natural environment. It is difficult to find fault with such objectives, but Feldman provides no concrete program for policy reform. Although he makes reference to political theory, particularly public choice theory, Feldman does not incorporate its lessons that interest group politics and short-term political goals will dominate in the decisions of politicians and agency officials. Just how a social contract for

water, as called for by Feldman, could be devised to avoid or mitigate these factors is never made clear.

GARY D. LIBECAP

California Institute of Technology
Pasadena

University of Arizona
Tucson

SEXTON, PATRICIA CAYO. *The War on Labor and the Left: Understanding America's Unique Conservatism*. Pp. ix, 325. Boulder, CO: Westview Press, 1991. $24.95.

In this very readable history of U.S. labor relations, Sexton seeks, as others have before her, to set out the underlying conditions that have resulted in the so-called American exceptionalism, that is, the inability of U.S. labor to fashion the unified, powerful political and social force that laboring women and men have achieved in other advanced capitalist economies. Sexton commences by rejecting the familiar answers to this question, including political consensus, the mitigating influence of open frontiers, the relative national and ethnic heterogeneity of the U.S. work force, and the divisive sectarianism of U.S. labor's would-be leaders. Instead, she argues that U.S. labor has been the enduring victim of both overt and subtle forms of repression brought about by a conservative hegemony in the United States. To sustain this position, one must demonstrate, first, that the alternative hypotheses are lacking; second, that comparable repression is not a feature of other industrial economies, and, third, that repression has indeed played a predominant role in shaping the U.S. labor movement. Sexton achieves greater success in establishing the last premise than the first and second.

One difficulty that prevails throughout the volume is Sexton's near total reliance upon secondary sources, which she quotes and paraphrases at some length. Unfortunately, she also offers the opinions of various like-minded scholars as authoritative substantiation of her perspective, a methodology that fails to convince even a sympathetic reader. Moreover, there is little here that cannot be found in more exhaustive detail elsewhere, which also raises questions as to who the intended audience is. Nevertheless, a virtue of this work is that it succeeds in collating a good deal of information into a coherent history of labor's repression in the United States, encompassing the several instruments of this repression, including the employers' private armies, the armed forces of the United States, the peculiar system of political stability and control, the legal and judicial system, macroeconomic policy, and the media. Still, establishing the contribution of repression to the undermining of labor's interests does not require the discrediting of complementary forces that might also be in play. Although Sexton resists any temptation to resort to conspiracy theories, she does not satisfactorily explain the convergence of repression from an apparent diversity of sources.

The reader may also be bothered by the implicit presumption that the repression of U.S. labor is largely exogenous to the developing historical relationship of capital to labor, which consequently represents this relationship with a strong suggestion of immutability. This contrasts markedly with the more endogenous, evolutionary model of social structures of accumulation, an alternative progressive perspective that Sexton does not address.

In the end, although Sexton's argument fails to carry the full burden of its provocative conclusion, the reader is presented with a very useful overview and extensive bibliography of the multifaceted forms of repression and violence that have been perpetrated upon U.S. labor from the formation of the Republic to the end of the twentieth century.

ALEXANDER M. THOMPSON III

Vassar College
New York

YAGO, GLENN. *Junk Bonds: How High Yield Securities Restructured Corporate America.* Pp. xi, 249. New York: Oxford University Press, 1991. $21.95.

This study extolls the high-yield securities that dominated the securities industry during the 1980s. Yago does a Herculean job of assembling and analyzing data to support his position. For example, he analyzes high-yield securities by overall use of proceeds, industry use of proceeds, industrial distribution of issuers, and so on. He compares employment behavior within specific industries for junk-bond-issuing firms with the industry as a whole and does similarly for sales per employee, total invested capital, and capital expenditures. Yago concludes that

high yield securities had a positive impact on corporate performance across a wide range of accepted performance measures. High yield firms evidenced a greater capacity than U.S. industry in general to create new jobs, retain old ones, and successfully manage employment reductions in industries that were losing jobs (p. 80).

Leveraged buyouts (LBOs) and corporate restructuring are examined with attempts to measure effects on productivity, profitability, capital expenditures, employment, and the like, and results are generally favorable. Thus Yago finds that LBOs enhanced industrial competitiveness.

At the public policy level, Yago laments state and federal actions hostile to junk bonds, especially antitakeover legislation and restrictions placed on junk bonds in savings and loan portfolios. Yago blames the collapse of the junk bond market in the summer and fall of 1989 on a "selling panic based on misguided regulation and fueled by ignorant media reports, all at a time when the market was least able to absorb the inventory: just after the government had taken $650 million out of Drexel Burnham."

This study suffers from being ideology driven, the ideology being that the market can do no wrong, only governments can. It is severely hampered because much of the analysis ends in 1986 and 1987 and some in 1989. Difficulties among junk bond issuers later exploded, so the statistical results would presumably have changed significantly. The *Wall Street Journal* on 9 January 1991 reported that junk bond defaults in 1990 were $24.6 billion, about 8.5 percent of the total outstanding. Nowhere is there reference to the impact of the business cycle on junk bond issuers. One misses reference to Connie Bruck's *Predators' Ball*, describing the tactics of Drexel Burnham's Michael Milken. Yago, moreover, seems to be little disturbed by unethical behavior. Concerning the Beatrice LBO, he states, "While the reshuffling of assets may be unsavory to some, most of the units that have been sold have continued to be productive and profitable under new management and ownership." Finally, missing is an analysis of the losses resulting from the junk bond and LBO orgy of the 1980s and their impact.

ERVIN MILLER

University of Pennsylvania
Philadelphia

OTHER BOOKS

AARON, HENRY J. and CHARLES L. SCHULTZE, eds. *Setting Domestic Priorities: What Can Government Do?* Pp. xii, 318. Washington, DC: Brookings, 1992. $32.95. Paperbound, $14.95.

ANDO, NISUKE. *Surrender, Occupation, and Private Property in International Law: An Evaluation of US Practice in Japan.* Pp. xvi, 208. New York: Oxford University Press, 1991. $69.00.

BANDOW, DOUG and TED GALEN CARPENTER, eds. *The U.S.-South Korean Alliance: Time for a Change.* Pp. xii, 217. New Brunswick, NJ: Transaction, 1992. $32.95. Paperbound, $19.95.

BARBER, JAMES DAVID. *The Pulse of Politics: Electing Presidents in the Media Age.* Pp. xi, 342. New Brunswick, NJ: Transaction, 1992. Paperbound, $21.95.

BERMAN, LINDA and MARY-ELLEN SIEGEL. *Behind the 8-Ball: A Guide for Families of Gamblers.* Pp. 285. New York: Simon & Schuster, 1992. Paperbound, $10.00.

BIENEN, HENRY, ed. *Power, Economics, and Security: The United States and Japan in Focus.* Pp. xii, 336. Boulder, CO: Westview Press, 1992. $65.00.

BOYDSTON, JEANNE. *Home and Work: Housework, Wages, and the Ideology of Labor in the Early Republic.* Pp. xx, 222. New York: Oxford University Press, 1990. $29.95.

BROD, HARRY. *Hegel's Philosophy of Politics: Idealism, Identity, and Modernity.* Pp. viii, 216. Boulder, CO: Westview Press, 1992. $45.00. Paperbound, $15.95.

BROWN, CHARLES J. and ARMANDO M. LAGO. *The Politics of Psychiatry in Revolutionary Cuba.* Pp. xiii, 217. New Brunswick, NJ: Transaction, 1992. $29.95. Paperbound, $17.95.

BURNS, JAMES MACGREGOR et al. *The Democrats Must Lead: The Case for a Progressive Democratic Party.* Pp. viii, 279. Boulder, CO: Westview Press, 1992. $49.95. Paperbound, $14.95.

CAVADINO, MICHAEL and JAMES DIGNAN. *The Penal System.* Pp. 298. Newbury Park, CA: Sage, 1992. $55.00. Paperbound, $21.95.

CHANDLER, DAVID P. *A History of Cambodia.* Pp. xv, 287. Boulder, CO: Westview Press, 1992. $29.95.

CHATTERJI, MANAS and LINDA RENNIE FORCEY, eds. *Disarmament, Economic Conversion, and Management of Peace.* Pp. xiv, 335. New York: Praeger, 1992. $65.00.

DANOPOULOS, CONSTANTINE P., ed. *Civilian Rule in the Developing World: Democracy on the March?* Pp. xiii, 273. Boulder, CO: Westview Press, 1992. Paperbound, $35.00.

EDSALL, THOMAS BYRNE and MARY D. EDSALL. *Chain Reaction: The Impact of Race, Rights, and Taxes on American Politics.* Pp. xii, 343. New York: Norton, 1992. Paperbound, $10.95.

FELKENES, GEORGE T. and PETER CHARLES UNSINGER. *Diversity, Affirmative Action and Law Enforcement.* Pp. xi, 212. Springfield, IL: Charles C Thomas, 1992. $42.75.

FERGE, ZSUZSA and JON EIVIND KOLBERG, eds. *Social Policy in a Changing Europe.* Pp. viii, 318. Boulder, CO: Westview Press, 1992. Paperbound, $44.50.

FESTE, KAREN A. *Expanding the Frontiers: Superpower Intervention in the Cold War.* Pp. xiv, 211. New York: Praeger, 1992. $45.00.

FINE, SEYMOUR H. *Marketing the Public Sector: Promoting the Causes of Public and Nonprofit Agencies.* Pp. xxiv, 360. New Brunswick, NJ: Transaction, 1992. Paperbound, $24.95.

FUNK, RAINER, ed. *Erich Fromm: The Revision of Psychoanalysis.* Pp. xiv,

149. Boulder, CO: Westview Press, 1992. $28.95.

FURINO, ANTONIO, ed. *Health Policy and the Hispanic.* Pp. viii, 240. Boulder, CO: Westview Press, 1992. Paperbound, $36.50.

GANZGLASS, EVELYN, ed. *Excellence at Work: Policy Option Papers for the National Governors' Association.* Pp. x, 187. Kalamazoo, MI: W. E. Upjohn, 1992. $24.00. Paperbound, $14.00.

GENOVESE, EUGENE D. *From Rebellion to Revolution: Afro-American Slave Revolts in the Making of the Modern World.* Pp. xxvi, 173. Baton Rouge: Louisiana State University Press, 1992. Paperbound, $9.95.

GEORGE, ALEXANDER I. *Forceful Persuasion: Coercive Diplomacy as an Alternative to War.* Pp. xv, 95. Washington, DC: United States Institute of Peace, 1991. Paperbound, $10.95.

GILL, G. J. *Seasonality and Agriculture in the Developing World: A Problem of the Poor and Powerless.* Pp. xvii, 343. New York: Cambridge University Press, 1991. $85.00.

GOLAN, GALIA. *Moscow and the Middle East.* Pp. 102. New York: Council on Foreign Relations Press, 1992. Paperbound, $14.95.

GOLDSCHEIDER, CALVIN, ed. *Population and Social Change in Israel.* Pp. xvi, 192. Boulder, CO: Westview Press, 1992. $30.00.

GONICK, LEV S. and EDWARD WEISBAND, eds. *Teaching World Politics: Contending Pedagogues for a New World Order.* Pp. x, 261. Boulder, CO: Westview Press, 1992. Paperbound, $29.95.

GRABER, MARK A. *Transforming Free Speech: The Ambiguous Legacy of Civil Libertarianism.* Pp. xi, 336. Berkeley: University of California Press, 1991. $39.95.

GREENAWALT, KENT. *Law and Objectivity.* Pp. x, 288. New York: Oxford University Press, 1992. No price.

GROFMAN, BERNARD and CHANDLER DAVIDSON, eds. *Controversies in Minority Voting.* Pp. xiv, 376. Washington, DC: Brookings, 1992. $36.95. Paperbound, $16.95.

GUY, MARY E., ed. *Women and Men of the States: Public Administrators at the State Level.* Pp. xx, 273. Armonk, NY: M. E. Sharpe, 1992. $42.50. Paperbound, $17.50.

HAGGARD, STEPHAN and ROBERT R. KAUFMAN, eds. *The Politics of Economic Adjustment.* Pp. xiv, 356. Princeton, NJ: Princeton University Press, 1992. $49.50. Paperbound, $16.95.

HOMANS, GEORGE C. *The Human Group.* Pp. xxxiv, 484. New Brunswick, NJ: Transaction, 1992. Paperbound, $24.95.

HOWARD, MICHAEL. *The Lessons of History.* Pp. 217. New Haven, CT: Yale University Press, 1992. $30.00. Paperbound, $11.00.

HURRELL, ANDREW and BENEDICT KINGSBURY, eds. *The International Politics of the Environment.* Pp. xiv, 492. New York: Oxford University Press, 1992. $72.00. Paperbound, $19.95.

JAMES, HAROLD and MARLA STONE, eds. *When the Wall Came Down: Reactions to German Unification.* Pp. xviii, 351. New York: Routledge, Chapman & Hall, 1992. $59.95. Paperbound, $17.95.

JAUBERTH, H. RODRIGO et al. *The Difficult Triangle: Mexico, Central America and the United States.* Pp. xvi, 192. Boulder, CO: Westview Press, 1992. $45.00. Paperbound, $15.95.

JOHNSON, CATHY MARIE. *The Dynamics of Conflict between Bureaucrats and Legislators.* Pp. xv, 179. Armonk, NY: M. E. Sharpe, 1992. $42.50.

JONES, J. R., ed. *Liberty Secured? Britain before and after 1688.* Pp. vi, 407. Stanford, CA: Stanford University Press, 1992. $42.50.

KAUFMANN, WALTER. *Freud, Adler and Jung: Discovering the Mind.* Vol. 3.

Pp. lviii, 494. New Brunswick, NJ: Transaction, 1992. Paperbound, $19.95.

KENIS, PATRICK. *The Social Construction of an Industry: A World of Chemical Fibres*. Pp. xix, 201. Boulder, CO: Westview Press, 1992. Paperbound, $45.00.

KENNEDY, PAUL M., ed. *Grand Strategies in War and Peace*. Pp. x, 228. New Haven, CT: Yale University Press, 1992. $27.00. Paperbound, $12.00.

KIM, YONG SHIN. *The Ego Ideal, Ideology, and Hallucination: A Psychoanalytic Interpretation of Political Violence*. Pp. ix, 223. Lanham, MD: University Press of America, 1992. $37.50. Paperbound, $19.50.

KIRK, RUSSELL. *The Conservative Constitution*. Pp. xi, 241. Washington, DC: Regnery Gateway, 1990. $22.95.

KOSTERS, MARVIN H., ed. *Fiscal Politics and the Budget Enforcement Act*. Pp. xii, 79. Lanham, MD: AEI Press, 1992. $24.95. Paperbound, $9.75.

KRITZ, MARY M. et al. *International Migration Systems: A Global Approach*. Pp. xii, 354. New York: Oxford University Press, 1992. $68.00.

KURTZ, MICHAEL L. and MORGAN D. PEOPLES. *Earl K. Long: The Saga of Uncle Earl and Louisiana Politics*. Pp. xvi, 312. Baton Rouge: Louisiana University Press, 1990. Paperbound, $9.95.

LAX, MARC D. *Selected Strategic Minerals: The Impending Crisis*. Pp. xvii, 337. Lanham, MD: University Press of America, 1992. $48.50.

LEBRA, TAKIE SUGIYAMA, ed. *Japanese Social Organization*. Pp. xi, 236. Honolulu: University of Hawaii Press, 1992. $34.00. Paperbound, $14.95.

LEVINE, ALAN J. *The Strategic Bombing of Germany, 1940-1945*. Pp. 235. Westport, CT: Greenwood Press, 1992. $45.00.

LISS, SHELDON B. *Radical Thought in Central America*. Pp. xi, 290. Boulder,

CO: Westview Press, 1991. $45.00. Paperbound, $16.95.

LUEBBERT, GREGORY M. *Liberalism, Fascism, or Social Democracy: Social Classes and the Political Origins of Regimes in Interwar Europe*. Pp. xi, 416. New York: Oxford University Press, 1991. Paperbound, $19.95.

LUNDAHL, MATS. *Apartheid in Theory and Practice: An Economic Analysis*. Pp. xii, 375. Boulder, CO: Westview Press, 1992. Paperbound, $34.85.

LUNDIN, S. J., ed. *Verification of Dual-Use Chemicals under the Chemical Weapons Convention: The Case of Thiodiglycol*. Pp. x, 144. New York: Oxford University Press, 1992. Paperbound, $35.00.

MASTNY, VOJTECH. *The Helsinki Process and the Reintegration of Europe 1986-1991: Analysis and Documentation*. Pp. xxi, 343. New York: New York University Press, 1992. $60.00. Paperbound, $25.00.

MATTOX, GALE A. and A. BRADLEY SHINGLETON, eds. *Germany at the Crossroads: Foreign and Domestic Policy Issues*. Pp. xxi, 217. Boulder, CO: Westview Press, 1992. $44.50.

MEHTA, UDAY SINGH. *The Anxiety of Freedom: Imagination and Individuality in Locke's Political Thought*. Pp. x, 186. Ithaca, NY: Cornell University Press, 1992. $24.50.

MENDEZ, RUBEN P. *International Public Finance*. Pp. xxii, 339. New York: Oxford University Press, 1992. $45.00. Paperbound, $24.95.

MESSINA, ANTHONY M. et al., eds. *Ethnic and Racial Minorities in Advanced Industrial Democracies*. Pp. xiv, 358. Westport, CT: Greenwood Press, 1992. $49.95.

MITCHELL, CHRISTOPHER, ed. *Western Hemisphere Immigration and United States Foreign Policy*. Pp. xii, 314. University Park: Pennsylvania State Press, 1992. $45.00. Paperbound, $14.95.

MONTAGUE, LUDWELL LEE. *General Walter Bedell Smith as Director of Central Intelligence October 1950-February 1953*. Pp. xxviii, 308. University Park: Pennsylvania State Press, 1992. $45.00. Paperbound, $14.95.

MOURITZEN, POUL ERIK, ed. *Managing Cities in Austerity: Urban Fiscal Stress in Ten Western Countries*. Pp. 242. Newbury Park, CA: Sage, 1992. $59.95.

MULLER, STEVEN and GEBHARD SCHWEIGLER, eds. *From Occupation to Cooperation: The United States and United Germany in a Changing World Order*. Pp. 288. New York: Norton, 1992. Paperbound, no price.

NELSON, DANIEL N., ed. *Romania after Tyranny*. Pp. viii, 311. Boulder, CO: Westview Press, 1992. Paperbound, $36.50.

PARET, PETER. *Understanding War: Essays on Clausewitz and the History of Military Power*. Pp. x, 229. Princeton, NJ: Princeton University Press, 1992. $24.95.

PEROT, ROSS. *United We Stand: How We Can Take Back Our Country*. Pp. x, 118. New York: Hyperion, 1992. Paperbound, $4.95.

PILON, JULIANA GERAN. *The Bloody Flag: Post-Communist Nationalism in Eastern Europe: Spotlight on Romania*. Pp. xi, 126. New Brunswick, NJ: Transaction, 1992. $29.95. Paperbound, $14.95.

PINDER, JOHN. *European Community: The Building of a Union*. Pp. 248. New York: Oxford University Press, 1991. $47.00. Paperbound, $13.95.

RAHE, PAUL A. *Republics Ancient and Modern: Classical Republicanism and the American Revolution*. Pp. xiv, 1201. Chapel Hill: University of North Carolina Press, 1992. $49.95.

RAMET, SABRINA P. *Nationalism and Federalism in Yugoslavia 1962-1991*. 2d ed. Pp. xviii, 346. Bloomington: Indiana University Press, 1992. $39.95. Paperbound, $17.95.

RAMET, SABRINA PETRA. *Balkan Babel: Politics, Culture, and Religion in Yugoslavia*. Pp. xvi, 230. Boulder, CO: Westview Press, 1992. $44.95.

RENZI, WILLIAM A. and MARK D. ROEHRS. *Never Look Back: A History of World War II in the Pacific*. Pp. xiii, 224. Armonk, NY: M. E. Sharpe, 1991. $21.95.

RICHTER, SANDOR, ed. *The Transition from Command to Market Economies in East-Central Europe*. Pp. x, 317. Boulder, CO: Westview Press, 1992. Paperbound, $35.95.

RIESENBERG, PETER. *Citizenship in the Western Tradition*. Pp. xxiv, 324. Chapel Hill: University of North Carolina Press, 1992. $42.50.

ROVERE, RICHARD H. and ARTHUR SCHLESINGER, JR. *General MacArthur and President Truman: The Struggle for Control of American Foreign Policy*. Pp. xvii, 344. New Brunswick, NJ: Transaction, 1992. $19.95.

RUMMEL, REINHARDT, ed. *Toward Political Union: Planning a Common Foreign and Security Policy in the European Community*. Pp. viii, 376. Boulder, CO: Westview Press, 1992. Paperbound, $45.00.

RUSSELL, JEFFREY BURTON. *The Prince of Darkness: Radical Evil and the Power of Good in History*. Pp. xii, 288. Ithaca, NY: Cornell University Press, 1992. Paperbound, $10.95.

SANDERS, ARTHUR. *Victory: How a Progressive Democratic Party Can Win and Govern*. Pp. xiv, 191. Armonk, NY: M. E. Sharpe, 1992. No price.

SCOTT, JAMES C. *Domination and the Arts of Resistance*. Pp. xviii, 251. New Haven, CT: Yale University Press, 1992. $32.00. Paperbound, $14.00.

SHAFRITZ, JAY M. et al. *Personnel Management in Government: Politics and Process*. Pp. xiv, 553. New York: Marcel Dekker, 1992. $49.75.

SIMON, JULIAN L. *Population and Development in Poor Countries*. Pp. xx,

463. Princeton, NJ: Princeton University Press, 1992. $45.00.

SKLAR, MARTIN J. *The United States as a Developing Country: Studies in U.S. History in the Progressive Era and the 1920s.* Pp. xi, 238. New York: Cambridge University Press, 1992. $49.95. Paperbound, $14.95.

SMITH, PETER H., ed. *Drug Policy in the Americas.* Pp. x, 366. Boulder, CO: Westview Press, 1992. $54.95. Paperbound, $18.95.

SOUTH, SCOTT J. and STEWART E. TOLNAY, eds. *The Changing American Family: Sociological and Demographic Perspectives.* Pp. vii, 304. Boulder, CO: Westview Press, 1992. $55.00.

STEPHANSON, ANDERS. *Kennan and the Art of Foreign Policy.* Pp. x, 380. Cambridge, MA: Harvard University Press, 1989. Paperbound, $15.95.

STEWART, JOHN B. *Opinion and Reform in Hume's Political Philosophy.* Pp. 325. Princeton, NJ: Princeton University Press, 1992. $45.00.

STONE, GEOFFREY R., RICHARD A. EPSTEIN, and CASS R. SUNSTEIN, eds. *The Bill of Rights in the Modern State.* Pp. viii, 583. Chicago: University of Chicago Press, 1992. $55.00. Paperbound, $19.95.

STRAUSS, WILLIAM and NEIL HOWE. *Generations: The History of America's Future, 1584 to 2069.* Pp. 538. New York: William Morrow, 1992. Paperbound, $12.00.

SWANN, DENNIS, ed. *The Single European Market and Beyond: A Study of the Wider Implications of the Single European Act.* Pp. xiv, 299. New York: Routledge, Chapman & Hall, 1992. $77.50. Paperbound, $22.00.

TAYLOR, BOB PEPPERMAN. *Our Limits Transgressed: Environmental Political Thought in America.* Pp. xiii, 184. Lawrence: University Press of Kansas, 1992. $25.00.

VARNIS, STEVEN L. *Reluctant Aid or Aiding the Reluctant? U.S. Food Aid Policy and Ethiopian Famine Relief.* Pp. xi, 229. New Brunswick, NJ: Transaction, 1990. $32.95.

WELLINGTON, HARRY H. *Interpreting the Constitution: The Supreme Court and Process of Adjudication.* Pp. xii, 196. New Haven, CT: Yale University Press, 1992. $25.00. Paperbound, $10.00.

WILSON, THOMAS. *The Power "to Coin" Money: The Exercise of Monetary Powers by the Congress.* Pp. xiii, 272. Armonk, NY: M. E. Sharpe, 1992. $37.50. Paperbound, $17.95.

WOLMAN, HAROLD and MICHAEL GOLDSMITH. *Urban Politics and Policy: A Comparative Approach.* Pp. xi, 256. Cambridge, MA: Basil Blackwell, 1992. $49.95. Paperbound, $19.95.

WOOLCOCK, STEPHEN. *Trading Partners or Trading Blows? Market Access in EC-U.S. Relations.* Pp. xi, 132. New York: Council on Foreign Relations Press, 1992. Paperbound, $14.95.

ZILE, ZIGURDS L., ed. *Ideas and Forces in Soviet Legal History: A Reader on the Soviet State and Law.* Pp. xxxi, 551. New York: Oxford University Press, 1992. Paperbound, $32.50.

ZIMMERMAN, SHIRLEY L. *Family Policies and Family Well-Being.* Pp. 201. Newbury Park, CA: Sage, 1992. $44.00. Paperbound, $21.95.

INDEX

STATEMENT OF OWNERSHIP, MANAGEMENT, AND CIRCULATION (See also attached P.S. Form 3526). 1A. TITLE: THE ANNALS OF THE AMERICAN ACADEMY OF POLITICAL AND SOCIAL SCIENCE. 1B. PUB. # 00027162. 2. DATE OF FILING: October 1, 1993. 3. FREQUENCY OF ISSUE: Bimonthly. 3A. # ISSUES ANNUALLY: 6. 3B. ANNUAL SUB. PRICE: Paper-inst. $145.00; Cloth-inst. $172.00; Paper-indiv. $45.00; Cloth-indiv. $65.00. 4. PUB. ADDRESS: 2455 Teller Road, Thousand Oaks, CA 91320. 5. HDQTRS. ADDRESS: 3937 Chestnut Street, Philadelphia, PA 19104. 6. PUBLISHER: Sara Miller McCune, 2979 Eucalyptus Hill Road, Montecito, CA 93108. EDITOR: Richard Lambert, The American Academy of Political and Social Science, 3937 Chestnut St., Philadelphia, PA 19104. MNG'NG EDITOR: Erica Ginsburg (same as editor). 7. OWNER: The American Academy of Political and Social Science, 3937 Chestnut Street, Philadelphia, PA 19104. 8. KNOWN BONDHOLDERS, ETC.: None. 9. NONPROFIT PURPOSE, FUNCTION, STATUS: Has not changed in preceding 12 months.

	Avg. No. Copies of Each Issue During Preceding 12 Months	Act. No. Copies of Single Issue Published Nearest to Filing Date
10. Extent & Nature of Circulation		
A. Total no. copies	5332	5625
B. Paid circulation		
1. Sales through dealers, etc.	979	1108
2. Mail subscription	3445	3392
C. Total paid circulation	4424	4500
D. Free distribution/free copies	150	133
E. Total distribution	4574	4633
F. Copies not distributed		
1. Office use, etc.	758	992
2. Return from news agents	0	0
G. Total	5332	5625

11. I certify that the statements made by me above are correct and complete.
Nancy Hammerman, Vice President and Director, Sage Periodicals Press

EUROPEAN ECONOMIC REVIEW

Journal of the European Economic Association

Editors:
François Bourguignon, *DELTA/ENS, Paris, France*
Francesco Giavazzi, *Università L. Bocconi, Milan, Italy*
Anthony J. Venables, *University of Southampton, UK*

AIMS AND SCOPE

Founded in 1969, the *European Economic Review* became as of 1986 the official Journal of the EUROPEAN ECONOMIC ASSOCIATION, (with an enlarged board of Editors and a new board of Associate Editors). As a broad-based professional and international journal, *European Economic Review* welcomes submission of theoretical and empirical papers, from both European and non-European authors. Being the official journal of the European Economic Association, it also seeks to support the EEA's aims to contribute to the development and application of economics as a science in Europe and to improve communication and exchange between economics teachers, researchers and students across the European continent. To this end the journal reflects the trends in European research and publishes papers of relevance to European problems. In particular, it invites papers from the younger generation of European economists.

Furthermore each year, the *EER* publishes the papers and proceedings of the Annual Congress of the EEA. These papers include the Marshall and Schumpeter Lectures, as well as brief papers summarizing contributions to the invited sessions of the Congress.

It has also become traditional for the journal to publish special issues (edited by Robert J. Gordon and Georges De Ménil) with a selection of papers from the International Seminar on Macroeconomics (ISOM). The most recent one contains papers presented and discussed at the 15th meeting (1992).

ABSTRACTED/INDEXED IN: ABI/INFORM, COREJ, ISI Current Contents, Journal of Economic Literature, Journal of Planning Literature, Social Sciences Citation Index, UMI Data Courier.

Subscription Information:
1994 Volume 38
(in 9 issues)
Price: Dfl. 1620.00 (US $ 876.00) incl. Postage and Handling
ISSN 0014-2921

Dutch Guilder price quoted applies worldwide, except in the Americas (North, Central and South America). US Dollar price quoted applies in the Americas only.

NORTH-HOLLAND
(An Imprint of Elsevier Science)

Coupon for a *FREE* inspection copy of European Economic Review

Elsevier Science
Attn: Ellen Momma-Vermaak
P.O. Box 1991
1000 BZ Amsterdam
The Netherlands

in the USA/Canada:
Attn: Judy Weislogel
P.O. Box 945, Madison Square Station
New York, NY 10160-0757

Name _____

Address _____

_____

City _____ Zip Code _____

Country _____

419\JJRNLS94

JOURNAL OF CONTEMPORARY HISTORY

This publication is available from UMI in one or more of the following formats:

- In **Microform**--from our collection of over 18,000 periodicals and 7,000 newspapers

- In **Paper**--by the article or full issues through UMI Article Clearinghouse

- **Electronically, on CD-ROM, online, and/or magnetic tape**--a broad range of ProQuest databases available, including abstract-and-index, ASCII full-text, and innovative full-image format

Call toll-free 800-521-0600, ext. 2888, for more information, or fill out the coupon below:

Name _____

Title _____

Company/Institution _____

Address _____

City/State/Zip _____

Phone (   ) _____

I'm interested in the following title(s): _____

UMI
A Bell & Howell Company
Box 78
300 North Zeeb Road
Ann Arbor, MI 48106

800-521-0600 toll-free
313-761-1203 fax

THIS PUBLICATION AVAILABLE FROM UMI

U·M·I